LOK ADALAT: AN EFFECTIVE ALTERNATIVE DISPUTE RESOLUTION MECHANISM

LOK ADALAT: AN EFFECTIVE ALTERNATIVE DISPUTE RESOLUTION MECHANISM

Sarfaraz Ahmed Khan

A P H PUBLISHING CORPORATION
5 ANSARI ROAD, DARYA GANJ
NEW DELHI-110 002

Published by
S.B. Nangia
A.P.H. Publishing Corporation
4435–36/7, Ansari Road, Darya Ganj,
New Delhi-110002
Phone: 011–23274050
e-mail: aphbooks@gmail.com

2026

Rs. 3995/-

Typeset by
Ideal Publishing Solutions
C-90, J.D. Cambridge School,
West Vinod Nagar, Delhi-110092

Printed at
RD DIGITAL PRINTERS
Ansari road , Daryaganj, Delhi-110002

Dedicated to the

Beloved Memory of

My Grand Mother

Late Anisa Khatoon

ACKNOWLEDGEMENTS

It is indeed my proud privilege to express my deep sense of gratitude and indebtedness to my Vice-Chancellor Prof. N. R. Madhava Menon for his inspirational guidance at every stage of my study. I thank Prof. Gangotri Chakraborty for her valuable guidance, scholarly inspiration and affectionate encouragement throughout the period of my research.

I take this opportunity to express my deep gratitude to Justice A. M. Bhattacharjee, Visiting faculty NUJS, Prof D. Banerjea, Head, School of Criminal Justice and Administration, NUJS and Prof V. Nagaraj for their valuable suggestions during my research study.

I am highly indebted to Judge N. Konar, Sr. Reasearch Fellow, SCJA, Judge Deepak.Kr Chatterjee, Research Fellow, SCJA, Mr. Bimal Chandra Biswas, Member Secretary, State Legal Services Authority West Bengal, Mr A. C. Joshi, Project officer (Programme & Publication) Gujarat Legal Services Authority, Justice Samaresh Banerjea, Chairman, State Legal Services Authority, Justice Dilip Kr. Basu, Chairman, LASWEB, Justice Malay Sengupta, Mr Mumtaj Ahmed Khan, Member Secretary, District Legal Services Authority, Alipore for their encouraging and valuable guidance and support.

I am also grateful to Amanullah Khan, Ms. Bindu Ronald, Ms. Sudarsana Sarkar, Mrs. Keya Ghosh, Advocate for their co-operation and encouragement.

I also thank Meena Di, Anirban Da, Joy Da, Shiju, Ram Mohan, Ajay, Partha and my friends Lovely Das Gupta, Ali Imam Siddiqui, Abdul Rashid and Anirban Chakraborty for their moral encouragement.

I am also thankful to the Librarians and to the staff of various libraries,, particularly, Mr Sanjib Lodh, Librarian of NUJS library along with the other staff, NLSIU library, National Library for their assistance rendered during my study.

I, express my immense gratitude to the learned authors whose works I have consulted and referred to many occasions.

I shall be failing in my duties in case I fail to express my thank to my wife, Reshama Khan, for the patience and forbearance exhibited by her during the completion of my study and sparing me the time which otherwise belongs to her. I must express my thank to Waqar, my son, Ejaz, Faiyaz, Imran, Nusrat, Rifat, Tarannum, my brothers and sisters, Md Jafiruddin, my cousin, for their moral support.

Over and above all, I owe, more than I could express, my immense gratitude towards my parents, Md Seraz Khan & Israt Bano, for their blessings, love, affection, inspiration, patience, moral and financial support.

NUJS **Sarfaraz Ahmed Khan**

Contents

Chapter 3
Emergence of Lok Adalat as an Effective ADR Mechanism

Chapter 4
Constitutional Directives for Lok-Adalat

Chapter 5
Legislative Mechanism for Lok-Adalat vis-a-vis scheme of Legal Services Authorities Act

Chapter 6
Role of Judiciary in strengthening Lok-Adalat

Chapter 7
Lok-Adalat in India: Study of the overall performance of the institution

Chapter 8
Study of the functioning of Lok-Adalat in West Bengal

List of Cases

LIST OF TABLES

List of Graphs

ABBREVIATIONS

AIR	All India Reporter.
CILAS	Committee for Implementation of Legal Aid Scheme
C.P.C	Code of Civil Procedure
Cr. P. C	Code of Criminal Procedure.
Crl Cases	Criminal Cases
DLSA	District Legal Services Authority
ed	Edition
HLR	Harvard Law Review
i.e	id est; that is
ibid	Ibidem.
Id.	Idem.
I.P.C	Indian Penal Code.
J.	Justice.
JILI	Journal of Indian Law Institute
Mat Suit	Matrimonial Suit
Misc	Miscellaneous
Misc App	Misc. Appeal
MACC	Motor Accident Compensation Claim
MACT	Motor Acident Claims Tribunal
No	Number
NGO	Non-Governmental Organisation
P.,PP	Page, Pages
Rs	Rupees
SC	Supreme Court
SCC	Supremem Court Cases
SLSA	State Legal Services Authority
U/S	Under Section
Viz	videlicet; namely
Vol	Volumne
V., Vs	Verus; Against

INTRODUCTION

LOK-ADALAT: AN EFFECTIVE ALTERNATIVE DISPUTE RESOLUTION MECHANISM STUDY OF THE FUNCTIONING OF THE INSTITUTION IN WEST BENGAL

The institution of Lok-Adalat has evolved as one of the alternative tools for dispute resolution. In the recent times Lok-Adalat has grown well as an Alternative Dispute Resolution Mechanism. It is steadily gaining popularity from last two decades, since its introduction in the present form in 1982 in village Una, under the district Junagarh, Gujarat. The seed, which was sown in early 80's, has now grown into a huge tree. Though this institution of Lok-Adalat, which is in vogue presently, is two decades old but the concept and process is entirely indigenous. This institution has been developed by the people themselves for providing equitable justice speedily and cost effectively. It is a system of dispensation of justice, which has come into existence to grapple with the problems of providing cheap and speedy justice to the people with a friendly spirit. This form of remedy is contrived for enabling the common people to ventilate their grievances against the state agencies or against other citizens and to seek an amicable settlement, if possible. It is based on morality and honesty, the real pillars of our traditional society.

Some people equate Lok-Adalat to conciliation or negotiation; yet others compare it with mediation and even arbitration. Those who find it different from all these call it "People's Court". The expression 'Lok-Adalat' literarily means "People's Court"; as the term, 'Lok' means 'People' and 'Adalat' means 'Court'. Thus, it can be understood as Court involving people, directly or indirectly, affected by the disputes or grievances and the people involve for remedying the grievances of such people. Though people equate it with Court but it hardly has any thing in common with the law Court with adjudicative proceedings except both are tools for resolution of grievances, and delivering of justice. While the former Court system deliver justice at its fixed place in the Court with specified hierarchy, where litigant with the utilisation of service of the lawyers and by exposition of documents and witnesses, verbatim expression tries to seek justice, the latter tries to provide justice at the people's place with the flexibility in the process by ways of amicable settlement. The system of Lok-Adalat is certainly different from the adjudication process. Participation, accommodation, fairness, speed, transparency, practically no cost, voluntariness, good neighbourliness, lack of rancour and ill will between the parties, and efficiency are all the distinctive features of this unique Indian institution rooted in Indian history and culture[1]. Lok-Adalat is a kind of institution provided by the people themselves or interested parties including social workers, legal aiders and public-spirited people belonging to every walk of life. Indeed a silent revolution is underway to set in motion an alternative style of dispute settlement in which lawyers will play a secondary role to social activists and opinion leaders.

Lok-Adalat is not a new concept in our country and evolution of this system can be traced back to Vedic times. For centuries, in private disputes in many parts of India's five hundred thousand villages, with some variation, "people's court" continued to exist imparting justice to millions of poor who had no access to formal

Courts. We find a reference of this system in the ancient classics of Kautilya, Gautama, Brihaspati and Yagnavalkya. The 'Lok-Adalat' or "People's Court" were functioning in those days by name of Kula Court, Sreni Court and Gana Court. Whatever may be the nomenclature of the system, the concept had been and continues to be substantially one and the same[2]. The Ancient Indian jurisprudence as well as the Islamic jurisprudence provides guidance for this form of alternative dispute resolution mechanism. The Lok-Adalat with different nomenclature effectively functioned through centuries and continued to exist even during Mughal regime. However, things changed with the advent of British regime and the similar institution to Lok-Adalat had eclipsed. The adversarial mode of dispute resolution mechanism replaced the ancient form of dispute resolution mechanism to a great extent. However, institutions similar to the Lok-Adalat were functioning effectively in some forms or other in almost all countryside villages in India.

The ill effect of the British mode of administration of Justice was the unmanageable docket of cases and alienation of large number of masses of the country from administration of justice because of its foreign origin, technicality, extreme formalism and rigid rules of procedures. The adversarial mode of dispute resolution mechanism failed to provide effective justice to the countryside people. The British administrators attempted to decentralize the administration of justice to give certain powers at village level and at the same time, they provided alternative means for resolution of commercial disputes. Nevertheless, such attempts did not change the situation. Even the independence of the country brings many new things for the people but it failed to provide access to justice to the majority of masses. The 'Made in England' administration of justice prevailing round the country, aggravated the situation further. The thrust was then on alternative means like Arbitration and Conciliation. However, such alternative means of resolution of disputes were utilised in some kinds of disputes but the benefit accrued out of such mechanism was unavailable to the millions of citizens in the country. Thus, on the one hand the adversarial mode of disputes resolution failed to provide access to justice to the village people, on the other hand the alternative mechanism failed to fulfil the hopes and aspirations of a large number of citizens.

The situation was aggravated to such an extent that several legal functionaries as well as the Law Commission observed that the administration of justice system is on the verge of collapse. It is acknowledged by the Law Commission that people are utilizing the services of the 'Underworld' in order to redress their grievances. The Adversarial system of administration of justice on the one hand failed to fulfil the Constitutional goal of access to justice and equal justice to all because of the docket of cases and on the other hand it becomes inaccessible because of the exorbitant cost of the proceedings, as prevailing in the country. The need was felt for revival of indigenous justice administration system. Three different Committees were constituted to provide ways for fulfilment of the Constitutional goal of access to justice to all. The report of those three Committees, namely the Report on Processual Justice To The People' 1973, The Report Of the Gujarat Legal Aid Committee' 1977 and The Judicare: Equal Justice Social Justice Report' 1977 laid the stones for the noble institution of Lok-Adalat. In order to implement the reports of the Committees and several Law Commission reports, the Committee for Implementation of Legal Aid Scheme was constituted under the chairmanship of Justice Bhagwati to evolve appropriate structure and procedure with a view to achieve easy access to justice and equal justice to all.

The first goal of providing cheap and speedy justice was achieved under the auspices of the Committee for Implementation of Legal Aid Scheme (CILAS) when the first Lok-Adalat was held in Gujarat in 1982. This noble institution is growing day by day since its birth and in the last two decades, it is providing access to justice to large number of people. Millions of cases were settled by utilizing the mechanism of Lok-Adalat. Though, the institution of Lok-Adalat initiated as legal aid strategy but the spirit behind the institution is to provide inexpensive and speedy justice to the masses. It revolves round the principle of creating awareness amongst the disputants to the effect that their welfare really, lies in arriving at an immediate and peaceful settlement of their disputes. The Judges of the Lok-Adalat make them realise their interest and well being in settlement of disputes instead of waiting for years in adversarial mechanism in which the ultimate outcome of the dispute is achieved after hierarchy of appeals. Thus the settlement not only bring the parties together and make both the parties winners but also cut litigation cost and time, which otherwise ought be borne by the parties concerned.

This supplementary means of dispute resolution mechanism effectively provides justice to millions of people of the country. The institution functioned effectively for more than a decade without any explicit legislative provision. Though Legal Services Authorities Act was passed in the year 1987 but it was enforced in the year 1995. The institution got further impetus by the judiciary. Judiciary acted as a watchdog for the institution. Judiciary even acted, as a policy maker for the institution. The Legal Services Authorities Amendment Act' 2002 is nothing but implementation of the judicial verdict[3]. The institution of Lok-Adalat has been grown with the constant efforts of Bar, Bench, Legislature, Social Activist, NGO's and a large portion of the masses. Their joint efforts made the institution an effective alternative means for disputes resolution.

The high magnitude of its performance can be highlighted from the fact that more than 97 million cases were settled upto the end of 1999 and more than Rs. 2306 crores awarded as compensation through out the country by this noble institution of Lok-Adalat[4]. Most of all States effectively utilized this alternative mode of dispute resolution. However, the performance of this institution is not similar in all the states. While some States have performed extremely well since the formation of the institution of Lok-Adalat, in some states the institution faded within the decade of its introduction. In the state of West Bengal it was introduced much later than the several other States. Until 1998, a little improvement has been seen in the functioning of the institution. A boom in the functioning of the institution has been registered in the year 1999 when the institution achieved a ten times increase in settlement of disputes. However, in recent times it has been seen that the number of settlements decreased in the State of West Bengal.

Keeping in mind the importance of the Lok-Adalat and the potentiality of this noble institution for dispensation of cost effective and time effective Justice, the researcher endeavour to find out the followings.

1. To assess the indigenous dispute resolution system and effectiveness of the Panchayat Justice during Ancient India and Medieval India and the genesis of Lok-Adalat, which we found in traditional Panchayat systems.
2. To find out the reasons for the gradual downfall of the ancient indigenous system of administration of justice during the British regime vis-a-vis the effect of the British system of administration of justice on the traditional People's Courts.
3. To understand the causes for exploring alternatives to adjudication by legal fraternity during post independence period and the out come of such search.
4. To find out the effectiveness of such alternatives dispute resolution mechanism during post independence period.
5. To find out the reasons and objectives behind the emergence of the institution of Lok-Adalat during 80's.
6. To find out the basic nature and characteristics of the institution of Lok-Adalat and the modalities of its functioning as well as the process of providing cheap and speedy justice to a large number of people.
7. To find out whether the institution of Lok-Adalat is a compromise on the part of the poor because superior quality justice in form of adjudicative proceeding is inaccessible to them.
8. To find out the legal instrumentalities for effective functioning of the institution of Lok-Adalat.
9. To find out whether the institution of Lok-Adalat has been evolved as an instrument to fulfil the constitutional obligation of providing equal justice to all.
10. To find out the effectiveness of the legislative mechanism for the institution of Lok-Adalat and if any changes required in the statute for making the institution more effective.
11. To find out the role of judiciary in strengthening the institution of Lok-Adalat.
12. To assess the benefit derived from the institution in the State of West Bengal by analysing the functioning of the institution in the State at High Court level as well as District and Taluk level.

13. To find out the reasons for effectiveness of the institution in certain category of cases and whether the institution of Lok-Adalat is a proper forum for only one or two category of cases.

14. To find out the role of Advocates, judges, para-lawyers, NGO's, social workers and the members of the different authorities and committees in making the institution a great success.

15. To gather the views of the people associated with the institution of Lok-Adalat as well as disputants about the functioning of the institution of the State of West Bengal.

16. To find out how far the institution of Lok-Adalat influenced at the sub-divisional levels and how far the institution of Lok-Adalat was effectively able to provide cheap and speedy justice to the masses.

17. To suggest ways and means to make the institution of Lok-Adalat more effective across the Country in general and West Bengal in particular, so that the access to justice become meaningful to the citizen of the Country.

REFERENCES

1. N.R. Madhava Menon, *Lok-Adalat: Indian contribution to world jurisprudence,* Nyaya Path, Souvenir, 56 (2000)
2. Justice P.S. Narayana, *Law Relating To Lok-Adalat,* 1, (2002)
3. *Abdul Hassan Delhi. Vidyut Board and others,* AIR 1999 Del 88.
4. *See the date published in,* Nyaya Path, Jan-Mar, 36, (2000)

CHAPTER 1

Panchayat System and Settlement Mechanism: A Path Provider for Lok-Adalat

INTRODUCTION

Administration of justice by people's Court is concomitant with people's participation in India and is as old as the village itself[1]. It is an old and long tradition in India of the encouragement of dispute resolution outside the formal legal system. Disputes ere quite obviously decided by the intervention of the elders or assemblies of learned men and other such bodies[2]. Such form of dispute resolution; Nyaya Panchayats, at grass root level were there even before teh advent of British System of Justice[3]. Their foundation in India seems to have been embedded in the Indian culture and civilization[4]. The system of Administration of Justice like Lok-Adalt, which we call today as Alternative System for Administration of Justice was traditionally the main system for justice administration.

ANCIENT PERIOD

The beginning of administration of Justice through popular Courst goes back to Vedic age. People's Courts or Popular Courts were for the first time mentioned in the Yajnavalkya Smriti[5]. According to scheme of the Manu as adlopted by Yajnavalkya, Brihaspati and Katyayan, the Sabha system formed the basis for forming and grading Courts. A headman was appointed over each village consisting of 10, 20, 100 and 1000 respectively. These Courts were known as popular Courts and terms such as the Kula, Sreni, and Gana Courts. They were within the easy reach of the masses. The idea behind these was to enable each and every person to receive proper justice without delay. The relationship between the King's Court and Popular Courts was well defined. Brihaspati states that Sabha occupied higher position than that of the Kulas, and the Adhyakshas were above the Sabhas and the King was above all[6].

The following Popular Courts were present in the ancient India.

Gana

Sreni and

Kula

Gana

The word 'PUGA' or 'GANA' appears to have denoted the local corporations of towns and villages during post Vedic period. In that period villagers had their own judicial system as observed by Lee in the following words, "The royal system did not harmonize with the spirit of the day. The villagers had a judicial system of their own at once familiar to and respected by them, the various traders and guilds had a similar system. The presiding officer of the popular courts or guild courts had office either by election or inheritance according to local custom. With him were associated three or five men. These apparently private courts settled the affairs of every day life. In the case of grave crimes or when the condemned party refused to obey the judgment of the local courts, the Court of the King was concerned with litigation[7]".

According to Altekar 'Puga Court', consist of members belonging to different caste and profession but staying in the same village or town. If the Sabha or village assembly of Vedic period was occasionally settling disputes, the Sabha Court would be the earlier prototype of the Puga Court[8]. The Puga Court or Gana Court were well known to the King and were empowered to decide the disputes of Civil and Criminal cases except Sahasa[9]. These Courts enjoyed appellate jurisdiction of the other two Courts namely Sreni Court and Kula Court.

Thus through out the ancient period, the Puga or Gana Courts, played a prominent role in resolving disputes with people participatory mechanism and so the administration of justice during such period were participatory forms of administration of justice.

Sreni

The Sreni form of Lok-Adatat was represented by companies, traders, or artisans of persons belonging to different tribes, but subsisting by the practice of the same profession[10]. These appeared to be the Courts of disciplinary bodies of different professions. The term Sreni was used to denote the Courts of Guilds, which became a prominent feature of the commercial life in ancient India. The Mahabharata reveals that these Courts were vested with the powers to decide matters relating to their special callings or trade[11]. The Dharamshastra and Nitishastra show to us that the Sreni Courts had jurisdiction to resolve disputes among their members. The Srenis had their own executive committees of four or five members and it was likely that these committees functioned as the Sreni Courts when the effort at the family arbitration failed[12]. According to Altekar, the Sreni Courts were the Courts of Guilds and became a prominent feature of commercial life in ancient India from 500 BC. These forms of Lok-Adalats continued to function down the eighteenth century and remained in existence through the length and breadth of India[13]. The powers vested with the Sreni Courts were to decide civil and criminal cases except those involving trial for an offence committed with violence[14]. However, they did not have authority to execute sentences of fines and corporal punishment, for which the matter had to go to the king, who alone could execute the sentences, if met with his approval[15]. The Courts of Sreni were appellate Courts and appeal from Kula Courts lay before these Courts.

Kula

The Kula Courts were mainly confined to personal and family laws and customs. Kula was meeting of persons collectively related by blood as of a family or tribe or even related distantly by marriage[16]. Kula was the lowest Court and it was the Court of informal body of family elders. Kulani has been interpreted as the officer who presided over the group of eight or ten villagers and received land grant proportional to one family[17].

Kula Courts were vested with the powers to discharge judicial functions and were considered to be the lowest popular Court in the entire strata of local Courts[18]. It was an arbitral tribunal of people or Lok-Adalat of today. The idea behind this Court was that the administration of justice was not the sole concern of the king alone but the people also shared the burden of the State in the administration of justice[19].

Hence, the Kula Court was the informal body of family elders taking cognisance of quarrel arising in the family. The popular elements with regard to the procedure of local Courts or Lok-Adalat was that the cultivators, artisans, trade guilds, artists, money lenders, religious mendicants and even robbers were empowered to resolve their disputes according to the rules of their own profession. Similarly, families, craft guilds and local assemblies were authorized by the king to dispose lawsuits among their members except some offence like violence[20].

Thus an effective form of people participatory dispute resolution mechanism, which we call Lok-Adalat today, was prevailing throughout the length and breadth of India. Such institutions had their specified hierarchy in functioning. The Kula Court was the lowest court and appeal from the Kula Courts lay before Sreni Court. The Gana or Puga Courts were higher Courts of Sreni and any appeal from Sreni Courts lay before such Gana Courts.

PRE-BRITISH PERIOD VIS-A-VIS MEDIEVAL PERIOD

The popular Court or in modern terms Lok-Adalat remained a distinct institution even during the Muslim rule in India. Such people participatory forum for disputants to resolve their dispute was effectively functioning throughout history until the advent of British. The unique characteristic of Mughal Administration in India was that it did not concern nearly three fourth of the total population because people of the rural areas had their own Courts which enjoyed civil and criminal jurisdiction[21]. A systematic classification and the gradation of the Courts were prevalent viz:

(i) Central Court or Royal Court at the highest level,

(ii) The Provincial Court at the State level or Province level,

(iii) District Court at the District level,

(iv) Pargana Court at Taluka level and

(v) lastly the Village Court at village level.

The result of such non-penetration of Muslim Rulers into the countryside was that the textual laws influenced but did not displace the local taws. The disputes in the villages and even in cities were not settled by Royal Court, but by the Lok-Adalat or Popular Court of the caste within which the dispute arose, or of guilds or associations of traders and artisans[22]. These tribunals were empowered to adjudicate in accordance with the custom and usage of locality, caste, trade or family[23].

According to Jadunath Sarkar, the Indian villagers had to settle their differences locally by appeal to the caste Court or the arbitration of an impartial umpire (Salis)[24]. The people's courts were vested with the power to dealt with both civil and criminal cases. The local courts enjoyed the power to decide local disputes and acted as an effective instrument for administration of justice, both civil and criminal. It is revealed that people were satisfied by the decision of the popular courts and relieved the government largely of its judicial functions[25]. It appears that the process of getting justice under the Mughals was not such a long drawn-out agony as it is at present. The decisions were quick. The lengthy and elaborate process through which a litigant had necessarily to pass was discouraged. There was no tedious brief of cases, no methodised form, and no harangues to keep the parties longer in suspense. The speedy decision of cases and the absence of long and intricate legal proceedings were admired by the rulers[26].

The decisions of the Panchayats or the Peoples Courts, on which today's Lok Adalat is based, were almost invariably unanimous and the punishments inflicted were fines, public degradation, or reprimands or ex-communication. No sentence of punishment of death was awarded, because there was no proper authority to execute these sentences, and because there was no jail in the villages. The fear of public opinion was one of the most potent factors responsible for the prevention of crimes and hardly anyone could go out of the boundaries of the village. Normally, cases involving even murders were settled locally. The law administered by the Panchayats or Peoples Court was usually caste and tribal usages and the customary law of the land[27].

One of the reasons for effective functioning of mediation or conciliation proceeding during the Mughal periods might be the guidelines of the Holy Quran, which prefer amicable settlement instead of adversarial system of disputes resolution. The Holy Quran on several occasion prescribed for amicable settlements. In family dispute, the Holy Quran mandate for appointment of mediator in order to bring compromise among the disputants. Directives for family disputes consist in following Arabic words of the Quran.

"WA IN KHIFTUM SHEQUAQA BAINEHEMA FAB ASHU

HAKAMUM NUN AHLEHI WA HAKAMAN MIN AHLEHA AIN

UREDA ESLAHAIN UOWAFIKIL LAHO BAILAHOMA"[28]

"And if you have apprehension of disbanding of husband and wife relationship, you appoint one mediator from the relatives of husband and one mediator from the relatives of wife. If they are eager to resolve the dispute, God will open the ways for resolution of dispute among them"

The Holy Quran instructed in this Ayat to appoint mediator so the family can be safe from dissolution and the dispute can be resolved within the boundary of family. Even the Court can refer the dispute for mediation so far as the family matter is concerned[29]. Though there are differences, of opinion between the Muslim legal scholars about the powers of the mediator/arbitrator as to whether they can pass an order but there are no differences of opinion about the appointment of mediator or arbitrator in family disputes[30].

Thus, the Panchayat system or the popular court/village court system was effectively functioning during the Muslim Rule. The people courts or village courts were resolving disputes through the people oriented dispute resolution mechanism.

PRE-INDEPENDENCE PERIOD VIS-A-VIS BRITISH REGIME

The people oriented dispute resolution, which was in existence since long, started eroding at grass root level due to the advent of British regime. Justice D. A. Desai highlighted the reason for induction of the alien system in India, and said[31], "Let it not be forgotten that for Pax-Britannica the colonial masters inducted in India by and large, the judicial system in vogue in their country. One does not build up an empire for some altruistic purpose. If charity begins at one's home, empire begins at the home of other people. Among various motivations, the one central to the empire building is economic exploitation, this economic exploitation necessitates internal peace and external security. Internal peace may be guaranteed by first maintaining the foreign military, loyal police and legal justice system which would keep the parties continuously litigating in the law courts with hierarchy of appeal so that the Indian illiterate, the victim of injustice struggles through labyrinths of Courts and loses all initiatives for settling the disputes".

However, the system of administration of justice was different during the initial British Period. In the beginning, they delegated the magisterial function to the native people for the reasons that the Britishers were unaware of the local language and the local laws. Nevertheless, after the reorganization of Courts in 1861, Justice was administered at higher level by judges trained in Common Law. The result of induction of British Judge in Indian judicial system shaped the entire working of the local courts. The people's court thus entered into an era of lessening importance, until, it went into eclipse, as a result of British Policy of feudalistic control of the countryside[32].

Gradually, the adjudicatory process became more and more formal with the introduction of Anglo-Saxon jurisprudence and when India came to be a part of British empire under the direct suzerainty of the Crown, a full fledged adjudicatory set up came into being. The result was the induction of technicalities in the process, which made it extremely difficult for the people to have access to justice without trained people in such technicalities. In effect worst sufferers were the poor people. On the effect of British system of Administration of Justice, Justice Bhagwati said, "*The British system of administration of justice in our country has not been an unmixed good.... it has also, at the lowest level, alienated the people from the system because foreign origin. technicality, extreme formalism, rigid rules of procedure and relevance and foreign language. It has, at village level, and even at the level of taluka towns, remained as alien system which has no living contact with the masses and is not meaningful to them*[33]".

The immediate effect of British system of administration of justice was dual in nature. First, it detaches the large number of masses from administration of justice that were traditionally followed. Secondly, it created a class of people called legal professionals who were experts in the technicalities as developed simultaneously in British system of administration of Justice. On such institution of legal profession Law Commission said, "When the British rulers by gradual doses introduced the institution of British justice in India, simultaneously the institution of Legal profession came along with it. Came the Barristers and Solicitors also. The form and organisation in which the institution of legal profession exists today has no relevance or connection with the period of Indian History prior to the advent of British rule in India[34]". The net effect was that the poor man found it difficult to enter into the portals of the Courts and the rich man was able to use the legal process as an instrument to harass his poor adversary[35]. Moreover, it became time consuming and the cost of litigation and lawyer's fees rose sharply making access to justice even more difficult[36]. The cost of litigation and process was not the problem in India only but was also existent in England. Lord Devlin, speaking about the legal methods in England, made a cryptic observation:[37]

"If our business methods were antiquated as our legal method, we should be a bankrupt country. There is a need for a comprehensive inquiry into the roots of our procedure, backed by a determination to adapt to fit the conditions of a welfare state".

However, it is not true that British rulers did not realize the effect of their alien justice administration system. They even tried to revive the functioning of people's court in the early 19th Country. To this end among several Commissions appointed by them, one Commission was The Royal Commission upon decentralization. The Royal Commission[38] recommended for formation of village organisations. It says:[39] *'It is most desirable to constitute and develop village Panchayats for the administration of certain local affairs within the villages. The system must, however be gradually and cautiously worked. The headman of the village, where one is recognized, should be ex-officio chairman of the Panchayat, other members should be obtained by a system of informed election by the villagers.... The function of Panchayats must be largely determined by local circumstances and experience'.* Relating to power of such Panchayats in relation to settlement cases, the Commission suggested that the Panchayat should have summary jurisdiction in petty civil and criminal cases[40]. Before the function of this Committee, two attempts were made by the Britishers to form Village Panchayat. In 1870, the Chowkidar Panchayat was introduced but it was only relating to village watch. Again, in 1885, The Bengal Local Self Government Act was passed as a sequel to the famous Ripon Resolution of 1882[41]. However, the system was abolished shortly. One reason was the number of nominated and ex-officio members in the Panchayat were higher than the elected members, which made the Panchayat unparticipatory in true sense[42]. On the failure of establishing a Panchayati Raj Gandhi said[43];

'Panchayat is our old and beautiful work, which has got the sweetness of ancient way of life. Its real meaning is that people of villages used to elect five persons for the Panchayat and they used to administer the whole village but the British ruler had crushed it. In 1921 an effort was made to revive the old Panchayat but could not succeed and even now it is not implemented in an organised and beautiful manner and with scientific approach'.

Thus the impact of English language and western literature, the British system of justice and the universal rationality of western law have combined to induce an inbuilt prejudice for any thing ancient[44]. Our traditional participatory form of dispute resolution mechanism became disuse in Indian Society.

POST-INDEPENDENCE PERIOD

The independence of the country brought many new things for the people of India, but it failed to change the 'Made in England' administration of justice system. The unmanageable backlog of cases, mounting arrears of cases and inordinate delay in disposal of cases in Courts at all level, lowest to highest, coupled with exorbitant expenses has become the fate of the consumer of justice, even in independent India.

Gandhi showed concern on the dilatory and inaccessible form of justice saying,[45] *"India lives in her villages and most of the countryside is smeared with poverty and social squalor. Today the poor and disadvantaged are cut off from the legal system.... They have distrust and are suspicious of the law, the law courts and the lawyers for several reasons. There is an air of excessive formalism in law courts, which over-awes them and sometimes scam them. They are completely mystified by the Court proceedings and this to a large extent alienate them from the legal and judicial process. The result is that it has failed to inspire the confidence in the poor and they have little faith in its capacity to do justice".*

It was realized by the wise founding fathers of the Constitution that the Anglo-Saxon judicial system must be reorganized as to make legal relief easily accessible to our people even to villagers, which Mahatma Gandhi considered as true India. Though it was the concern of all to provide justice, which will be accessible to all and accordingly the Preamble of Constitution enshrine the aims to provide 'Justice; Social, Economic & Political' but the means to provide justice, which Mahatma Gandhi saw in Village Panchayat, was absent from the Constitution initially. On such absence of guidelines for formation of village Panchayat, Mahatma Gandhi said[46]; 'I must confess; that I have not been able to follow the proceedings of the Constituent Assembly... there is no mention or direction about village Panchayats and decentralization in the foreshadowed Constitution. It is certainly an omission calling for immediate attention, if our independence is to reflect the people's voice. The greater the power of the Panchayat, the better will be for the people'. However, in recognition of the significance and relevance of the village Panchayat, Art. 31A has been inserted in the Indian Constitution[47], which is now numbered as Art. 40 in our Constitution. The provisions mandate the State for organization of village Panchayat and to equip them with necessary powers. One of the reasons behind the directives was to revive and recognize our indigenous judicial system, to ensure people's participation in the administration of justice at the lowest level, which will ultimately help In delivery of justice to the poor, and the backward in rural areas without any delay and practically at no cost.

However, till now the legal fraternities are struggling for providing administration of justice in a manner as prescribed by National Charter. The question then arises; how can justice be provided to the people? What does justice mean to them? How can they access to justice? Does the entire justice system require changing or has any alternative method to evolve?

How will the villagers sitting in remote villages get justice? How the centralised system of administration of justice can be decentralised? How traditional system of administration of justice can revive? These are the numerous questions, which arose because of the failure of judicial system to provide justice. This prompted thinking in the Government of India that a judicial reform committee may set up to find out the ways. However, the task was assigned to the Law Commission. The term of reference included the setting up of a system of participatory justice and formation of Nyaya Panchayat[48]. Due to consciousness of the fact that the system is highly centralized, which contributed in making the system dysfunctional, the Law Commission tried to find out the ways for decentralization of the system of administration of justice[49].

Thus in independent India, when the British system of administration of justice failed to provide access to justice to all as per the guide lines and mandate enumerated in Indian Constitution, the search started for the alternative mechanism for administration of justice taking clue from our ancient heritage. A similar situation was also prevailing even in other developed Countries where people are marching towards alternative modes of dispute resolution. Among such alternative form of dispute resolution, some are Arbitration, Conciliation, Mediation, Med-Arb, and Lok-Adalat.

CONCLUSION

There is no debate so far that the People's Court, today's Lok-Adalat was in existence in our country from time immemorial. The system was effectively functioning and providing justice through village Courts or People's Courts, with variation of name, through out the history. The ancient periods as well as medieval period were the period of Lok-Adalat. However, the advent of British regime made all such people oriented and participatory forms of dispute resolution dysfunctional. Even in independent India, the system was not changed and legal fraternities are still searching ways for providing speedier justice. Law Commission in its several reports have suggested for the alternative systems for providing justice and to revive the traditional form of dispute resolution mechanism[50]. The Gandhian philosophy of Gram Swaraj is still a distant dream. We are still far behind the goal of providing justice to all.

Now with the aim of providing justice, the legal fraternity is marching towards the participatory form of dispute resolution. There are several such mechanisms, which are functioning all over the globe including Arbitration, Conciliation, Mediation and Med-Arb. In all these alternative systems of providing justice, some we have borrowed from others and some were in our ethos. However, in reality the Indian contribution to World jurisprudence of ADR is the system of Lok-Adalat[51]. This system of Lok-Adalat is established, taking clue from our traditional dispute resolution system.

Thus in reality, if we have to provide justice in true terms we should have to revive our traditional Panchayat system, may be with certain variations, otherwise the word justice will become meaningless for a large number of people in the Country.

REFERENCES

1. R.Sahai, *Panchayat Raj in India.* 95. (1968), P 12.

2. K. Jayachandra Reddy, *Alternative Dispute Resolution, In* P.C.Rao. *ADR: What it is and how it works, 79 (1997).*

3. K. Jayachandra Reddy, id. P 79.
4. M.N.Moorje, *Lok-Nyalaya: A place for common man in a changing society,* AIR 1984, Journal 68.
5. Sunil Deshta, *Lok-Adalat in India: Genesis and Functioning,* 12 (1995).
6. Birendra Nath, *Judicial Administration in Ancient India,* (1979), Pg 71.
7. M.K. Sharan, *Court Procedure in Ancient India,* 24-25, (1978). Quoted in Supra 5, P20
8. Supra 5, P 74.
9. The term 'Sahasa' means any grievance offences with violence, including Murder, See Justice M. Rama Jois, *Legal and Constitutional History of India,* 348 (2001).
10. id, P 490
11. Shraddhakar Supakar, *Law of Procedure and justice in Ancient India,* (1986), Pg 17. See also, Supra 5, P 16-22.
12. id
13. Dr A. S. Altekar, *State And The Government to Ancient India,* 252 (1979).
14. Justice M. Rama Jois, Supra 9, P 491
15. Supra 5. P 23
16. M. G. Chitkara, *Lok Adalat and Poor,* (1993), P 37, See also id.
17. P. V. Kane, *History of Dharmashastra,* 280 (1973), referred in Supra 15, P 23.
18. S.D.Sharma, *Administration of justice in ancient India,* 167(1988),
19. id pg 167.
20. Brindra Nath, *Judicial Administration in Ancient India,* 145 (1979).
21. R. C. Majumdar, *The History and Culture of Indian People: The Mughal Empire,* Vol.- VII, P549-550(1974).
22. Upendra Bakshi and Marc Gatanter, *Panchayat Justice : An Indian Experience in Legal Acces,* In M. Cappellitti (Ed), 344. Vol III (1979), see Supra 15 P 29.
23. id.
24. Sir Jadunath Sarkar, *Mughal Administration,* (1935). P-251
25. id.
26. Supra 15 P-33
27. R.C. Majumdar, *The History and Culture of Indian People: The Mughal Empire,* (1974), Vol. - VII, P-545, see also, A.L. Srivastava, *Akbar the Great,* P 279, Vol-II (1972) Supra 15, P 35.
28. Ayat 35, Al-Nisha 4, Para 5, Referred in Syed Abul Ala Moududi, *Tafhimul Quran,* vol-1, P 350.
29. It can be estabilished by the fact that Hazrat Usman (RA) appointed mediator/arbitrator in family disputes. Once a matter of Hazrat Aquil (s/o Abu Talib) and his wife Fatma (D/O Utba) appeared in the Court of Hazrat Usman (RA). He appointed Ibn Abbas as mediator/arbitrator from the family of the husband and Hazrat Mauia (S/O Abu Sufia) from the family of the wife. The Hajrat Usman (RA) empowered the arbitrator to decide the dispute. He also said that if the separation is better for them separate them. See Syed Abul Ate Moududi, Tafhimul Quran, vol.-1, P 350
30. The scholar belongs to Hanif School and Shafi school belief that the mediator or arbitrator do not have power to decide the dispute. They can only suggest the agreeable terms for resolution of deputes and it is on the paries to accept or not. However, If both the parties empowered the mediator or arbitrator to decide then they can pass their verdict and it is the duty of the parties to obey the order. Other scholar of separate school feels that the mediator or arbitrator have power to decide the dispute. In India most of the Muslim's follows the Hanif School. See Syed Abul Ala Moududi, Tathimul Quran, vol-1, P 350
31. Law Commission of India, *Alternative Forum For Resolution of Disputes at Grass-roots Level,* 114th (12-8-1986), P48.
32. R.C. Majumdar *An Advanced History of India: The Delhi Sultanate And The Mughal Empire,* (1977) P 553, See also, Supra 15, P 35.

33. Report of the Legal Aid Committee, (Govt of Gujarat) 1971 para 13.12, pg -209, Quoted in 114th LCI Report, P48, Para 1.4
34. Law Commision of India, the rate of legal profession to strengthening the system of administration of justice, 131st Report, P 11 Para 1.4.
35. Legal Aid News letter. Vol X (Part 1 & 11) May- August 1990 P-14, See also Sunil Deshta, Supra 15, P-36.
36. Justice A.M. Ahmed, *'Access to justice in India'* Legal Aid News Letter, vol XI, page 4, January- March 1992 P -17.
37. 131st Law Commission Report P-4 Para 1.16.
38. The Royal Commission upon decentralization in India was appointed by warrant of the King and Emperor Edward VII under the Royal Sign Manual on 7th September' 1907, under the chairmanship of Mr. C.E.H. Hobhouee. See, M. Anees Chisti, Committees and Commission in pre-Independent India, (2001), Mittal Publication
39. M. Anees Chisti, Committees and Commission in pre-independent India Volume 4, P 79, (2001), Mittal Publication.
40. id
41. Swapan Kr. Pramanik & Prabhat Datta, Panchayat and people- The West Bangal Experience, 1(1994),
42. At the close of 1891-92 of the total 790 member in 38 district of Bengal, 168 were exofficio members, 313 were nominated and 309 were elected by local Boards. In the local Boards of the total 1248 members, 40 were ex-officio member, 730 members nominated by the Govt. and other 469 were elected. See id
43. H.M.Vyas, M.K. Gandhi, Village Swaraj, P 6-8, Navjivan Publishing House, Ahmedabad, see alslo Janardhan Pandey, Gandhi & Panchayat Raj, In Anil Dutta Mishra & Madhev Shivappa Dadage, Panchatey Raj-Gandhian Perspective, P-59, (2002)
44. 114th LCI Report, Supra 39, P16, Para-5.8.
45. Mahatma Gandhi, quoted in Judicare: Equal justice - Social justice report, (1977) P-32, see also Sunil Deshta, Supra 15, P-37
46. Harijan, 21.12.1947, P- 473, see also G. Veerraju, Panchayati Raj-A Gandhian Perspective. In, Anil Dutta Mishra, Mahadav Shivappa Dadaye, Panchayati Raj - Gandhian perspective, 106 (2202), Mittal Publication.
47. "that after Art. 31, the following new articles be added (31 A- The State shall take steps to organize village Panchayats and endow them with such powers and authority as may be necessary to enable tham to function as units of self-govenment See Jay Prakash Narayan, *Panchyat Raj*: as *the basis of India policy,* P-12, see also ibid Pg-106.
48. Law Commission of India, Urban Litigation: Mediation As Alternative to Adjudication, P 1, 129th Report. The terms of Reference was,

    "1. The need for decentralzation of the system of administration of Justice by,

    (i) establishing, extending and strengthening in rural areas the institution of Nyaya Panchayats or other mechanisms for resolving disputes;

    (ii) Setting up of a system of participatory justice with defined Jurisdiction and powers in suitable areas and Centres;

    (ii) Establishing other tiers or systems within the Judicial hierarchy to reduce the volume of work in the Supreme Court and High Courts. 57
49. 129th law commission report on Urban Litigation, Pg-1.
50. See 14th Law Commission Report 114 Law Commission Report on Nyaya-Panchayat, 124th Law Commission Report on The High Court Arrears: A fresh look, 129th Report on Urban litigation, 131st Report. The Role of legal profession in strengthening the system of Administration of Justice.

51 N.R. Madhav Menon, Lok-Adalat: An Indian Contribution to world Jurisprudence, 56, Nyaya-Path. Souvenir (2000).

CHAPTER 2

Emerging Trend of Dispute Resolution: ADR

INTRODUCTION

It is now widely acknowledged that our litigation system requires drastic spring-cleaning. This is not to minimize the role of our Court but to supplement the functioning of the Courts with different alternative means. Generally speaking, except litigants who stand to gain by delaying the process of justice, others do not perhaps enjoy taking recourse to litigation that consume innumerable number of years and considerable amounts by way of expenses. This is true in all types of cases. There is always a great rush for interim order of Courts. Not many in India can afford litigation. This state of affairs makes people cynical about the judicial process, often subjecting it to ridicule. Where do we go from here[1]?

The inappropriateness of the inherited judicial system and its alienation from the common people coupled with the apparently intractable problem of delay and arrears compelled the legal fraternity to look for alternatives to the formal Courts particularly to resolve the simple disputes of common folks[2]. The Law Commission in its several reports recommended for participatory justice system. The Commission's recommendation was for decentralization of administration of justice. Long back in 1958, the Minister for Law and Justice said[3]; '*There is no doubt the system of justice which obtains today is too expensive for the common man. The small dispute must necessarily be left to be decided by a system of Panchayat justice. Call it people's Court, call it popular Court, call it any thing - but it would certainly be subject to such safeguards as we may devise - the Common man can be assured of a system of judicial administration which would not be too expensive for him and which would not be too dilatory for him*'.

The non-participatory British model of administration of justice has certainly alienated the people from the system, because of its foreign origin, technicality, extreme formalism and rigid rules of procedure. The effect of the Anglo-Saxon jurisprudence was the rule and procedure oriented adversarial administration of justice. The adversarial system fails to provide justice quickly and effectively. Several conferences have been held in India, including a conference of Chief Minister of the various states and Chief Justice of the High Courts, to devise appropriate strategies for dealing with the exploding docket problem[4]. The backlog of cases reached at an alarming level, as some print media declared it to be 24 million. Referring this back log, Justice S. B. Sinha said; '*with an average time to settle each case being put at 20 years, We require 324 years to clear the legal backlog. Is it a cause for despair? Should we ignore this backlog and still adhere to traditional adjudicate process in the Civil Court[5]?* Some argues that the proportionate number of judges is much lower in India than other developed countries, which is the root cause of such problem[6]. However, it might have some effect but it cannot be the sole reason. Though USA has 107 judges per million-population compared to 10.5 judges per million in India, the similar situation is subsisting in their justice administration system[7].

Thus, such exploring docket of cases, inability of adversarial system to cope up with the problem, inability of Justice Administration system to provide equal justice to all raised several issues as; where do we go from here? How can we solve the problems? How can we cope with this alarming docket of cases? What other alternatives are available to us for providing Justice? What then is our choice? Finding alternatives was the concern of all members of the legal fraternity because in the end we have no other choice but to vigorously and quickly devise effective alternative option to litigation.

Therefore, such findings provide different alternative mechanisms namely arbitration, conciliation, mediation and several other hybrid processes. However, it is experienced that such alternative mechanism does not enable to fulfill the hope and aspiration of the people at large. The large number of masses unable to access such ADR institutions and the fruit of the institutions were available to few classes of people.

This chapter is divided into four parts. In Part 1, I have tried to find out the reasons for the emergence of different alternative disputes resolution mechanism. Whether, the docket of cases is the only reason for emergence of ADR mechanism or for some other forms of disputes, the ADR is the best forum for resolution.

In the second part, I have discussed the emergence of different alternative disputes resolution mechanisms and the different forms of ADR mechanism and their ways of functioning.

In the third part, different advantages of the Alternative Disputes Resolution have been discussed and in the last part, I have tried to find out the performance of such ADR mechanism in India.

NEED FOR ALTERNATIVE

In our applied adversarial system for adjudication of any grievances, the only mode of participation consists in the opportunity to present proofs and arguments. Hence, issues tried before adjudication tends to become claim of right or accusations of fault[8]. Thus in the adversarial system prevalent in the Courts, the Judge allows the opposing parties represented by Counsel to place, in the best manner possible, all relevant facts in the shape of evidence based on their legal pleas. From that manner of evidence brought before the Court by the parties opposing each other, the Judge tries to search the truth in order to come to a decision in accordance with law and to do justice in the case[9].

With the passage of time and decline of moral values in the Society, the adversarial system has degenerated into a sham or false trial where parties and their witnesses, even on oath, place false evidence before the judge. They attempts to suppress the truth, as distortion of facts and falsehood, which may many times suit their plans. The attempt of the parties in the adversarial system of trial is to win a case in their favour through the art and skill of lawyers engaged by them[10]. In the ideal adversarial system, the expectation from the parties that they would place truthfully all evidence and legal pleas available to them to render help to the judge, so that he might come to a just conclusion, is frustrated when the parties take oath and yet bring false evidences, distort the facts and suppress the weak points[11]. Thus the traditional adversarial system has degenerated due to fall of morality in the society. The judge is not equipped with correct facts to apply the law correctly and thus be able to do justice in the cause brought before him[12]. Thus, the main aim to discover facts for doing justice is frustrated.

The other problem lies in the technicalities, which made the justice system inaccessible to millions of masses. The corruption and high cost of the litigation in adversarial system made the system detached from 70% of country's population living in the rural areas. Once Justice M.G. Chitkara said on denial of accessibility of justice to poor people, 'In view of the corruption in Courts also the access to justice has become meaningless. The justice cannot be achieved by the poor who cannot afford to purchase it. For accessibility to Court, we have to keep the streams of justice pure and clean[13]'.

The problems with litigation are well recognized. Apart from injunctive procedures or other means of rapid relief available in special cases, litigation usually involves parties in delay, costs, distraction from day to day management affair and loss of control of the conduct of the case, once the case is handed over to the lawyer[14]. Quite apart from procedural defects of litigation process, there are certain substantive or jurisprudential questions, which arises as to whether adjudication is the proper forum for the resolution of all types of cases? Lon. L. Fuller argues that there are certain categories of cases, which are not proper to adjudicate[15]. In such cases when the task is assigned for adjudicative treatment, will it be possible to preserve the meaning of the affected party's participation through proof and arguments?[16]

The out come in the adversarial system are determined by the evidence and arguments put before the Court. The Court's duty is therefore not to decide on grounds, sense or improved business relationship, but purely on the basis of the evidence and argument put before it. Many disputes are not black and white in character, yet judges must tend towards such assessment on the balance of probabilities. In some cases, this 'balance' may be inclined one way by rather narrow aspects of the case or strict legal principles. It is therefore not surprising that many a litigant may feel aggrieved by 'losing'[17].

In addition to these apparent defects, the system also embodies a way of multiplying the cost, delay, uncertainty of the outcome, and potential for gamesmanship through the level of appeal, which may be available depending on the nature of the case. The Court system setup by British rulers has continued to be operative until today with minor modifications. The model is of a State Court, presided over by professionally trained lawyers who enter judicial service. This model is in vogue for over 150 years. This model has practically become dysfunctional. The system is in total disarray[18]. This system is not able to cope-up with ever-increasing burden of litigation. The problem is not of bad alone. The deficiency lies in the adversarial nature of judicial process, which is time consuming and procedure oriented. Thus, it is common thought that in bulk of cases Court action is not an appropriate recourse for seeking justice[19].

The Law Commission in its report said[20], "*The law Commission is guided by the fact that till now the present monolithic system of administration of justice offered the same model for resolution of disputes by the same prolix procedure even though the disputes arising in rural areas are comparatively simple in character compared to the disputes in urban areas. A very simple dispute arising in rural areas would have been dealt with by the judges of civil or the criminal Courts, as the case may be, in the same manner as the dispute would be dealt with in highly developed urban areas, with the consequence is that a simple dispute remains unresolved for years, may be decades, causing misery to the disputants, imposing an unbearable load on the system and rendering the system highly expensive'. Law Commission again observed that it is admitted on all hands that this monolithic approach requires to be largely abandoned and Law Commission recommended a participatory mode*[21].

The Law Commission in its several reports, suggested for alternative forum of dispute resolution[22]. The Commission's, alternative model envisages de-professionalisation of dispute settlement at the grass root level not only by associating lay people but also by invoking their sense of justice and fairplay. Appearance of parties through Lawyers is not prohibited though in the scheme of things, it may be unnecessary and impractical. Unnecessary because the adversary process is discounted and a simple summary procedure in the local language at the door step of the litigants recommended and, impractical because the venue of the Court is not to be urban centres where lawyers are settled and there is to be no adjournment or change of venue to accommodate lawyer[23].

Finding alternatives of the adjudication process became concern of all. While assigning work of judicial reform to the Law Commission, the Minister for Law and Justice informed[24], *'The problem of delays and arrears in trial and appellate Courts has, over the years, assumed serious proportions. The extent of pendency of cases in various Courts in the country is very high. Increase in the number of judges has not been able to halt the mounting arrears in the Courts. The recommendation made in past by various bodies, like Law Commission and the High Court Arrears Committee, have been found to be inadequate to effectively deal with the rigidities and dilatoriness of Court procedures. A fresh approach is necessary to examine to which extent decentralization and other changes in the constitution and functioning of the Courts should be brought about and what basic changes in structure and procedures should be devised to eliminate delay in the disposal of cases of all categories pending before all Courts'.*

Thus, the alternative disputes resolution mechanism emerges not only because the adversarial dispute resolution mechanisms fail to provide justice to a large number of masses but also because the adversarial system is not a proper mechanism for certain classes of cases, for which the ADR is the best mode for dispute resolution.

Hence, the terrible experience of the past and numerous issues concerning the forms for providing dispute resolution mechanism, had led to search for the alternatives. Accordingly, the search provided us with the mechanisms like arbitration, conciliation, mediation, ombudsman and several other forms of alternative dispute resolution. Of course, India is not the only country, which is buffeted by arrear of Court cases. Even the developed countries such as the United State of America and the United Kingdom suffer from such problems, albeit on a lesser scale. The USA and, following its inspiration, several countries, including Australia, Canada, Germany, Holland, Hong Kong, New Zealand, South Africa, Switzerland and United Kingdom have been using over the last 20 years or so, what is popularly known as "Alternative Dispute Resolution" (ADR) that encourage the disputants to arrive at a negotiated understanding with a minimum of outside help. The primary object of ADR movement is avoidance of vexation, expenses and delay and promotion of the ideal of 'access to justice' for all. In other word ADR system seeks to provide cheap simple, quick and accessible justice[25].

The ADR procedures consist of negotiation, conciliation, mediation, arbitration and an array of hybrid procedures, including mediation and last offer arbitration, mini trial, med-arb and neutral evaluation. In the countries like USA, several Federal and State judges have incorporated ADR techniques in their Courtroom practice and are calling upon litigants to utilize them. Legislation was also enacted to promote the use of ADR by State instrumentalities[26]. Recently a message was issued by the judges of the U.S. District Court (northern District of California) wherein the Court pledged to do everything it can to help parties to resolve their disputes as fairly, quickly and efficiently as possible. They urged the litigants to consider using an ADR process, which is faster, less expensive, more creative and better tailored to all parties[27]. However, professional mediators in USA came on the scene for collective bargaining disputes in a few sittings early in last century and more broadly in 1940s, but it took the shape of a broad based ADR movement in 1970s[28]. In 1980s in the USA the priorities based program was taken having following guidelines[29].

- To lower Court case loads and expenses
- To reduce the parties' expenses and time,
- To provide speedy settlement of those disputes which were disruptive of community or the lives of the party families.
- To improve the public's satisfaction with the justice system,
- To encourage resolutions those were suited to the parties' needs.
- To increase voluntary compliance with resolutions,
- To restore the influence of neighbourhood and community values and the cohesiveness of communities,
- To provide accessible forums to people with disputes, and
- To teach the public to try more effective processes than violence or litigation for settling disputes.

In USA and other developed countries, tremendous progress has been made concerning the use of ADR during the past three decades. At the midpoint of the twentieth century ADR was used primarily in specialized settings, such as labour disputes, but their use now extend to almost every sector of the society. In many places it is even required as a precondition for going to the Court. In India too the system of arbitration, which is one form of ADR, was used in the past but was concentrated on the specific category of cases, where financial transactions were involved, mainly between the Government and Jamindars, in the initial period[30]. Until 70s, the arbitration and conciliation were utilized in only commercial and labour disputes but subsequently the ambit was expanded. Before discussing the advantages and disadvantages, it is essential to discuss about ADR and its forms.

ALTERNATIVE DISPUTE RESOLUTION AND ITS FORM

ADR is an activist alternative to litigating justice through public co-operation, creative professional intervention and constructive involvement of officials concerned. The objective of ADR is to make justice quicker and less expensive, justice delivery system less cumbersome and easily accessible to the illiterate and indigent, and to check litigation explosion. The focus is to avoid feud and to harmonise the relationship between the disputing parties for an amicable settlement, out of Court, using mediation, conciliation, motivation and negotiation as dispute resolving techniques. The positive aspects of ADR are that it involves parties directly, and the parties themselves address their needs, it fosters joint problem solving, enables the parties to use their energy creatively, and establishes a frame work for developing options for finding solutions. ADR makes people responsible for their own decision rather than having decisions imposed upon them. As a result, the enmity or antagonism between or among the parties and bitterness within the parties get lessened considerably. The process and procedure for ADR are expeditious and are done with minimum cost and thus it saves time and money. ADR is informal and it enables accessibility of justice to everyone who is in need of it[31].

Alternative disputes Resolution is not intended to supplant altogether the adjudicatory process but it offers only alternative options to litigation. There are still a large number of cases of important areas, including criminal law, in respect of which there is no substitute for Court decisions. ADR may not be appropriate for every dispute even in other areas; even if appropriate it cannot be invoked unless both parties are genuinely interested in a settlement.

There are four basic forms of dispute resolutions including adjudication. If we exclude the adjudicating process then only three forms are functioning as alternative to the adjudicating process. These are (i) negotiation, (ii) mediation or conciliation and (iii) arbitration. However, different scholars count arbitration under the range of adjudicative processes[32]. There are other varieties of ADR processes, which are elements of these primary processes namely negotiation, mediation and adjudication including arbitration have combined in a number of ways and produces a rich variety of hybrid dispute resolution mechanisms. These processes are (i) Mini-Trial, (ii) Medola, (iii) Med-Arb (iv) Ombudsman and others, which are in vogue in different parts of the World.

Negotiation

Negotiation is the second most powerful method, besides unilateral action[33], for a party in terms of their control of process, subject only to constraint imposed by the other party. This is a common method that can be used more than any others, and with good cause. It is most flexible, informal, and party directed, closest to the parties circumstances and control, and can be geared to each party's own concerns[34]. It is a nonbinding process in which discussion between the parties is initiated without the intervention of any third party with the objective of arriving at a negotiated settlement. Although it is a non-binding process, the out come of the process in the form of mutually acceptable agreement can be enforced as contract.

Conciliation/Mediation

It is a non-binding procedure in which an impartial third party, the conciliator or mediator, assists the parties to a dispute in reaching a mutually satisfactory and agreed settlement of the dispute. The most critical aspect of dispute resolution is where the final decision making authority resides. In mediation, the decision always rests with the parties themselves. In other proceeding such as arbitration, the decision is made by the third party[35]. In mediation process, mediators, all operate differently, but one thing all mediators have in common is that they have learnt to listen to both sides to determine the true source of the dispute and the real stumbling blocks to settlements. While each mediator proceeds differently, most mediators start a session by discussing ground rules for the sessions[36]. In practice mediation functions in dual ways. Firstly as a facilitating mediator and secondly as evaluative mediator. In the process of facilitative mediation, the mediator facilitates the parties negotiating towards a settlement, and in evaluative mediation process, mediator assists the parties to settle their disputes by introducing a third party view of the merits of the case or of some of the issues between the parties[37].

The concept of mediation is not broadly recognized in the Indian Statutes except for the few references that exist[38]. However, conciliation got statutory recognition and settlement reached in the conciliation equates the decree of the Court[39] The process of mediation is also described as conciliation[40]. Some times both the processes can be issued interchangeably. Practically both have the same process as well as the same results.

The distinction between both the forms lies in the process leading to legal recommendation or to more active interventions in terms of making settlement proposals[41]. It was considered that mediation process is more informal than conciliation, and so mediator can play more active role than the conciliator. However, the formalities came into existence with the legal instrumentalities which accepted the forum and mediation is a new forum than conciliation; the formalities will also encroach these modalities as soon as legal instrumentalities begin to recognize fully their outcome. Thus, we proceed onward with the premise that both areas, if not same, are similar. In both processes control lies with parties concerned.

Arbitration

Arbitration has been the traditional private alternative to Court with parties contracting to be bound by a third party private award that is normally legally enforceable as a Court judgment[42]. The Arbitration & Conciliation Act 1996 includes both forms of arbitration whether administered by permanent arbitral institution or not[43]. Arbitration is the most successful dispute resolution mechanism in the Commercial World. Even in labour disputes, it was widely utilized. Disputants in the commercial world need resolution systems where they can get justice quickly because almost all cases involve huge financial transaction and resolution in decades is good for nothing. The voluntary nature of most binding arbitration enables the parties to stipulate the procedural rules and evidentiary rules used during arbitration[44] and the process for selecting the arbitrator[45]. Because the parties usually control the selection of arbitrator, they are able to choose someone with the expertise necessary to understand the dispute[46].

Arbitration proceedings are more informal than the pure adjudicative proceeding. In arbitration the rules of evidence applies flexibly. Binding arbitration offers several advantages when compared with court proceedings. It is generally speedier and more informal, and it usually avoids, the series of motions, hearings, extensive discovery and the protracted wait for a trial date that is typical in civil litigation. Parties also may agree that unlike trials, arbitration proceedings are confidential. Confidentiality may be an important incentive for a party concerned about adverse publicity, or disclosure of trade secrets involved in a dispute[47].

In England, over the years, however, the arbitration's reputation has suffered, mainly because it has become increasingly costly and proceedings have extended to as much as Court time tables. Also parties are not always as free to choose their arbitrator as they would wish, and often become upset on losing their case unjustifiably due to what they consider a poor quality arbitrator, as compared to the judicial standards[48]. In India, too, a similar situation persists. Supreme Court in several cases cautioned about the process of its functioning. In fact in one case, Supreme Court said[49], *"The way in which the proceeding under the Act conducted and without an exception challenged in Courts, has made lawyers laugh and legal philosophers weep. Experience shows and law reports bear ample testimony that the proceedings under the Act became highly technical accompanied by unending prolixity at every stage providing a legal trap to be unwary. Informal forum chosen by the parties for expeditious disposal of their case disputes has by the decision of the Courts have been clothed with leg-lese of unforeseeable complexity".*

Once the arbitration process started, very little control of the parties subsists in the process, unless both parties mutually agree during the parleys. The comparative Table 2.1 below will show the process and control of the parties on the three basic forms of ADR and Adjudication.

Table -2.1[50]
"Primary" Dispute Resolution Processes

Characteristic Voluntary/In-Voluntary	Adjudication Voluntary	Arbitration* Voluntary	Mediation Voluntary	Negotiation Voluntary
1	2	3	4	5
Binding/Non-binding	Binding: Subject to appeal	Binding, subject to review on limited grounds	If agreement, enforceable as contract	If agreement, enforceable as contract

1	2	3	4	5
Third Party	Imposed, third party neutral decision maker.	Party-selected third-party as Arbitrator to decide often specialized in subject concern.	Party-selected out-side facilitator called Mediator.	No third party facilitator.
Degree of formality	Formalised and highly structured by predetermined, rigid rules	Procedurally less formal, procedural rules and substantive law may be set by parties.	Usually Informal, unstructured	Usually informal, unstructured
Nature of proceeding	Opportunity for each party to present proofs and arguments.	Opportunity for each party to present proofs and arguments.	Unbounded presentation of evidence, arguments and interests	Unbounded presentation of evidence, arguments and interests
Outcome	Principled decision supported by reasoned opinion	Sometimes principled decision supported by reasoned opinion; sometimes compromise without opinion	Mutually acceptable agreement sought	Mutually acceptable agreement sought
Private/Public	Public	Private, unless judicial review sought	Private	Private

The ADR movement has spawned or revitalized a variety of hybrid processes. These hybrids are variants of the primary processes namely negotiation, mediation and adjudication which includes arbitration developed to resolve a dispute not amenable to the primary processes[51]. Some of these are as follows:

Mini-Trial

This is a non-binding procedure. The disputing parties present the summaries of their case in order to assess the strength, weakness, and prospects of their case. Then they get the opportunity to negotiate a settlement with the assistance of a neutral adviser[52]. This is a more formal type of mediation practice and associated clearly with an evaluative approach. The neutral adviser may give a view on the likely outcome if the case went to trial or arbitration in order to facilitate settlement.

In America, there is an organization for conducting such trials known as Centre for Public Resources and in U.K. The Centre for Dispute Resolution. In India too an organization has recently come into existence known as International Centre for Alternative Dispute Resolution[53].

Medola

It is a procedure wherein if the parties fail to reach agreement through mediation, a neutral person who may be the original mediator or an arbitrator will select between the final offer of parties, such selection being binding on all the parties. The process of medola, Mediation followed by last offer arbitration, as promoted by American Arbitration Association. According to them it is an exciting and innovative idea.

Med-Arb

It is a hybrid of Mediation and Arbitration. It is a procedure, which combines sequentially, conciliation/ mediation within a period of time agreed in advance by the parties to arbitration. A person may be appointed in such a procedure both to mediate, and if that is unsuccessful, then arbitrate a dispute. An arbitrator thus may use mediation initially and upon discovery of the strength and weakness of a party, he may sort out the differences. Upon failure of mediation he may act as an arbitrator.

Ombudsman

The Ombudsman system has evolved as a successful approach for the citizen or consumer complaints to protect Public Sector or Industry reputations and to provide quick redress to the aggrieved. The Ombudsman office is established as an independent agency to review and adjudicate on complaints. Usually fact-finding and adjudication are involved, and sometimes efforts made for mediation at the inquiry stage[54]. In the U.K. the Ombudsman has been established even when the administration is said to have maintained a high standard of integrity and impartiality. The Ombudsman therefore is regarded as the manifestation of the society's respect for rule of law, social justice, equality before law, and democratic ideate. In India too attempts were made to operate similar institutions by name of Lok-Pal and Lok-Ayukt but til now it has not materialized[55].

Now before discussing about the applicability of aforesaid form of dispute Resolution, we should look at a glance the different advantages of ADR.

ADVANTAGES OF ADR

There are numerous advantages of the ADR in which these are the few examples of such advantages[56].

(a) The first advantage of the process of ADR is that it can be used at any time, even when a case is pending before a Court of law. Though recourse to ADR confer maximum advantage on the parties as soon as the dispute arises, it can be used at later stage to reduce the number of contentious issues between the parties, and it, except in the case of binding arbitration, can be terminated at any stage by any one of the disputing parties,

(b) It can provide better solution to disputes more expeditiously and at less cost than litigation. It helps in keeping the dispute a private matter and promotes creative and realistic business solutions, since the parties are in control of the ADR proceedings. ADR procedures take only a day or a few days to arrive at a settlement.

(c) The ADR programs are flexible and not afflicted with rigors of rules of procedure.

(d) The freedom of the parties to litigation is not affected by ADR proceedings. Even a failed ADR proceeding is never a waste either in terms of money or time spent on it, since it helps the parties to appreciate each other's case better.

(e) ADR can be used with or without lawyers. A lawyer, however, plays a very useful role in identification of the contentious issues, exposition of the strong and weak points in a case, rendering advice during negotiation and overall presentation of his client's case.

(f) ADR procedures help in the reduction of the workload of the Courts and thereby help them to focus attention on the cases which ought to be decided by the Courts.

(g) ADR procedures permit parties to choose neutrals who are specialists in the subject matter of the disputes. This does not mean that there will be a diminished role for lawyers. They will continue to play a central role in ADR processes; however they will have to adopt themselves to ADR requirements.

ALTERNATIVE DISPUTE RESOLUTION: FUNCTIONING IN INDIA

In India the origin of ADR could be traced to the origin of political institution on the one hand and commerce and trade on the other[57]. The system of ADR is functioning in some form or other since time immemorial.

However, the modern concept of ADR as it has developed in some developed countries, and spread over the rest of the World in institutional form is not practiced by such names except the arbitration and conciliation. The hybrid forms, which are themselves newborn institutions in developed countries, are not intercepted in our legal mechanism as forms of dispute resolution. The other three basic alternative forms are in practice for a long time namely negotiation, Conciliation/mediation and arbitration.

The negotiation, which we practised in our day-to-day life, has not been institutionalised as a separate institution of dispute resolution. However, the basic characteristic of negotiation exists in the processes of conciliation or mediation and even in arbitration. Therefore, negotiation became part of other two alternative dispute resolution mechanisms. The legal instruments recognize the negotiated settlements[58]. Thus in practice, two forms of alternative dispute mechanisms were functioning in an institutionalised manner namely arbitration and conciliation, before the advent of the system of Lok-Adalat.

Arbitration

Arbitration as one of the ADR mechanisms is functioning in India during the last three centuries. The legislative reference for arbitration found in the Bengal Regulation of 1772 and subsequently all Regulations had references regarding arbitration. However, during that period arbitration was utilized only in monetary disputes between Government and other agencies or Jamindars and on few occasions by the commercial world[59]. In the post-independence scenario, arbitration was governed by the Arbitration Act, 1940. During the long period of operation of 1940s Act, it was noticed that there were widespread abuses of arbitral processes under the Act. Supreme Court, in a number of cases, adversely commented on its functioning and recommended for an Arbitration law, which will be simple, less technical and more responsible to the actual reality of the situation[60]. In this background the Arbitration and Conciliation Act, 1996 was enacted.

Arbitration is functioning as the most successful ADR mechanism in the Commercial world. Several institutions cropped up to provide institutional arbitration at national as well as international level[61]. The institution is working well, at least compared to other mechanisms, but the problem lies in its technicalities, which made it judiciary centric dispute resolution mechanism. On such functioning of arbitration F.S. Nariman said, *"There is much prosperity in arbitration — certainty, for arbitrators and the arbitral institutions. But arbitration must also be popular with user. Whilst in the past commercial men chose arbitration because it seemed a good way of resolving disputes, in the present it is selected mainly through habit and only because all other methods seem even worse! The current preoccupation with Alternative Disputes Resolution is a symptom to this, and demonstrates a growing sentiment that there is need, not for alternative to national Courts, for that does exist — in most places — in the shape of (Court structure) arbitration; but a need, for some alternative to judicial arbitration[62]".*

Though in the commercial world, people accepted arbitration as a means of dispute resolution, yet there are difficulties and shortfalls, which lie in the arbitration process, for which it did not become popular among the large number of people.

Firstly, arbitration is used mainly in commercial disputes and a large number of people are not able to access the process in different cases. This is mainly because the arbitration proceedings are conducted only on prior agreement. Therefore, the people in the commercial world made it a part of their contract to refer the dispute for arbitration. Courts, where a large number of cases were instituted do not have the power to refer the case for Arbitration[63].

Secondly, the arbitration procedure is not at all cheap, as it exists today, which deprived the poor people and even small businessmen from utilizing the institution for resolution of their disputes.

Thirdly, the process is not a quick process, as it was expected to. However, compared to the adjudicative process as functioning in the Courts, it is much faster.

Fourthly, the process is one form of adjudicative process where the disputant does not have any control. Accordingly, the end result, which came out makes one party winner and other loser. Therefore, the party who won the match tried to impose it and the party who lost the game tried his best to make it lengthy by filing appeal on different grounds.

Thus, the aforesaid short-comings in the process has made it aloof from the general masses and the need was felt to evolve people participatory form of dispute resolution, a dispute resolution mechanism, which will not concentrate only among a class of people but will provide justice to all, if accessibilty of justice for all have any meaning. Thus, this ADR mechanism fails to fulfil the Constitutional goal of accessibility of justice for all.

Conciliation

The process of conciliation was mainly used in two forms of disputes. First, in respect of labour disputes and second in family disputes. However, the recently enacted Arbitration and Conciliation Act has elaborated the provisions for conciliation. The Industrial Disputes Act, 1947, created independent agency of conciliation officer charged with the duty to mediate in disputes and promote the settlement in industrial disputes[64]. The Act also empowered the Government to constitute the Board of Conciliators consisting of one chairman and 2 or 4 members representing the disputant parties[65]. It prescribed the duty for conciliator officer and Board[66]. The settlement awards not only have binding effect on the disputant but also to the co-employee, newcomer and heirs[67]. To make the conciliation proceedings more effective, the Act vested the Board and the Conciliation officer with powers similar to Civil Court in respect of enforcing attendance, examining documents etc.[68]

Thus, the alternative mechanism of conciliation was being utilized in labour dispute for a long time. It was also utilized in family disputes. The Hindu Marriage Act prescribes settlement through conciliation[69]. The preamble of Family Court Act, 1984 highlights the importance of conciliation in family disputes[70]. The Family Courts Act, 1984 addresses itself to two types of remedies to family disputes those being (i) employment of alternative therapy to arrive at a conciliated settlement thereby maintaining family as a cohesive unit, and (ii) speedier adjudication of cases where the differences between the parties are irreconcilable[71]. The Act empowers the Government to appoint counsellor to assist the Family Court in discharging its functions, having the prime goal of promoting conciliation and settling disputes[72]. Further the Code of Civil Procedure, 1908 made binding and unapealable all settlement agreements, which either reaches through conciliation or negotiation[73].

Conciliation was used in family disputes effectively in all the states. However, the study snows a mixed picture about its functioning in most places. The rates of settlement vary from State to State. Not more than 10% cases being settled in Family Courts through conciliation in Maharastra, where the pay scale of counsellor is highest among all the States, while the settlement rate is around 50% in Tamil Nadu[74]. However, the low result of settlement does not make the institution as unworthy because it depends on different factors like the performance of conciliators, legal instrumentality, persuasion of conciliators, forms of dispute and the available alternatives to the parties.

The process of Conciliation was not gaining much popularity as an ADR mechanism, as it was required. There are certain other reasons for which this form of ADR could not become a popular alternative mechanism for dispute resolution.

(1) First, the conciliation processes were available only in family disputes, labour disputes, and few commercial disputes. Therefore, concentration of the process in only few sectors made it aloof from general masses.

(2) Secondly, the enactment of Arbitration & Conciliation Act, 1996 made no big changes in functioning except to provide legal recognition to the process. In conciliation also, the matters are referred on the basis of prior agreement. Therefore, any case of disputes, which does not have prior agreement, cannot be resolved by this mechanism.

(3) Thirdly, the process becomes procedure oriented, though theoretically it is required to be flexible. Such procedure orientation is also somehow responsible for the effect, which takes the process away from the general people, and the large number of masses do not have access to it except in few forms of disputes.

Thus, this form of alternative dispute resolution also failed to fulfill the aspirations of the people, although it is in vogue.

CONCLUSION

The emergence of vast varieties of alternative dispute resolution mechanisms were made due to the failure of the adversarial system to provide justice effectively. Indeed, it is also manifest from the above study that on jurisprudential aspect, the institution of ADR is more appropriate for resolution of certain category of cases. The ADR processes are effectively functioning in almost all places, with a little variation, in the procedures. A large number of disputes are settled through ADR. It is also exhibited that the ADR forum is not only appropriate for the commercial cases[75], family disputes[76], compensation Cases[77] but also technical forms of disputes like Intellectual property disputes[78]. Even the biggest case of Intellectual property disputes was resolved through ADR[79]. It is apparent that though a large variety of dispute resolution mechanisms emerged, in India, the mechanism of conciliation and arbitration are utilized effectively in certain types of disputes.

However, study reveals some short falls in the functioning of conciliation and arbitration, which made both the institutions aloof from the general masses. It is exhibit that the arbitration was effectively utilized in commercial disputes but was and still not popular among large number of masses. Similarly, the conciliation process was also unable to intercept among large number of people. Therefore, both the process of ADR failed to provide justice to a large number of people. In such circumstances, it was deeply considered by legal fraternity for evolving participatory form of dispute resolution mechanism, because all the other forms failed to reach the large number of downtrodden masses. People are eagerly waiting for cheap, speedy, informal form of dispute resolution where every one will have access to justice.

REFERENCES

1. P.C. Rao, Alternative to litigation in India, in P.C.Rao & William Sheffield, ADR- what it is and how it works, P24, (1997)
2. N.R.Madhava Menon, Law Commission and grass root level justice. Indian Bar Review, Vol 12(4), (1985 Editorial).
3. Law Commission of India, Alternative Forum for Resolution of Disputes, at grass-roots level, P 42, 114th Report.
4. P.C. Rao, Alternative to litigation In India, in P.C.Rao & William Sheffield, A.D.R. what It is and how it works, P 24 (1997).
5. Justice S. B. Sinha, ADR with Spl. Reference to C.P.C. (Amendment) Act, 1999, Souvenir of ADR work shop, LASWEB, P 9 (2001).
6. In India we have 10.5 judges per million population, while the corresponding figure in England is 50.9, Australia 57.7, Canada 75.2 and USA 107. See Justice M. Jagannadha Rao, Laws delay world over- need for change in our mindset- towards permanent Lok-AdalaL Nyaya Path, April-June 1999. P 24.
7. Even, ten States in USA had to close their court house door for civil cases in order to provide speedy justice in criminal proceeding. This example highlights the gravity of situation even in America. See id.
8. Lon-L, Fuller, The forms and limits of Adjudication, Harvard Law Review, P 369, Vol 92:353, (1978). As fuller spell out four steps of argument in an adjudication process, (1) Adjudication is a process of decision that grants to the affected party a form of participation that consists in the opportunity to present proofs and reasoned arguments, (2) The litigants must therefore, if his participation is to be meaningful, assert some principle or principles by which his arguments are sound and his proofs relevant. (3) A naked demand is distinguished from a claim of right by the fact that latter is a demand supported by a principle, likewise (4) a mere expression of displeasure or resentment is distinguished from an accusation by the fact that the letter rests upon some principle. Hence, issues tried before an adjudication tend to become claims of right or accusations of fault
9. Justice D. M. Dharmadhikari, Lok-Adalat, P30, Nyaya Path, Souvenir (2000).
10. id
11. id
12. id
13. Justice M.G. Chitkara, Accessibility of Justice, Nyaya Path, Souvenir-2000, Pg-82

14. Karl Mackie, David Mites & William Marsh, Commercial Dispute resolution : An ADR Practice Guide, (1995) pg. 4, Better-worth Publication.

15. Lon. L. Fuller, The Forms and limits of Adjudication, P 393, HLR (1978) Vol : 92 :353: Fuller given example of certain category of cases where adjudication is not a proper forum. He stated an example, "Some months ago a wealthy lady by name of Timken died in New York leaving a valuable, but somewhat miscellaneous, collection of paintings to the Metropolitan Museum and the National gallery in equal shares. Her will indicating no particular apportionment. When the will was probated the judge remarked something to the effect that the parties seemed to be confronted with a real problem". He says that in such situation it became impossible to provide justice as to distribute paintings among two organizations, it lies in the fact that the disposition of any single painting has implications for proper disposition of every other painting.

    However in this case one of the Museum attorneys informs the Court that both litigants will work it out. Thus in such situation any judge assigned to hear such an argument would be tempted to assume the rote of mediator.

16. id

17. Karl Mackies, supra 14.

18. Law Commission of India, 129th Report on Urban Litigation, P 32 Para- 3.14

19. Sarvesh Chandra, ADR: Is Conciliation the Best Choice?, in, P.C. Rao & Wulliam Sheffelds, ADR, What it is & How It works, P83 (1997).

20. 129th LCI Report, P 5

21. See. 129th LCI Report, on urban litigation.

22. See 114th LCI Report on Nyaya Panchayat 129th report an Urban Litigation : Mediation as best alternative for litigation, 124th report on "The High Court Arrear" and also. 131st report on "The rote of legal profession in strengthening the system of Administration.

23. N. R. Madhava Menon, Supra. 3.

24. 114 Law Commission Report, Pg-42.

25. P.C. Rao, Supra 4.

26. Id

27. Justice S.B.Sinha, (C.P.C.Amemdment), Supra 5.

28. Stephen B Goldberg. Frank-E.A. Sander, & Nancy -H. Rogers, Dispute Resolution: Negotiation, Mediation and other processes, P6-9 (1992), Little Brown & Co

29. Id.

30. The Bengal Regulation of 1772 threw light on the legislative provisions for arbitration. The Regulation said, in all cases of disputed accounts etc, it shall be recommended to the parties to submit the decision of the cause to arbitration, the award of which shall become a decree of Court. Then the Regulation of 1787, Bengal Regulation 1793, Regulation VI of 1813, Madras Regulation of 1816, and Bombay Regulation IV & VII also provided provision for Arbitration. These provisions were enforced till the enactment of Code of Civil Procedure 1859, which was repealed by Code of Civil Procedure, 1882. In 1889 Arbitration Act was enacted. The Code of Civil Procedure, 1908 provide elaborate provisions in Secs. 89 & 104 in the original Code. However this provision of C.P.C. was repealed and a separate Arbitration Act, 1940 was enacted. See for detail, V.A. Mohta, Arbitration and Conciliation, Introduction (2001), AIR Publication.

31. See www.councilforjustice.orglfunction.htm

32. See Karl Mackie, David Miles and William Marsh, Commercial Dispute Resolution. An ADR practice Guide, (1995) pg- 10-12, Butterworth Publication.

33. The process of unilateral action has not been mentioned as a process of dispute resolution because it is not a process of dispute resolution under rule of law and it cannot be valid in any civil society. However, it is used by powerful party on the other who does not have power to resist it is arbitrary action taken by one and imposed on other. In other words, the other party avoids the dispute. In this process, the protagonist has complete control over his action.

34. See P.O. Rao. Supra 4, P-26

35. See LASWEB, Study material on Mediation skills, 24-29th Sep 2001, Kolkata.

36. The ground rule may include an agreement that neither side will interrupt the other during their statement session, each party will treat other with respect, that the parties will agree not to call the mediator as a witness in a Court of law and a the like. See id

37. Supra 32.

38. The first reference for mediation we got in sec. 4 of the Industrial Disputes Act, 1947. The Act created independent agency of Conciliation Officers charged with the duty of mediating in and promoting the settlement of industrial disputes. Recently the C.P.C. 1999 Amendment inserted sec. 89, which made it mandatory to refer the dispute for alternative mechanism and one of such alternative forums is the institution of Mediation.

39. Sec. 74 of the Arbitration and Conciliation Act, 1996, equate the settlement reached in conciliation proceeding with the settlement reached during arbitral proceedings under Sec 30 and is enforceable as decree of the Court under sec. 36 of the Act.

40. See Karl Mackie, Supra 30 P-9 Para 1.3.3

41. id P 10

42. id p 47

43. See Sec. 2 (1a) of Arbitration of Conciliation Act, 1996.

44. S.19 of the Arbitration Act 1996 specifically debar the application of Evidence Act or Code of Civil Procedure. The sub-clause (2) authorize the party to freely agree on the procedure to be followed by the Arbitral Tribunal in conducting it proceeding.

45. S10 & S11 of the Act authorize parties to select their own arbitrator and in failing to appoint arbitrator court can appoint, if any arbitration agreement is exist.

46. Donald, G. Gifford, Legal Negotiation : Theory and Application, 211 (1989), West Publishing Co.

47. id,

48. This view was expressed by Karl Machie, Supra 40

49. M/S Guru Nanak Foundation -VS- M/S Ratan Singh & others, AIR 1981 SC 2075 at 1076

50. Stephen B Goldberg, Frank. E. A. Sander, & Nancy, H. Rogers, Disputes Resolution: Negotiation, Mediation and other processes, #4 (second edition). Little Brown & Co. N.B. Court-annexed arbitration is involuntary, nonbonding, and public.

51. Stephen B. Goldberg, Supra 28, P233.

52. P.C. Rao Supra 19

53. Study Material on ADR, Prepared by Legal Aid Services, West Bengal. Supra 94.

54. See Karl Meckie, David Miles & William Marsh, Commercial Dispute Resolution. An ADR Practice Guide, (1995) Butterworth Publication pg-49

55. Subhash Chandra Gupta, OMBUDSMAN ; AN Indian Perspective, 1995), Manak Publication.

56. P.O. Rao, in Supra 110, P- 25 -26, mentioned the advantages.

57. Sarvesh Chandra, ADR : Is Conciliation the Best Choice, in P.C. Rao & William Sheffield, ADR, what it is & how it works, (1997) Pg-85

58. Order 24 Rule 3 of the Code of Civil Procedure uphold the Compromise agreement on which basis Court can pass order. Even Rule 3A debar the Court to set aside such compromise on the ground that the compromise was unlawful and Sec 96(3) read with Order XLI made It unappealable.

59. For full history see V.A. Mohta, Arbitration and Conciliation Act, 1996, Introduction, AIR Publication, See also. Nripendra Nath Sirkar, The Law of Arbitration in British India. Tagore Law Lecture (1942) Calcutta University.

60. See Guru Nanak Foundation V. Rattan Singh. AIR 1981 SC 2075, Food Corporation of India V. Goginder Pal. AIR 1981 SC 2075, See also 76th Law Commission Report & Consultation Paper an review of the working of Arbitration and Conciliation Act. 1996.

61. Indian Chamber of Commerce, Bengal Chamber of Commerce, ICADR are the few examples of such Institution at national level and ICA, AAA, WIPO are the few examples of International level institution.

62. F.S. Nariman, Arbitration and ADR In India, in P.C. RAO, ADR what It is and how it works, (1997) Pg 45, Universal Law Publication.

63. However Recent Amendment of C.P.C. in 1999 made it possible for Court to refer the dispute for arbitration u/s. 89 C.P.C. See Sec. 4 of the Industrial Disputes Act, 1947.

64. See Sec. 4 of the Industrial Disputes Act 1947.

65. See Sec. 5 of the Industiral Disputes Act 1947.

66. See Secs. 12 & 13 of Industrial Disputes Act respectively.

67. Sec 18 of the Act. See also, Binny & Buckingham & Carnatic Co. Employee Union V. Commissioner of labour and Chief Conciliator Officer - AIR 1964 Madras 538, All India Textile Janata Union V. The Labour Commissioner, 1994 LLR 204 (P& H).

68. Sec 11 of the Industrial Disputes Act, 1947.

69. See Hindu Marriage Act, 1955.

70. The preamble reads, "An Act to provide for the Settlement in Family Court with a view to promote conciliation in and secure speedy settlement of disputes relating the marriage and family affairs and for matters connected therewith.

71. M.V. S. Sitalaxmi, Family Court and the Goal of Speedy Settlement of Matrimonial Disputes ; LLM Dissertation, NLSIU, 1992.

72. Sec 9 of Family Court Act. 1984.

73. Sec 96(3) of C.P.C, Which says that no appeal lay against the order which was passed by the consent of parties.

74. Supra 79.

75. Supra 54.

76. John H. Wade, Arbitration of Matrimonial Dispute, Bond Law Review, P 395 (1999X11).

77. P.C. RAO Supra 52.

78. Peter Grove, Mediation & Arbitration: Alternatives for intellectual property disputes, http://www.beicac.com/cfm/index/cfm?L=157&P=167,down loaded on 24.11.01, See also. Carman Collar & Gerry Spotter, International I.P. Dispute.Resolution: Is Mediation a Sleeping Giants? LL.M ADR Study Material. Bond University.

79. id

CHAPTER 3

EMERGENCE OF LOK ADALAT AS AN EFFECTIVE ADR MECHANISM

INTRODUCTION

While on the one hand the justice administration system failed to provide access to justice to all irrespective of their resources, on the other hand alternative forum like arbitration and conciliation failed to fulfil the aspiration of the masses, no other option was left but to find alternatives. Alternatives, not only to adjudicative systems but also to so-called alternatives like arbitration and conciliation. Law Commission observed; to quote[1], "if professionalized model of justice delivery thus cannot be extended to meet the legal needs of the Indian masses, it becomes incumbent to consider alternatives. The alternative is de-professionalized model of justice. In this model the indigenous juristic potential of the people, including their own sense of justice, is allowed room for development. This has been sought to be done through people's participation in administration of justice". Several Law Commission Reports recommended for the participatory form of administration of justice.[2] Frankly admitting the existing legal system has remained unfortunately alien having no living contact with the masses and is not at all meaningful to them.[3]

The judicial system, which is continuously getting overburdened by the mounting arrears, repeatedly attracted the attention of the Law Commission. In the year 1974, the Commission after eulogizing the Supreme Court of India for making 'the concept of rule of law relevant, coherent and stable in this country, could not shut its eyes to the problem of growing arrears in the administration of justice. It was noticed long ago by Law Commission of India (LCI) that these arrears have now assumed a somewhat alarming dimension.[4] The docket of cases in reality becomes challenge for legal fraternity. It exists at all levels from lowest court to apex court. Even the disposal of cases is much less than the institution of cases each year, which can be established by table 3.1 hereunder. In 1982 while cases instituted was 6,63,183 the number of disposal of cases was 5,51,785, as a result of which a number of pending cases reached to 9,76,781. In 1985 while 731,543 cases were instituted the number of disposals were 6,05,698 and the backlog reached at 13,77 790.

Table 3.1[5]
High Court Arrear

Year	Institution	Disposal	Pending
1982	6,63,183	5,51,785	9,76,781
1983	6,71,195	5,40,357	11,09,188
1984	7,07,912	5,75,451	12,51,945
1985	7,31,543	6,05,698	13,77,790

Similar situations persist in the District Courts also. The Courts at District level also fail to dispose of the number of cases instituted in the year and as a result the pendency of cases increased rapidly[6]. Thus, such an aggravated situation denied access to justice to large numbers of people in practical sense. Even in the Supreme Court where arrears of cases, which stood at 2319 in 1960 went up six fold in 1975 to 15000. The record of another sixteen years shows that the arrears of pending cases in Supreme Court of Indian touched the mark of 2,30.000[7]. However, the Supreme Court was able to bring down the pending cases merely to 20483 as on 1st May 2000. In 1999, 34683 cases were instituted in the Supreme Court and 34707 cases were disposed of[8]. The arrears of cases reached an alarming level of 3.5 million in the high courts[9]. The number of arrears is still increasing and the situation instead of improving is becoming worse. During 1998, in different High Courts of India 15,01,227, cases were instituted and 13,72,270 cases were disposed of[10]. The situation is becoming worse every day.

Once former Chief Justice E.S. Venkataramiah rightly observed[11]; The problem of delay and backlog was likely to put the functioning of Constitutional Government in disarray. This warning of the former Chief Justice carries really great weight when examined in the light of piling arrears and accumulated workload of different courts. The mounting arrears of cases in the Supreme Court and in various High Courts in India prove it beyond the shadow of doubt that the position of arrears is quite alarming and as a matter of fact the whole system is likely to crumble down under the weight of pending cases which go on increasing every day[12]. Such a prevailing situation looses faith of the general people on the justice administration mechanism as it was functioning. As a result, in some places, the people prefer to hire antisocials or utilize the service of the underworld for obtaining his rights instead of filling cases in the Court and waiting for justice for a decade[13].

The 129th LCI report while recommending the mediation in Urban Disputers made a thorough analysis of different alternative mechanisms for resolution of dispute in urban civil cases.[14] First, the Commission analysed the concepts, which 114th Law Commission recommended for the semi urban areas and villages, dispute being settled by Nyaya Panchayat where one professional judge interacting with two lay judges from the society decides the disputes. Secondly, where there will be two judges instead of one judge who, will decide the cases, and no appeal will lie against their decision. Thirdly, the neighbourhood justice system in which neighbourhood justice centre should be set up[15], where petty civil disputes like disputes under Rent Act can be decided. The Commission referred that by 1980 about one hundred neighbourhood centres have been set up in different parts of United State of America[16]. Such neighbourhood centres may consist of three local residents and if a retired judge is residing in the area, preferably he should be included. The fourth was the introduction of Conciliation Courts as was working in Himachal Pradesh. Ultimately the Commission prefers the Himachal Pradesh model where Court will function as a Conciliatory Court. The case pending in one Court can be referred to another Court for conciliation where the other Court will function as a conciliator in the case[17].

Truly speaking, the way the mechanism of justice was functioning under the umbrella of adversarial administration of justice, the Constitutional goal of equality and equal justice became meaningless. Once justice Krishna Iyer said that if the people find that there is nothing to expect from law, they will find reasons to fight against law[18]. Supreme Court in a series of cases highlighted the need of speedy and equitable justice system and equate the legal aid with basic fundamental rights[19]. A similar view was expressed by the U.S Supreme Court, which held that the failure of according benefit of counsel, would amount to denying the due process of law[20]. In England too, the Economic Opportunity Act, 1964 and the Access to Justice Act, 1999 were planned to provide access to equal justice to all[21].

Government of India is committed to legal aid as enshrined in the Constitution. The restructuring of the judicial system forms a part of an effective legal service program, as it tends to include every form of legal assistance, which bring justice nearer to the people, particularly to the rural people. The poor and disadvantaged are cut off from the legal system because of its expensiveness and dilatoriness and because of the nature of the judicial system[22]. To implement the Constitutional mandate the Government of India appointed a Committee for Implementation of Legal Aid Scheme (CILAS) in 1980 under the chairmanship of Justice Bhagwati. In view of the commendable efforts made by CILAS, legal aid scheme is being administered through out the country as per the guidelines circulated by it. One of the strategic legal aid programmes adopted by the Committee for Implementation of Legal Aid Scheme (CILAS), pertains to the holding of Lok-Adalat for settlement of disputes through conciliation[23]. Thus the modern version of Lok-Adalat, arose out of concern expressed by the Committees, setup to report on organizing legal aid to the poor and the alarm generated by judicial circles on the mounting arrears of cases pending for long at different levels in the court system[24].

In India, the institution of Lok-Adalat has been gaining popularity quite steadily since its initiation in March 1982, when the first Lok-Adalat was held at village 'Una' in Junagarh, Gujarat as an experiment. The first Lok-Adalat was held successfully and the observation made there by Justice Desai, while inaugurating the Lok-Adalat is noteworthy. The learned judge said, "It was a novel experiment in the direction of amicably resolving legal dispute between parties. If it is succeeded it might be repeated, if not, it be forgotten."[25] Fortunately, for the State of Gujarat as well as for the Country, this experiment instead of failing became more successful and got deep rooted. The seed, which was sown in early 1980's, has now grown into a huge tree.[26] Thus, the Lok-Adalat is the brainchild of necessity. The accumulated frustration of the people desirous of quick disposal of their cases is the biggest single reason, for the people having responded with hope, excitement and zeal, in holding Lok-Adalat for dispute ending of pending disputes.[27]

The basic principles that underline the idea of Lok-Adalat are to provide cheaper and quicker justice at the doorsteps of the people. It would not only relieve the workload on the regular Courts, but also go a long way in settling disputes outside the fora of Courts.[28] Our present judicial system has badly failed to keep pace with the aspirations of the people. The system is cracking and is on the verge of collapse. Now the blind-folded Dike, the Greek Goddess of Justice, cannot be the symbol of 21st century Goddess of Justice. Twenty first century Goddess of Justice holding a scale of justice in her hand cannot and need not be blind-folded. Her eyes must be wide open so as to see that justice is being done between the parties and no one turns his back to justice with bitterness.[29]

Therefore, it is the result of social philosophy of judges, jurists and eminent scholars that judiciary has entered in a new age with a new alternative forum in the form of Lok-Adalat.

LOK-ADALAT: WHAT IS IT?

Lok-Adalat is a forum where voluntary efforts are made to bring about the settlement of disputes. Though there is no standardized or statutory definition of the term, it is now widely accepted as an informal, voluntary, dispute settlement agency involving the people and public-spirited lawyers and citizens.[30] It is informal because it is held out side the Court with a conciliatory mechanism without any formalism as in vogue in the adversarial system of justice. It is voluntary because people have control over the process as to agree or not to agree on any issue and they, themselves, have the right to settle disputes. Lok-Adalat is not a 'Court' in its accepted connotation[31] though people may find attributes of a Court in it and may even call it by that name.[32] It is just a forum provided by the people themselves or by interested parties including social activists, legal aiders and public-spirited people belonging to every walk of life.[33] Here voluntary efforts are aimed to bring about settlement of disputes between the parties through conciliatory and persuasive efforts.

Generally speaking, Lok-Adalat is a para-Judicial institution being developed by the people themselves.[34] These are not akin to regularly constituted Law Courts and are to supplement and not to supplant the existing adjudicatory machinery.[35] One of the important aspects of Lok-Adalat is that it provides speedy and inexpensive justice at the very doorsteps of the people.[36] It is born out of belief that even if State-supported programmes of legal aid were able to provide legal assistance to every indigent client, that is not going to solve the problems of the poor vis-a-vis the administration of justice. The poor do not have the staying power which litigation inevitably involves; nor can they expect equal justice in all stages of the complicated and technical procedures of the law. Even the not-so-poor find it prudent to invoke informal processes if available to settle their disputes. In other words, Lok-Adalat phenomenon is an expression of the disgust and disenchantment of the poor and the middle class people in respect of the Court system as it functions today.[37]

The basic objective of Lok-Adalat coming into existence is a sound rationale which tells us that an adversarial adjudication ending up in one party being declared victorious and the other the vanquished does not remove the dispute from the society and may lead to further disputes or social tension. It is perhaps based on a sound historical experience, which shows us that Indian people are disposed to conciliated settlements with community intervention rather than adjudicated decisions through adversarial process of formal Courts.[38] The spirit behind the Lok-Adalat is 'live' and 'let live', 'give' and 'take'. There is neither a victor nor a vanquished in the cases settled through Lok-Adalat.[39] In a dispute, which comes to Court, seldom it is found that any one of the parties is totally wrong or right. The Justice like a 'golden mean' lies 'in between' and in the procedure of Lok-Adalat the attempt is to reach that 'mean'.[40]

About Lok-Adalat, Justice S.M. Dharmadhikari said[41]; 'Lok-Adalat is, Indianisation of the system of dispensation of justice based on the customs and tradition found in the villages and societies of India. I also call it humanization of justice delivery system as there is more and more participation of human beings involved with larger consideration to the human aspects in the course of resolving disputes. I have also given it another description calling it spiritualization of justice delivery system because it is a process to uplift the society by educating its members to do justice to each other'.

However, where as on one hand the common people welcome Lok-Adalat as a relief, to some it is an otherwise oppressive system under which justice remains uncertain, costly and time consuming, on the other hand a small percentage of lawyers are taken unawares by the development, suspect the motive and possible impact of it on their profession[42]. Some even criticize it by saying; 'it is a substandard substitute for the regular Courts and has been introduced because Courts find it impossible in the present cumbersome system to deliver justice in long pending cases before them in a reasonable period of time'[43]. On the above premise, one may also doubt whether it is not a compromise on the part of the poor, for a system of justice inferior in quality because the superior variety is just not accessible?

These misconceptions about Lok-Adalat are required to be removed from the minds of such public and legal fraternity who pre-supposes the system as sub standard. One's concept of justice and the function of law in an unequal society may be open to question, if the debate is logically extended. It can also be argued on the contrary that when judges tried to find the truth out of evidences and logical arguments placed before them by the disputants, and the disputants, out of their resources and capabilities tried to impress the judge even by placing false evidence on oath and associating renowned lawyers to utilize their technicalities, which is not possible without sufficient resources, can in reality adjudicatory proceedings provide equal justice in such situation? Is it not the aim of 'discover truth and provide justice frustrated' when the party by utilizing resources tried to establish their cases by placing false evidences? Compared to the adversarial system, Lok-Adalat is a revolutionary justice delivery system. Here the parties, their counsels, conciliators cum judges on the panel, all with one single aim are negotiating and co-operating with each other to bring the parties to amicable settlement so as to initially satisfy both the parties and bring the disputes to a final end[44]. Mr. D.K. Sampath from his own experience as mediator reiterated the need tor mediation in certain disputes for the people in general and for countryside poor man in particular. According to him poor are much more co-operative on the mediation table. He said[45], 'the poor are better off for coming to the negotiation table. Resources are important in dealing with a conflict in terms of confrontation. The poor have no resources. As a consequence, they have no-ability to use the facilities that are made available as a substitute for their own resources. They lack the will to sway the situation in their favour. This creates frustration, when they are up against the problem. The poor cannot ride out the crisis. This frustration disintegrates their personality. They lack motivation when it is needed most. This is evident when one sees how helpless poor suitors are, even when lawyers are allotted to them free by the Legal Aid Boards. The tendered assistance is of no use to them unless it is absorbed. They do not have the self-confidence and faith in their own cause. They are often ignorant of their rights and threat to them. To redress the situation, it is possible only in mediation, which is both informal and flexible'.

The procedure for settlement of disputes as followed in Lok-Adalat by mediation or conciliation was exactly followed by our nation's father Mahatma Gandhi. He said,[46] 'I had learned the true practice of law. I had learnt to find out the better side of human nature and to enter hearts, I realised that the true function of the lawyer was to unite parties given as under. The lesson was so indelibly burnt into me that the large part of my time during the twenty years of my practice as a lawyer was occupied in bringing about private compromises of hundreds of cases. I lost nothing thereby, not even money, certainly not my soul'.

So, in the relevant situation what would be the better form of providing justice other than that the people themselves decide and settle their disputes? Is there any other better way to provide justice qualitatively when the people themselves control the process and decided the case by mutual understanding? In the process of negotiation, which runs on the principle of 'give and take' one may give more or take less, the other may take more while give less, but it does not make the process sub-standard. At least qualitatively, because the decision was their own. In one Calcutta case, one 76 yrs. old man had some grievances against his son who was running his shop but would not maintain him or pay maintenance. The son was in possession of the shop and residence, which he had made out of his whole life income and the old man was deprived of every thing. He, on advice, appeared before High Court Legal Services Committee. The High Court Legal Services Committee summoned his son. The matter was settled in Lok-Adalat. The terms of the settlement was that the son would pay Rs. 1500 per month to the old father and on the other hand, the father would change the trade license in the name of the son. Thus, the dispute was settled without any case being instituted in the Court of law. Does any one consider that the decision is of low quality? Do any of them father or the son loses any thing? Is it not better that such cases be filed before conciliatory forum like Lok-Adalat, instead of going to the court and showing proof and reasoning argument against the son and on the other hand son will repeat this against the father? I consider that no decision can be better qualitatively than the settlement reached by and between the parties themselves.

Lok-Adalat is, thus, not a sub-standard substitute for the regular Courts. It is an innovative form of dispute resolution form. It is a para-judicial organ organized primarily by judiciary as a form for conciliation and adjudication involving little cost and no delay with an informal procedure confirming only to the requirements of natural justice where the keynote is justice rather than law. In fact the whole emphasis and proceeding becomes an instrument to prevent frustration.

Functioning of Lok Adalat

Until the enforcement of the Legal Services Authority Act the functioning of the Lok-Adalats were based on the guidelines given by the Committee for Implementation of Legal Aid Scheme. The Lok-Adalats were generally organized in that period by the State Legal Aid and Advice Boards or the District Legal Aid Committee and on such a date and time, fixed about a month in advance by the Legal Board[47]. Now the Lok Adalats are held as per the guidelines provided in Legal Services Authority Act, 1987 and Rules made thereunder. The Lok-Adalats at District level and taluka level are organized by the District Legal Service Authority and Taluka Level Legal Services Committee. The Lok Adalat in different High Court and Supreme Court are organized by High Court Legal Services Committee and Supreme Court Legal Services Committee. Normally the Lok-Adalats are held during holidays, either on Saturdays or Sundays. However, now several District Authorities and Taluka Level Committees are organizing permanent Lok-Adalats at respective places in different States. Information about holding of a Lok Adalat is given wide publicity through press, poster, and where possible, through, radio, television and cinema slides. However, the process of advertisement is not similar in all places. Initially, civil revenue and criminal disputes, which were compoundable, were taken up by the Lok-Adalat. With the success of Lok Adalat in bringing about settlement of such disputes and the co-operation extended by the Chairman of the General Insurance Corporation of India, CILAS requested the State Legal Aid and Advice Board to take up motor accident compensation claim cases also at the Lok-Adalat. This has resulted in settlement of a large number of long pending Motor Accident Claim Tribunal cases, which would have otherwise taken years for adjudication[48]. Today motor accident compensation cases are most successful forms of disputes as settled in different Lok Adalats in the Country. In addition to the aforesaid cases, Lok Adalat is also taking up cases involving mutation of lands, land pattas, forest lands, bonded labour case, land acquisition cases, matrimonial and family disputes and bank Loan cases etc.

COMPOSITION, ORGANIZATION, AND PROCEDURE OF LOK-ADALAT

Lok-Adalat consists of not just those few lawyers and judges who have volunteered to act as conciliators or mediators between the disputants who brought their problem to the Lok-Adalat. They are of course an important segment of what we conceive as Lok-Adalat. It also includes a large number of social workers, legal aiders, law students, village elders and public men who, concerned with social tensions arising from denial of justice and conscious of the limitations of the justice system mobilize people to agree to fair settlement, educate them of their respective rights and duties under law, help organize the forum for discussion and settlement and render paralegal assistance for fair, expeditious settlement, if the parties are so disposed[49]. Lok-Adalat may even include social organizations, media, and influential sections of the local populace who either because of their charitable motives or personal interests give varied services.[50]

The panel of the judges in Lok-Adalat consists of three persons, one from the judiciary, either in service or retired, one from the Bar (Advocate) and one social worker. In West Bengal it is customarily followed to appoint retired judges as conciliator in order to utilize their long experience, which will help in pursuing the parties for settlement. Earlier, if conciliation in such Lok-Adalat resulted in settlement of a dispute, a compromise deed would have to be drawn up and after obtaining signature of the parties and their advocates, if present, the compromise deed was presented to the presiding officer of the competent Court, who used to be present where Lok-Adalats were organized, for passing a decree in terms of compromise.

However, such hurdle is being eliminated through Legal Service Authority Act, which equates the settlement reached at Lok-Adalat with the decree of the Court[51]. Normally cases are referred to Lok-Adalat in three circumstances. First, if both the parties agreed to transfer the case for settlement in Lok-Adalat and the Court is satisfied that there is chance of settlement. Secondly, if one party applies to the Court for reference of the case to the Lok-Adalat and the Courts are satisfied that there are chances of settlement if the case was referred to the Lok-Adalat. Thirdly, when Court itself is satisfied that particular cases could be settled in the Lok-Adalat. All the above circumstances appeared when the case is pending before any Court. However, the Lok-Adalat can also take cognisance in the pre-litigation case if the concerned authority organizing the Lok-Adalat refers such a case for taking cognisance in order to arrive at a settlement.

The Lok-Adalat functions purely on democratic basis on which Justice D.M. Dharmadhikari said; 'Lok-Adalat is democratisation of the judicial system in the sense that in its process there is free and large participation of the people, apart from the parties to the dispute and the witnesses. There is no technical inhibition imposed by any strict procedural law. In this system, justice is done by the concerted effort of people, parties and witnesses. The outcome is justice by consensus[52]. There is no compulsion to settle the disputes through Lok-Adalat. If the parties agree to decide their disputes mutually on the basis of their free will and in a voluntary manner, only then Lok-Adalat comes to their assistance. The presence of a lawyer is not required in the process of conciliation and settlement; they are however, not debarred from attending Lok-Adalat. The role of Advocate in the Lok-Adalat is simply of advisory nature and helps their clients to arrive at a compromise through their sweet efforts. The process of conciliation starts in the Lok-Adalat when both the parties make their presence before the judge[53]. Once the settlement is arrived between the parties, the Lok-Adalat reduces it into black and white on the spot and passes the compromise order.

The process of Lok-Adalat is voluntary though the Court has power to refer the matter before Lok-Adalat and the C.P.C mandates for choosing one of ADR mechanism, the decision making authority lies with the party concerned. The process although structured and public in nature, it is a less formal process compared to adjudication. Even in most occasions it is an informal process except on the occasion where the production of documents, examination of witness, or the things like these, are needed, which makes it formal. The third party consisting of the three members' Court intervenes as conciliator and helps the party to settle their dispute amicably. Even on such intervention the decision making power lies with the party concerned and the conciliator (Lok-Adalat) only functions as the facilitator. The out come of the process is an amicably settled resolution of disputes. A comparison chart, Table 3.2, will show the comparative value of the different processes.

Table-3.2
Comparative Chart of the Dispute Resolution Process

Characteristic Voluntary/In-Voluntary	Adjudication Voluntary	Arbitration* Voluntary	Mediation Voluntary	Lok-Adalat Voluntary
1	2	3	4	5
Binding/Non-binding	Bidning: subject to appeal	Binding, subject to review on limited grounds.	If agreement, enforceable as contact.	All orders are binding a/nd unappeable.
Third Party	Imposed, third-party neutral decision maker.	Party-selected third-party as Arbitrator to	Party-selected out-side facilitator called	Three member panel of judge function as

1	2	3	4	5
		decide. Often specialized in subject.	Mediator	conciliators.
Degree of formality	Formalized and highly structured by predetermined, rigid rules	Procedurally less formal, procedural rules and substantive law may be set by parties	Usually informal, unstructured.	Though structured but process are mostly informal and flexible.
Nature of proceeding	Opportunity for each party to present proofs and arguments	Opportunity for each party to present proofs and arguments.	Unbounded presentation of evidence, arguments and interests	Unbounded presentation of evidence, arguments. Basically negotiation between parties
Outcome	Principled decision supported by reasoned opinion	Sometimes principled decision supported by reasoned opinion, sometimes, compromise without opinion	Mutually acceptable agreement sought	Mutually agreed order by the panel of judges. So both the party became winners in the process. In case of permanent Lok-Adalat, court can pass an order on merit, if parties failed to settle the disputes.
Private/Public	Public	Private, unless judicial review sought	Private	Public

ADVANTAGE OF LOK-ADALAT OVER OTHER DISPUTE RESOLUTION MECHANISM

These are the few examples among the enormous advantages of the Lok-Adalat as an alternative mechanism for dispute resolution.

1. Lok-Adalat is the only institutionalised dispute resolution mechanism where the parties do not have to bear any expenses. Even the incentives have been provided in the form of return of Court fee, which the concerned disputant has paid at the time of institution of the case.

2. The lawyers are not essential during the process. However a lawyer can help the parties to understand contentious issues and judge available alternatives and accordingly can settle the dispute. The lawyer also functions as a facilitator during the process.

3. The institution can be used any time irrespective of whether the case is instituted in the Court of law or not. However, recourse to any such conciliatory forum as soon as the dispute arises may

confer maximum advantage, because till that period relations between the parties are not totally broken.

4. It can be terminated at any time if the parties fail to settle their disputes are willing to terminate the process.

5. It can provide better solution to the parties expeditiously. In a single day, the parties can settle their dispute. So it is the most time saving process compared to any other processes.

6. It helps in keeping the business secret or other private matter undisclosed if the parties can settle their dispute accordingly.

7. The procedures in the Lok-Adalat are flexible and not afflicted with rigors of rules and procedures.

8. The control of the process and authority to decisions lay in the hands of the party concerned and judges will function only as facilitators through the process of conciliation.

9. The freedom of parties to litigate does not affect through the process of Lok-Adalat. If the parties are able to settle their disputes, it is a binding order, and if fails to settle they are free to decide the fate of their case through adjudication. However, in case of a permanent Lok-Adalat, the judges can pass order on merit if the parties fail to settle their disputes amicably.

10. The process of Lok-Adalat helps in the reduction of the work load of the Courts and thereby help them to focus attention on the cases for which adjudication is a fit process.

CONCLUSION

In a situation where a large number of people are deprived of the institution of justice, to access it, the emergence of Lok-Adalat is a welcome approach. Once Abraham Lincoln observed; 'Discourage litigation, persuade your neighbours to compromise whenever you can. Point out to them the nominal winner is often a real loser; in fees, expenses and waste of time. As a peacemaker, the lawyer has a superior opportunity of being a good person'. The institution of Lok-Adalat evolves as an institution to bring the parties to compromise and eliminate enmity. The institution of Lok Adalat has numerous advantages and the people have enormous faith in it not only as an institution of resolution of disputes but also as an instrument of social change. According to Prof Menon[54], 'Lok-Adalat has the potential for social reconstruction and legal mobilization for social change. It can influence the style of administration of justice and the role, of lawyer and judge in it. It can take law closer to the life of the people and reduce disparity between law in books and law in action'.

At a time when the Country is in search of suitable reforms in judicial administration and better access to justice for the common people, the advent of Lok-Adalat is indeed a welcome development. Similar institutions had existed in the ancient period and were effectively functioning till it went into to eclipse during the British period. Till the advent of British regime it was functioning by different names in almost all parts of the country but the British administration of justice cast a gloom on the institution. In the post British period we adopted some form of alternative mechanism for providing justice but those also did not fit with the Indian culture and ethos. They also had the taste of foreign culture and ethos and did not have an Indianised flavour, which was unable to provide justice to members of the ordinary folk. However such alternatives were popular in the commercial world. Thus, need was felt not only for alternative to the adjudication process but also the alternative to the so called alternative's processes, compatible to the Indian ethos and culture and to fulfill the gap as exists in the alternative dispute resolution mechanism.

It is here, worth noting, the observation made by former Prime Minister, Sri P. V. Narasimha Rao, while inaugurating the International Centre for Alternative Dispute Resolution. He said[55];

"Any democracy worth the name must provide for adequate and effective means of dispute-resolution at a reasonable cost; otherwise, the rule of law becomes a platitude and people may take law in their own hands, disrupting peace, order and good government. Effective dispute resolution is also necessary to secure the smooth functioning of trade and commerce". He again said; "Law is not a static concept. The effectiveness of the legal process depends upon its ability to mould itself to the requirements of the society from time to time. I find no reason why we should not ourselves experience with new methods of dispute-resolution. Passivity and conservatism have to give way to dynamism, adoptability and resurgence. A properly conceived alternative dispute resolution movement will ensure wide access to justice to all section of the people".

In such situation the Lok-Adalat appeared as a messiah for the ordinary folk in order to provide them access to justice. It is apparent from the aforesaid study that the Lok-Adalat is a brainchild of necessity. The emergence of Lok-Adalat as a new instrument for dispensation of justice is a result of social philosophy of judges, jurists, and eminent scholars who were always engrossed in the thought of providing a new forum for dispute resolution which can provide justice cost effectively and time effectively and should be accessible to all. Needless to say in the present scenario, the alternative dispute resolution system of Lok-Adalat movement appeared as one of its component, has assumed great importance. The Lok-Adalat system has become a regular feature and has become a living and continuous movement. Day by day, large numbers of litigants are resolving their dispute in form of settlement through this institution of Lok-Adalat. People have become conscious of their rights and are availing this alternative institution of Lok-Adalat for expeditious and inexpensive disposal of their cases.

The reason of its success lies in its process, which is simple, less formal, cheap, and expeditious. In the entire process, the decision making power lies with the disputants, which make it more consumer friendly. Though graph wise the Lok-Adalat is settling disputes effectively but it is not entirely a success story. The system is still in its growing stage. It has not been developed in all States in a similar way. Though different category of cases has been referred before Lok-Adalat but it is effectively successful only in few forms of cases. Though a large number of consumers of justice take benefit out of it but still a majority of litigants are not aware of this institution and even on transfer of cases they do not bother to appear before the forum. The legal profession on the other hand has not taken keen interest to this alternative mechanism, which affects its performance, and now need arises for a radical change in the style of advocacy.

Justice S. B. Majumdar describes five jewels of Lok-Adalat namely Advocates, Judicial officers, the members of staff associated with the process, conciliators and litigants. Among these, the Lawyers can play a vital role in any proceeding, specially when the people are poor and illiterate they have blind faith in their lawyers, and thus in any proceeding the first jewel namely the Advocate can play a vital role. It is evident from the fact that lawyers taking keen interest in the depute relating to the Motor Accident Compensation Claim, made the process most successful in such category of cases.

Thus if the institution is required to function effectively all the five jewels of Lok-Adalat have to be effective. The public to be made aware about the proceedings and to educate them on the advantages of the proceedings. NGOs have to involve themselves in the proceedings of educating the litigants. Lawyers have to come forward to discharge their social responsibility and appreciate the advantages of the institution neutrally. The executive has to function as co-operators between the different functionaries of the institution of Lok-Adalat. The judiciary have to discharge their responsibilities in a fruitful manner. They have the vital power of reference of disputes.

The challenge for legal fraternity today is to adopt this participatory and conciliatory institution and provide new encouragement so as to provide access to justice to all and can deliver justice qualitatively and quantitatively through the instrument of Lok-Adalat.

REFERENCES

1. Law Commission of India, *Alternative forum for Resolution of dispute at Grass root level,* 114th Report. Para 5.6
2. See Id, Report suggests for formation of Nyaya Panchayat, 129th Law Commission report suggest for alternative

mechanism like mediation, in urban litigation 124th report on High Court arrear 131st report on the role of legal profession in strengthening of administration of justice.

3. *See*. Legal Aid Committee Report (Government of Gujarat), 1971 para 13.12
4. 99th report of LCI, Quoted in LCI 124th report on High Court arrears Pg-5, para 1.15
5. 124th Report of LCI High Court Arrear: A Fresh Look. P2
6. *See* the data provided in 129th LCI report on Urban Litigation.
7. Lok Sabha USQ No. 1464 August 2, 1991.
8. Justice Dr A.S.Ananad, Fifty years of Indian Judiciary: Its achievement and failures, Nyaya Path, April-June, 2000, P8.
9. The data has been shown in the programme telecast in Star News Channel on 6-7-02 in the programme 'Big Fight' where three renowned lawyers of country, namely F. Nariman, Arun Jaitely, and Venu Gopal were participated as panelist.
10. Justice Dr A. S. Anand, Supra 8
11. Shrinivash Gupta, *'Judicial delays versus Right to speedy trial'*, May 24, 1992, P32, referred in Sunil Deshta, Lok-Adalat in India: Genesis and Functioning, P. 97
12. id
13. see 129th LCI report pg. 32 para 3-14.
14. id P 34 to 41 pare 3.16 to 3.21.
15. id.
16. Roman Tomasic & Malcolm M. Feelay, *Neighbourhood Justice: Assessment of an Emerging Idea* (1982) *Quoted In Id* Para 3.20.
17. Supra-15.
18. V.R. Krishna Iyer, *A Constitution Missllany*- P 179
19. Hussainara Khatoon case AIR 1979 SC 1360, Khatri Case AIR 1981 SC 928, Sukhdas's Case AIR 1986 SC 991, *Gopalachari* V. *State of Kerala* AIR 1981 SC 674.
20. *Zeve Powell* V. *State of Alabama* 287 US (1932), See, Justice P.S. Narayana, Law Relating to Lok-Adalet,(2002) P 2.
21. Justice P.S. Narayana, *Law Relating to Lok-Adalat*, P2 (2002).
22. K. Ramaswamy, *Settlement of Disputes Through Lok-Adalat, is one of the effective ADR on statutory basis*, P 96, in P.C. Rao, ADR: What it is and how its works, (1997).
23. id
24. N.R. Madhava Menon, Lok-Adalat in Delhi: *A Report from a legal educational perspective*, Indian Bar Review. Vol 12 (4) 1985, P 416, The different committees, which shows concern on the way of the functioning of Administation of Justice and recommended for such programme for legal aid includes The Gujrat Legal Aid Committee, 1971, The Report on Processual Justice to the people (1973), Juridicare: Equal Justice-Social Justice Report (1977). and Committee for Implementation of Legal Aid Scheme(1980).
25. Justice S. B. Majumdar; *Profile of legal aid scheme in India: Past and Present*, Nyaya Path, Souvenir-P38,2000.
26. id.
27. Justice M. G. Chitkara, *Accessibility of Justice*, P 83. Nyaya Path, Souvenir 2000.
28. id.
29. id.
30. N.R. Madhava Menon, Supra 24.
31. K. Gupteshwar, *"The Statutory Lok-Adalat: Its Structure and Role'*, June, vol.-30, April-June, 1988, Pg.-174.
32. N. R. Madhava Menon, *Lok-Adalat, People's Programme for speedy justice*, Indian Bar Review, Vol. 13(2): 1986, Pg.- 132 71id

33. id
34. id
35. K. Ramaswamy, *Supra* 60, P96
36. id
37. N. R. Madhav Menon, supra -171
38. id
39. K. Ramaswamy, Supra 173, P 98.
40. Justice D. M. Dharmadhikari, Lok-Adalat, Nyaya Path - Souvenir 2000, P. 31.
41. id.
42. N.R. Madhava Menon Supra 171.
43. *Supra* 178.
44. Justice D. M. Dharmadhakari, id.
45. D. K. Sampath, *Mediation*, (1991) NLSIU Publication, P. 9.
46. Justice M. Jagannadha Rao, *Law's delays world over-need for a change in our mindset-Towards permanent Lok-Adalat,* Nyaya Deep- April - June'2000 P. 23 at 25.
47. Legal-Aid news letter, May-August, 1990, P. 15.
48. K. Ramaswamy, Supra 39. P. 96.
49. N. R. Madhava Menon, *Lok-Adalat: People Programme for speedy Justice,* Indian Bar Review, Vol. 13(2): 1996 P. 134.
50. id.
51. Sec. 21 of The Legal Services Authority Act, 1987.
52. Justice D.M. Dharmadhikari, 44.
53. Sunil Desta, Lok-Adalat in India: Genesis and Functioning, P. 112.
54. N. R. Madhava Menon, *Lok-Adalat: People Programme for speedy justice,* Indian Bar Review, Vol. 13(2): 1996 P. 134.
55. Justice K. Ramaswamy, *Settlement of Disputes through Lok-Adalat is one of lhe effective Alternative Dispute Resolution on statutory basis,* In P.C.Rao, ADR: What it is and how it works, (1997) P. 101.

CHAPTER 4

CONSTITUTIONAL DIRECTIVES FOR THE LOK-ADALAT

INTRODUCTION

Equal justice for all is a cardinal principle on which entire system of administration of justice is based. It is so deep rooted in the body and spirit of Common Law as well as Civil Law jurisprudence that the very meaning, which we ascribe to the word, justice, embraces it[1]. We cannot conceive of justice that is not fair and equal, which is given to one and denied to another. This idea has always stirred the hearts of men since the dawn of civilization and so far as Anglo-Saxon legal history is concerned, we find it manifested in the earliest laws, which continually directed that justice be done alike to rich and poor. It is embedded in Indian ethos of justice - Dharma - equally. It was asserted in the charter of liberties of Henry II and it received its classic statement, its most glorious enunciation, in the fortieth paragraph of Magna-Carta, where it is inscribed:

"To no man will we deny, to no man will we sell, or delay, justice or right[2]"

Do the goal of providing justice with the fundamental principle of equality achieved? Has the Constitutional mandate of providing justice equally irrespective of rich, poor, caste, creed, achieved? Are the Constitutional mandate for providing legal aid, which is also embedded in Articles 7, 8, 10 of Universal Declaration of Human Rights being provided to the needy?

No one can deny the fact that the great principle of justice as inscribed in the Magna Carta and which is the basic principle of all National Charter has not been translated into reality. It did not inaugurate an era of absolute freedom and equality of justice[3]. Even in England, the author of the 'Justice And The Poor in England' felt so strongly about the non-fulfilment of the promise of providing equitable justice, that he printed an appendix to his book, a draft bill, to repeal the aforesaid section of the 'Magna-Carta' in so far as the poor persons were concerned[4].

Rendering justice to the people is an obligation on the State to provide a judicial system where its people are able to redress their grievances and have justice without any delay. Today, in order to provide justice equally and without any delay to every person, high or low, the philosophy of social justice under Art. 39A requires a radical change in the judicial process. Justice Krishna Iyer said on such requirement of judicial activism; 'We want revolutionary judicial system which will fight for people's sake, even the Cabinet's policy - not a dependant creature funded and controlled by the administration. We want legal social research lobbying for legislations, new models of mobile, people oriented tribunals. We want justice to be a proletarian estate. This is the preambular tryst'[5]

Indian Constitution is first and foremost a social document that symbolizes the hopes and aspirations of the people. Granville Austin called it a corner stone of social change[6]. In order to provide equal justice, the framers of the Constitution inscribed the mandate for social, economic and political justice in the national charter. While the Chapter on Fundamental Rights incorporates the idea of political and equal justice the Chapter on Directive Principles of State Policy along with Preamble incorporates economic, social and cultural justice. These provisions make it a Constitutional duty of all the three organs of the State to participate in the Constitutional march towards securing equal justice and social justice for all.

Thus, in order to fulfil the Constitutional mandate of providing equal justice, all machineries of State attempted to find out the means of providing justice. The ways and forms of providing justice, particularly in disputes, by the means of adversarial mechanism, made justice inaccessible to large number of masses. Such performance of adversarial system made despair to legal fraternity. If the constitutional mandates have to fulfil, which is fundamental to governance, the means for providing justice has to evolve. In order to provide justice to all by making it accessible to all, the institution of Lok-Adalat evolved, as one of the instruments to fulfil the Constitutional obligation. Thus, a clear mandate and directive for such instrument subsist in the Constitution.

PREAMBULAR SPIRIT OF JUSTICE AND LOK-ADALAT

A Government founded on anything except liberty and justice cannot stand[7]. It is intended by the members of the Constitution that the largesse of law must belong to all, not as now, to those who use the Constitution for unconstitutional ends. The Preamble of the Constitution itself represents the aspirations of the people. However, for the materialization of such aspiration, the Government has to march towards the cherished goal of justice, as enshrined in the Preamble of the Constitution. The Preamble of the national charter solemnly resolves to constitute India as a Sovereign, Socialist, Secular, Democratic, Republic. It commands for securing justice, not only social justice but economic and political justice too, for the citizens of the country. It enshrines the liberty of thought, expression, belief, faith and worship. It mandates for equality of status and opportunity. It also proscribed for promoting fraternity, dignity of every citizen and the unity and integrity of nation.

The test of the Preamble makes it abundantly clear that Government should aim to achieve justice, Social, economic and political. The philosophy of Justice enshrined in Preamble of our Constitution is based on the spirit contained in clause (5) of Objective Resolution of Nehru which was adopted by the Constituent Assembly on 22nd June 1947 and which inspire the shaping of the Constitution through all its subsequent changes. It says, "This Constituent Assembly declare its firm and solemn resolve to proclaim India as an independent Sovereign Republic and to draw up for her future governance a Constitution wherein shall be guaranteed and secured to all the people of India Justice, Social, Economic and political, Equality of Status, Opportunity and before the law; Freedom of thought, Expression, Belief, Faith, Worship, Vocation, Association and Action subject to law and Public Morality[8].

This spirit of justice has not materialized till today for a large number of citizens of this country. The aim was that the Constitution makers would wipe every tear from every eye and it is expected that law must do the same and not compel the litigant to reach an urban lawyer and a judge. But sadly the same has not been achieved in the true sense.

Article 14 of the Constitution[9] enshrines the philosophy of equality. It directs the State not to deny equal protection of laws within its territory. Justice Bhagwati said: "Article 14 shines like a beacon light pointing towards the goal of classless egalitarian socio- economic order which we promised to build for ourselves when we made a tryst with destiny..........when we adopted our Constitution[10]".

This philosophy of equality of justice based on the last clause of 14th amendment of American Constitution, which enjoins that the equal protection shall be secured to all such persons in the enjoyment of their rights and liberties without discrimination or favoritism. Though the philosophy of equality is enshrined in the Art of the Constitution, today it is a most difficult challenge before the legal fraternity and Governmental machinery to provide equal justice.

It is an established reality that the guarantee of equality before law does not mean anything to the poor if there is no one to tell him what the law is or that the Courts are open to him on equal terms with every other person. Solely this, will not able to take care of the economic status. Even after having information, there are rare chances for the poor to get equal justice because inequality exists in the economic status of the litigant. Acknowledging the fact of inequality in the society Dr.Ambedkar said that on the social plane, we have in India a society based on the principles of graded inequality, which means elevation of some people as against the general elevation of the community or social up-gradation.[11]

So long as socio-economic and other forms of inequality exists, the implementation of national charter becomes impossible, until or unless we evolve the process of administration of justice where the economic differences is not a factor for getting justice. Expenses, which can only be affordable by parties with strong economic capacities, create an unfortunate situation for the poor litigants where they are getting priced out of Court. The dispensation of justice has thus become lopsided. The economically disadvantaged litigant is overwhelmed by his opponents who can engage senior Counsels with best of legal talents. Even if the Courts try to keep the scale even, an impression is created that the legal system in India is only for economically advantaged litigants. This gives rise to a sense of hopelessness among the general people of India.

It is a stark reality today that a large number of men, women and children who constitute the bulk of our population are living in sub-human conditions. They accept social and economic exploitation and denial of legal rights as their fate. As a result, millions of people of the Country have badly lost their trust over the existing legal system. Therefore, the basic rights as enshrines in the national charter became meaning less to those millions of people of the Country. Thus, in reality equal justice for them is nothing but a formal promise.

Supreme Court showing concern about these dark realities said,[12] "The rule of law does not mean that the protection of laws must be available only to a fortunate few or that the law should be allowed to be prostituted by the vested interests for protecting and upholding the status quo under the guise of enforcement of their civil and political rights. The poor too have civil and political rights and the rule of law is meant for them also, though today it exists only on papers and not in reality... so far the Courts have been used only for the purpose of vindicating the rights of the wealthy and the affluent. It is only those privileged classes who have been able to approach the Courts for protecting their vested interests. It is only the moneyed who have so far had the golden key to unlock the door of justice.... They (poor) have been crying for justice but their cries have so far been in the wildness: They have been suffering injustice silently.... But time has now come when the Courts must become the Court for poor and struggling masses of this country... It is true that there are large arrears pending in the Courts, but that can not be any reason for denying access to justice to the poor and weaker sections of the community. No state has right to tell its citizens that because a number of cases of the rich and the well-to-do are pending in our Courts, we will not help the poor to come to the Courts for seeking justice until the staggering load of cases of people who can afford, is disposed of".

Thus, in the present scenario, if goal of providing equal justice has to be fulfilled, we require to evolve a participatory form of justice dispensation system. Lok Adalat is one such instrument, if utilized in the right direction. Although Lok-Adalat has not been mentioned explicitly under the provisions enumerated in the Constitution, it is implicit in it because of its philosophy of providing justice equally to all irrespective of their status, which can only be achieved by participatory form of dispute resolution mechanism.

LEGAL AID DICTATE, PANCHAYAT JUSTICE AND LOK-ADALAT

Since long it was felt necessary to enjoin the legislatures to get clear guidelines from the Constitution as to how they should function as Legislature to remove disparity in the context between litigants in the Courts of law so that the poor litigants may not feel helpless and priced out of justice, at all levels[13]. With this goal, Directive Principles of State Policy was added as part IV and by way of 42nd Amendment of the Constitution Article 39A[14] was inserted, which directs the State to establish such legal machineries by which justice can be provided based on equal opportunity. It also mandates that free legal aid shall be provided so that the opportunity of securing justice are not denied to any citizen by reason of their economic and other disabilities.

Article 40 of the Constitution[15] provides directives for the state to organise village panchayat and to empower them in such a manner that they can function as a self-governing unit. One hundred and fourteenth report of the law commission suggests the formation of Gram Nayalay (Nyaya Panchayat) for decentralization of the system of administration of justice and to make effective the participatory form of dispute settlement mechanism[16].

The 42nd Amendment, which made explicit the guidelines providing opportunity to secure justice on the basis of equality, was implicit in the Article 14 and Preamble of the Constitution. Though Article 39A is a directive on the State which is unjusticiable[17] but once it is read with Article 21 and Article 14 which guarantees a fundamental right of equality before law and equal protection of laws within the territories of India to all its citizens, it can easily be visualized that provision for free legal aid to needy litigants cannot remain an idle direction[18]. Its enforceability may be guaranteed by issuing Part III, Articles 14 & 21, of the Constitution.

Several judicial pronouncements have made this right of legal aid a fundamental right[19]. Long ago in Keshvananda Bharti[20], Justice Dwivedi observed that the Constitution is not intended to be the arena of legal quibbling for men with long purses. It is made for the common people. Learned Judge again said; "It is really the poor, starved and mindless millions who need the Court's protection for sewing to themselves the enjoyment of human rights[21].

This justice order is vibrantly implicit in Part III and Part IV of the Constitution, both of which are fundamental in the governance of the Country. The judiciary in India is expected to be the sentinel, sword and shield of rights of the humblest millions with an assurance to bring social salvation of the weaker section. That is why Article 39A likewise obligates the State, which includes the Judiciary, to secure that the operation of legal system promotes justice on the basis of equal opportunity to ensure that the opportunities for securing justice are not denied to any citizen by reason of economic and other disabilities[22].

Legal aid is not only human right enshrined in the Constitution but also a recognised international human right. Legal aid as human right is also implicit in Articles 7, 8, and 10 of the Universal Declaration of Human Right and more particularly it flows clearly and inevitably from clause 3(d) of the International Covenant on civil and political rights[23].

Articte 14(3) of the International Covenant on Civil and Political rights prescribes: 'The right to be tried in his presence, and to defend himself in person or through legal assistance of his own choosing, to be informed, if he does not have legal assistance, of his right, and to have legal assistance assigned to him in any case where the interest of justice shall require, and without payment by him in any such case if he does not have sufficient means to pay for it'.

The developed countries have begun to discuss the subject of access to law as of grave concern. The Massachusetts Constitution adopted in 1780 declared to provide equal justice to all[24]. Even in England, Access to justice Act was passed in order to provide access to all the judicial administration system and no one can be denied access due to lack of financial resources[25].

Traditionally, legal aid is conceived as the representation by the counsel in Court proceedings. However, the Indian concept of 'legal aid' is much wider in scope and application. All types of legal services including public legal education (legal awareness), legal advice and counselling, public interest litigation, legal clinics in law teaching institutions, Lok-Adalat and settlements through similar alternative dispute resolution system in the community, legal mobilization for social justice, para legal and preventive legal services, law reform initiatives intended to help the poor are brought within the meaning of legal aid[26]. Several expert committees on legal aid were appointed by the Central Government. Justice Krishna Iyer Committee on Processual Justice (1973) advocated for implementation of effective legal aid schemes and the Committee for Implementing Legal Aid Scheme (CILAS) in 1980 popularised such wide meaning to legal aid, taking into consideration the socio economic condition of the people of India and the inability of the formal legal system to penetrate into the rural countryside where poor people live. They canvassed for a pro-active, people-friendly scheme of legal aid for providing meaningful access to justice[27]. The CILAS, successfully attempted to provide access to justice to large number of people by holding Lok-Adalat. Thus under the directives and guidelines of the CILAS, different Legal Aid and Advice Boards were constituted and started holding Lok-Adalat as legal aid strategy. Thus the institution of Lok-Adalat evolved as an instrument to provide access to justice to all in equal terms and to provide justice quickly and without any cost. So the institution of Lok-Adalat as evolved by CILAS is nothing but an instrument to fulfil the Constitutional obligation, for which the Constitution has clear directives.

It will be worthy here to mention that Delhi High Court, while directing different Governmental agencies like Delhi Vidyut Board, Municipal Corporation of Delhi, Mahanagar Telephone Nigam Limited, General Insurance Corporation to constitute permanent Lok-Adalats to redress the disputes between general public and such companies or between employees and companies through negotiated settlement, highlighted the great principles enshrined in Article 39A. The Court says, "The language of Article 39A is couched in mandatory terms. This is made more than clear by the use of the twice occurring word "shall" in Article 39A. It is emphasized that the legal system should be able to deliver justice expeditiously on the basis of equal opportunity and provide free legal aid to ensure that opportunities of securing justice are not denied to any citizen by reason of economic and other disabilities[28]".

Though Article 39A has not said any thing about Lok-Adalat but to fulfil the goal, enshrined in Article 39A, Lok Adalat is being effectively used as an instrument to provide equal justice, based on negotiated settlement through participatory form of judicial administration system.

CONCLUSION

The genesis of Lok Adalat can be found in our traditional Panchayat system[29]. Article 40 of the constitution provides directives for the state to organise village panchayat and to empower them in such a manner that they can function as a self-government unit. The philosophy behind Article 40 is that village Panchayat as a unit of self-government would go a long way in ensuring democratic decentralization and creating an exhilarating feeling and sense of confidence among the villages in the sphere of decision making[30]. The statement made by the Law Minister in the Parliament in 1959 also reminds us of the fact that small disputes must be left to be decided by the system of Panchayat Justice, the People's Courts or institutions like Lok Adalat. To quote,[31] "There is no doubt that the system of justice which obtained today is too expensive for the common man. The small disputes must necessarily be left to be decided by a system of panchayat justice call it people's Court, call it popular Court, call it any thing - but it would be certainly subject to such safeguards as we may desire in the village level that the common man can be assured of a system of judicial administration which would not be too expensive for him and which would not be too dilatory for him".

The modern concept of Lok Adalat appeared on the concern shows by different bodies on failure of Anglo-Saxon judicial system to provide justice to a larger number of people and on the recommendation of different Committees for promoting participatory form of administration of justice, particularly the CILAS. The Constitutional directives for forming Lok-Adalat, for the people and by the people, are implicit in the Preamble, Articles 14, 39A, 40 and other provisions of the Constitution. Thus it is crystal clear from the aforesaid study that the organisation of the Lok-Adalat is a mandate provided by the Constitution. The march towards making Lok-Adalat a great success is a Constitutional goal, for which every one has obligation to fulfil.

REFERENCES

1. Justice K. Ramaswamy, *Settlement of disputes through Lok Adalat is one of the effective dispute resolution on statutory basis*, In, P.C.Rao, A.D.R: What it is and How its works, (1997), P 93.

2. id.

3. K. Ramaswamy, *Settlement of disputes through Lok-Adalat is one of the effective ADR on statutory basis*, P 93, in P.C.Rao, ADR: *What it is and how its works, (1997).*

4. id, 93.

5. V.R. Krishna Iyer, *Our Courts on Trial, (1987)*, quoted in. Sunil Deshta, Lok-Adalat India: Genesis and Functioning, 63 (1995).

6. Granville Austin. *The Indian Constitution: Cornerstone of a Nation*, (1966).

7. V. R. Krishna Iyer, *Law Versus Justice: Problems and Solutions* 16 (1981), in, Sunil Deshta, *Lok-Adalat in India: Genesis and Functioning*, 51 (1995).

8. Constituent Assembly Debate, C-59 (moved by Pt. Nehru) of the Resolution. Book No. 1, 59 (1947), dt 13.12.1946.

9. Indian Const. art. 14: Equality before the law *"The state shall not deny to any person equality before the law or equal protection of the law within the territory of India."*

10. *Maganlal Chhaganlal* V. *Municipal Corporation*. 435-436, 1974 (2) SCC 402.

11. *State of Kerala* V. *N. H. Thomas*. AIR 1976 SC490 at 513

12. *Peoples Union for Democratic right & other* V. *UOI & other* AIR 1982 SC 1473 at P 1478, *Bandhua Mukti Morcha* V. *Union of India*. AIR 1984 SC 802

13. Justice S. B. Majumder, *Profile of legal Aid Scheme in India post and presents* Nyaya Path. Souvenir, 37 (2000)

14. Indian Constitution. Art 39A: *Equal justice and free legal aid:* The state shall secure that the operation of the legal system promotes justice, on a basis of equal opportunity, and shall in particular provide free legal aid, by suitable legislation or schemes or in any other way, to ensure that the opportunities for securing justice are not denied to any citizen by reason of economic and other disabilities.

15. Article 40 of the Constitution: *Organisation of village Panchayat:* The State shall take steps to organise Village Panchayats and endow them with such powers and authority as may be necessary to enable them to function as unit of self government.

16. Justice D.A. Desai was the Chairman of the Law Commission and submitted its report on 12th August 1986. The Law Commission suggested that at village level the 'Nyaya Panchayat' shall be constituted so that large number of disputants can get justice quickly through such Panchayat Courts. Commission suggested for formation of three member Nyaya Panchayat in which one person should be trained judicial personnel and other two would be lay men of village. Such three member Court will provide justice at lowest level even on the spot enquiry they can verdict immediately.

17. Art 37 of Constitution: *Application of the principles contained in this Part. The provision contained in this Part shall not be enforceable by any Court, but the Principles therein laid down are nevertheless fundamental in the governance of the country and it shall be the duty of the State to apply these Principles in making laws.*

18. Justice S. B. Majumdar *Supra* 13, P. - 37.

19. See *Hussainara Khatoon* V. *Home Secretary Bihar*. AIR 1979 SC V. 1360, *Khetri and others* V. *State of Bihar* AIR 1981 SC 928, *Sukhdas and other* V. *Union Territory of Arunachal Pradesh*. AIR 1986 SC 991, *M.H. Hosket* V. *State of Maharstra* - 1978(3) SCC 544.
20. *Keshvananda Bharati* V. *State of Kerala*. 1973(4) SCC 225 at P-947, Para 1947.
21. id at 949, para 1947.
22. Sunil Deshta. *Lok-Adalat in India; genesis and functioning*, 63 (1995).
23. The Universal Declaration reads: *"Every one has right to an effective remedy by the competent national tribunals for acts violating the fundamental rights granted by the Constitution or by law". See* K. Ramaswamy, Settlement of Dispute Through Lok Adalat, In, P.C. Rao & William Sheffield, ADR what it is and how its works, 94, (1997).
24. The Massachusetts Constitutional provisions reads, *"Every subject of the Commonwealth ought to find a certain remedy, by having recourse to the laws, for all injuries or wrongs which he may receive in his person, property, or character. He ought to obtain right and justice freely and without being obliged to purchase it; completely, and without any denial, promptly, and without delay; conformably to the laws"*. See K. Ramaswamy, id at 95.
25. Access to Justice Act, 1999. The Act was enforced on 27th July, 1999.
26. N. R. Madhava Menon. An Indian Contribution to world jurisprudence, Nyaya Path, Souvenir 2000 Pg. 57.
27. See N.R. Madhava Menon, id.
28. *Abul Hasan* V. *Delhi Vidyut Board*. AIR 1999 Del. 88 at 89.
29. Justice M.B. Shah, *effective fast Track Court*, Nyaya Path, Souvenir (2000), P 25.
30. Sibnath Bhattacharya, *Rural Poverty in India*, 137 (1989).
31. RAJYA SABHA. DEB, 1959 Vol. 27, No. 3, Col 388. See also Supra 26. 71 - 72.

CHAPTER 5

Legislative Mechanism for Lok-Adalat vis-a-vis scheme of Legal Services Authorities Act

INTRODUCTION

The initiation of Lok-Adalat was not done with any statutory backing but it was devised and developed by people themselves as a participatory instrument of democratic Judicial making[1]. The institution of Lok-Adalat was functioning as a voluntary and conciliatory agency without any statutory backing for more than one decade. Initially, with the object of providing free legal aid the Government appointed a Committee by the name of Committee for Implementation of Legal Aid Scheme (CILAS) under the Chairmanship of Justice Bhagwati, on 26th September 1980. It was realised that providing legal aid solely to poor disputants cannot solve the problem of a large number of masses who do not have access to justice. CILAS started to organise Lok Adalat as a Legal Aid strategy. The institution of Lok-Adalat proved to be very popular in providing for a speedier system of administration of justice. But on a review of the working of the CILAS, certain deficiencies were noticed. There was a demand from all corners for providing statutory backing to the institution of Lok-Adalat. It was also felt that it would be desirable to constitute Statutory Legal Services Authority at National, State and District Level. Accordingly, the Legal Services Authority Act was passed in 1987[2]. However, it took 7 yrs for enforcement[3]. Chapter III of the Act, which is concerning the establishment of the State Legal Services Authority, was enforced under different notifications in different States during the period from 1995 to 1998[4].

One of the reasons and objects for the enactment of this Statute was to provide speedy and inexpensive justice, as it appeared from statement and reasons accompanying the Bill, which said, "for some time now, Lok-Adalats are being constituted at various places in the Country for the disposal, in a summary way and through the process of arbitration and settlement, between the parties, of a large number of cases, expeditiously and with lesser costs. The institution of Lok Adalat is at present functioning as a voluntary and conciliatory agency without any statutory backing for its decisions. It has proved to be very popular in providing a speedier system of administration of justice. In view of its growing popularity, there has been a demand for providing a statutory backing to this institution and awards given by Lok-Adalats. It is felt that such a statutory support would not only reduce the burden of arrears of work in regular Courts, but would also take justice to the door-steps of the poor and needy and make justice quicker and less expensive".

Thus, in a situation where the whole justice administration system is likely to crumble down under the weight of pending cases, which goes on increasing everyday and the access to justice denied to the large number of masses, the enactment of this legislation for strengthening the institution of Lok-Adalat is a welcome step to provide access to justice to all. In fact, the preamble of the Act has also made it clear that the basic object of the Act is to provide free and competent legal services to the weaker sections of the society to ensure that opportunities for securing justice are not denied to any citizen by reasons of economic or other disabilities, and to organize Lok-Adalats to secure that the operation of the legal system promotes justice on a basis of equal opportunity.

Three fold objectives of the Act are, (1) to provide free and competent legal services to the weaker sections of the society, (ii) to ensure security of justice to all despite their economic or other disabilities, and (iii) to organise Lok-Adalat with a view to promote justice on a basis of equal opportunity. The remarkable features of the Act is that, while giving statutory authority to both Legal Aid and Lok-Adalat, it enlarges the scope of the former in coverage along with the beneficial effects flowing from it. With an enthusiasm to provide wider powers to Lok-Adalat, wider jurisdiction has been conferred on it, in the sense that it can deal with any matter, whatever be its legal character and in whatever Court or Tribunal it might be pending, provided they were within the jurisdiction of such areas where Lok-Adalat is going to be held[5]. However, such unlimited power in respect of jurisdiction would likely to lead to absurd situations in some cases, mainly in Criminal cases of grievous nature, where the forum of Lok-Adalat is not an appropriate one. Therefore, this anomalous and undesirable situation created by original Sub-Sec. (3) of Sec. 19 was duly taken note by the Parliament and a suitable amendment thereof has been brought in by the Legal Services Authorities Amendment Act, 1994[6]. The Legal Services Authority Act, 1987 provides ample opportunity to all to have easy access to justice available at the doorsteps of litigants through Lok-Adalat. It has virtually given birth to participatory justice system and has fulfilled the need to work as an alternative forum to quench the thirst of justice. The very objective of the Act is to evolve a mechanism to deal with arrears of cases, expeditiously, by resorting to the device of Lok-Adalat by means of participatory form of justice.

Recent amendments of the Legal Services Authority Act have provided for a new model of Lok-Adalat, which will make an utmost attempt for settlement but on failure to settle the case between the parties, it can pass order on merit. Such an order of the Lok-Adalat is unappealable. Basically this model will deal with the cases, which are related to public utility services. This model of Lok-Adalat will be called as permanent Lok-Adalat. However, Legislature equates the process with adversarial system and there is apprehension about the losing of basic characteristic of Lok-Adalat itself. To discuss elaborately about the Legislative mechanism I have divided this Chapter into five sub-parts. In the first part, I have discussed about the formation of different Legal Services Authorities and Committees and their powers and responsibilities. In the second part, I have discussed about the formation of Lok-Adalat. In the third part, I have discussed about the power of the Lok-Adalat. In the fourth part, I have tried to find out the impact of the 2002 Amendment of Legal Services Authorities Act and the formation of permanent Lok-Adalat and in the fifth part I have analysed the effect of C.P.C on the Alternative Dispute Resolution vis-a-vis Lok-Adalat.

FORMATION OF LEGAL SERVICES AUTHORITIES AND COMMITTEES

The Legal Services Authority Act, 1997 creates three hierarchical Legal Services Authorities and three Legal Services Committees in order to provide Legal Aid and for holding Lok-Adalat from Apex Court at Central Level to the Sub-Divisional Court at the Lowest Level. It creates National Legal Services Authority[7] at Central level as the apex body in order to provide Legal Aid and holding Lok-Adalat. Under the direct supervision of National Authority, two bodies are constituted viz. Supreme Court Legal Services Committee[8] and State Legal Services Authority[9] as functioning in different States at the State level, (iii) High Court Legal Services Committee[10] and District Legal Services Authority[11] are obliged to function under the guidelines and direct supervision of the State Legal Services Authority. The Taluk or Sub-Divisional Legal Services Committee[12] is constituted to work at the grass root level, under the direct control and supervision of District Legal Services Authority, subject to over all supervision of the State Legal Services Authority. So the hierarchy of the legal services authorities and Committees are as hereunder:

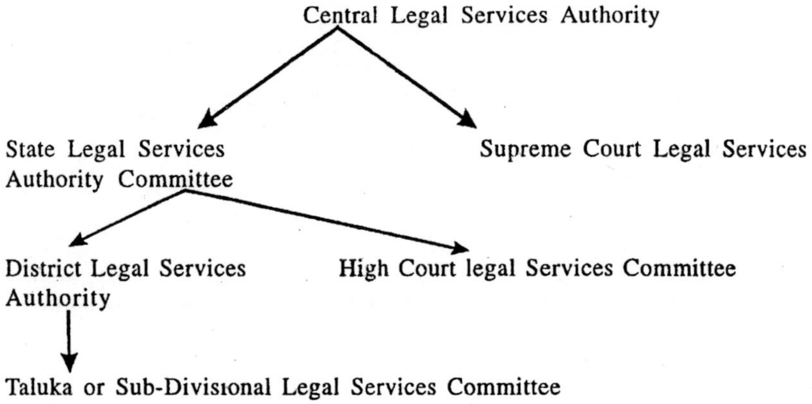

National Legal Services Authority

The Act empowers the Central Government to constitute National Legal Services Authority to exercise the powers and perform such functions as conferred by the Act. The Act also empowers the Central Government to frame rules to carryout the provisions as enumerated in the Act[13]. Sec. 3 (2) of the Act prescribed that the Central Authority shall consist of: (a) The Chief Justice of India who shall be the Patron-in-Chief of the Authority, (b) a serving or retired judge of the Supreme Court to be nominated by the President, in Consultation with the Chief Justice of India to function as Executive Chairman of the Authority and (c) such number of other members, possessing such experience and qualifications, as may be prescribed by the Central Government, to be nominated by that Government in consultation with the Chief Justice of India.

Further clause (3) of Sec. 3 empowers the Central Government to appoint Member Secretary of the Central Authority in consultation with the Chief Justice of India to exercise powers and perform duties under the executive chairman. The elaborate provision relating to the power and function of the Member Secretary are in Rule 6[14], which includes, to workout the modalities of the Legal Services Schemes and Programme and to ensure their effective monitoring and implementation throughout the country, to liaise with the social action groups and State Legal Services Authorities, to maintain up-to-date and complete statistical information including progress made in the implementation of various legal services programme etc. The Rule[15] also prescribes that the Central Authority shall consist of not more than 12 members including the Secretary, Department of Legal Affairs under the Ministry of Law Justice and Company affairs or his nominee and Secretary, Department of Expenditure under the Ministry of Finance or his, nominee. Finance is backbone of any organization. The Act has made it clear that all the administrative expenses of the Central Authority shall be defrayed out of the Consolidated Fund of India[16]. The Act has also prescribed that the Central Authority should work in co-ordination with other agencies. It also provides, that in the discharge of its functions under this Act, the Central Authority should, whenever appropriate, act in co-ordination with other Governmental and Non-Governmental Agencies, Universities and others engaged in the work of promotion of the cause of Legal Services to the poor[17].

The Act has made it obligatory on the part of the Central Authority to perform the following functions[18]:- (a) to lay down policies and principles for making legal services available, (b) to frame the most effective and economical schemes for the purpose of making legal services available; (c) distribution of fund at its disposal among the State Authorities and District Authorities; (d) to take necessary steps by way of Social Justice Litigation with regard to Consumer Protection, Environmental Protection or any other matter of special concern to the weaker sections of the society and in order to achieve the goal as prescribed in the Act, it mandates to give training to social workers in legal skills, (e) to organize legal aid camps, especially in rural areas, slums or labour colonies with the dual purposes of educating the weaker sections of the society as to their rights as well as encouraging the settlement of disputes through Lok Adalats, (f) to encourage the settlement of disputes by way of negotiation, arbitration and conciliation; (g) to undertake and promote research in the field of legal services with special reference to the need for such services among the poor, (h) to do all things necessary for the purpose of ensuring commitment to the Fundamental Duties of the citizens under Part IVA of the Constitution; (i) to monitor and evaluate implementation of the legal aid programmes at periodic intervals and provide for independent evaluation of programmes and schemes implemented in whole or in part by funds provided under the Act; (j) to provide grants in aid for specific schemes to various voluntary and social services institutions and the State and District Authorities, (k)to develop, in consultation with the Bar Council of India, programmes for clinical and legal education and promotion of guidance and supervising the establishment and working of legal services clinics in Universities, Law Colleges and other institutions; (I) to take appropriate measures for spreading legal literacy and legal awareness amongst the people and, in particular, to educate weaker sections of the society about the rights, benefits and privileges guaranteed by social welfare Legislations; (m) to make special efforts to enlist the support of voluntary social welfare institutions working at the grass root level, particularly among the Scheduled Castes and the Scheduled Tribes, women and rural and urban labour, and (n) to co-ordinate and monitor the functioning of State Authorities, District Authorities, Supreme Court Legal Services Committees, High Court Legal Service Committees, Taluk Legal Services Committees and voluntary social service institutions and other legal services organizations and give general directions for the proper implementation of the legal services programme. The Act also mandates the National Authority for formation of National Legal Aid fund. The expenditure incurred on legal aid provided by National Authority and Supreme Court Legal Services Committee shall be made out of this Fund[19].

Thus elaborate provisions have been made for the National Authority and being the apex body a supervisory role has been entrusted upon the Authority.

Supreme Court Legal Services Committee

The Supreme Court Legal Services Committee was constituted by virtue of the guide lines prescribed in Sec. 3A of the Act. The Act empowered the Central Authority to constitute the Committee at the apex level of the judicial hierarchy in order to provide access to justice to the large number of people at the Apex Court level. Provision for formation of Supreme Court Legal Services Committee was not there in the beginning and was inserted subsequently in the year 1994. The Act prescribed for the formation of a Committee consisting of one serving or retired judge of the Supreme Court and other members possessing such experience and qualifications as would be prescribed by the Regulation. The Supreme Court Legal Services Committee Regulations 1996 prescribe the detailed guidelines for the functioning of the Committee at the apex level[20]. The Regulation prescribed that one of the functions of the Committee is to administer and implement legal services programme in so far as it relates to Supreme Court of India. It further provides a free hand to the Committee to take all such necessary steps, which is required to take for the proper implementation of such Legal Services Programme[21]. Though the word 'Lok-Adalat' has not been mentioned in the Regulation, yet it is implicit in the definition of Legal Services Programme. However, it would be better to have the goal in black and white so that it will be easier to achieve. If so, then a small amendment in the provision will suffice the need of making it obligatory on the Supreme Court Legal Services Committee to organize Lok-Adalat in order to explore the possibility of negotiated settlement.

State Legal Services Authority

The Act has empowered the State Government to constitute State Legal Services Authority for the State to exercise the power and perform the functions conferred on the State Authority under the Act[22]. The Act prescribe that the State Legal Services Authority shall consist of:

(a) the Chief Justice of the High Court who shall be the Patron-in-Chief;

(b) a serving or retired Judge of the High Court, to be nominated by the Governor, in consultation with the Chief Justice of the High Court, who shall be the Executive Chairman, and

(c) such number of members possessing such experience and qualifications as may be prescribed by the State Government to be nominated by that Government in consultation with the Chief Justice of the High Court.

The Act also provides guidelines for appointment of the Member-Secretary of the State Authority, from persons belonging to the Higher Judicial Service of the State[23]. The State Governments have been empowered to provide the terms of office and other conditions relating to the Members and Member Secretary and appoint such number of officers and employees required for the efficient functioning of the Authority to discharge its functions under the Act[24]. It has also specified that all administrative expenditure of the State Legal Services Authority should be defrayed out of the Consolidated Fund of the State[25]. It is made obligatory on the part of the State Authority to give effect to the policy and direction of the Central Authority. The Act also provides for the State Authority to perform these functions:

(a) give legal services to the eligible persons,

(b) conduct Lok-Adalats,

(c) undertake preventive and strategic legal aid programmes, and

(d) perform such other functions as are prescribed by the Regulations[26].

The West Bengal State Legal Services Rules, 1994 have made elaborate provisions relating to powers and functions of the Member Secretary. Such vast powers of the Member Secretary includes[27]:

(a) providing free legal services to the eligible people,

(b) to work out modalities of the Legal Services Schemes and Programmes and ensure their effective monitoring and implementation;

(c) to exercise powers in respect of Administrative House keeping, Finance and Budget matters as Head of the Department in the State Government,

(d) to manage the properties, records and funds of the State Authority;

(e) to maintain true and proper accounts of the State Authority including checking and auditing in respect thereof periodically;

(f) to prepare Annual Income and Expenditure Account and Balance-sheet of the said Authority,

(g) to liaise with the Social Action Groups and District and Sub-Divisional Legal Services Committees,

(h) to maintain up-to-date and complete statistical information including progress made in the implementation of various Legal Services Programmes,

(i) to process proposals for financial assistance,

(j) to organize various Legal Services Programmes as approved by the State Authority and convene Meetings/Seminars and Workshops connected with Legal Services Programmes and preparation of reports and follow up action thereon;

(k) to produce video/documentary films, publicity material, literature and other publications to inform general public about the various aspects of the Legal Services Programmes;

(l) to lay stress on the resolution of rural disputes and to take extra measures to draw schemes for effective and meaningful legal services for settling rural disputes at the door step of the rural people,

(m) to perform such of the functions as are assigned under the Schemes formulated under Sec. 4(b) of the Act, and

(n) to perform such other functions as may be expedient for efficient functioning of the State Authority.

The Act has mandated the State Authority to act in co-ordination with other Governmental Agencies, Non Governmental voluntary social service institutions, Universities and other bodies engaged in the work of promoting the cause of legal services to the poor, while discharging its functions[28]. The Act also provides guidelines for the State Authority to form State Legal Aid Fund and such Fund can be utilized for providing legal aid and grant to different District Authorities for the purpose[29].

High Court Legal Services Committee

The Act also provides for State Government to constitute High Court Legal Services Committee, which shall consist of a sitting Judge of the High Court, who shall be the Chairman, and such number of other members as may be determined by the State Government[30]. Initially the provision for formation of the High Court Legal Services Authority was not there and was subsequently incorporated[31]. Elaborate provisions relating to the powers and functions of the High Court Legal Services Committee of the Calcutta High Court have been made in Regulation 3 of the West Bengal Legal Services Authority Regulation 1998. The power and functions of the High Court Committee enumerated in the Regulation, includes

(a) Rendering legal service to eligible person,

(b) Conducting Lok-Adalat for High Court cases,

(c) To encourage the settlement of disputes by way of negotiation, arbitration and conciliation,

(d) Conducting legal literacy campaign and legal awareness programmes. Thus a clear guideline has been prescribed for the functioning of the Committee at High Court level.

District Legal Services Authority

The Act empowers State Government to constitute District Legal Services Authority for each district in consultation with the Chief Justice of the High Court. It also prescribed that the District Authority shall consist of (a) the District Judge who will function as the Chairman of the Authority, and (b) other such members as prescribed by the State Government. It authorised the State Authority to appoint Member Secretary for each District from among the Members of the State Judicial Service, not below the rank of a sub ordinate judge or Civil judge[32]. Administrative expenses of every District

Authority shall be defrayed out of the Consolidated Fund of the State[33]. It is obligatory on the part of the District Authority to perform such functions of the State Authority in the District as may be delegated to it by the State Authority[34]. Sub-Section (2) of Section 10 of the Act specified the function of District Authority, (a) to Co-ordinate the activities of the Taluk Legal Services Committee and other Legal Services in the District, (b) to organise Lok-Adalats within the District, and (c) to perform such other functions as the State Authority may fix by Regulation. In order to fulfil the mandate of providing legal aid, the Act made the provision for formation of District Legal Aid Fund at district level and the legal aid can be provided out of this Fund[35].

Taluk Legal Services Committee

In order to provide the fruit of institution of Lok-Adalat at the lowest level at Taluk and to provide legal aid to the needy, so that the goal of providing access to justice to all can be achieved, the Taluk Legal Services Committee was constituted. This provision for formation of such Committee was not there in the original 1987 Act but subsequently the provision was incorporated so as provide access to justice at the grass root level. The provision relating to formation of Taluk Legal Services Committee is enumerated in Sec. 11A of the Act. It mandates State Authority to constitute Taluka or Sub-Divisional Committee consisting of a senior Civil Judge operating within the jurisdiction of such Committee who shall function as an ex-officio Chairman of the Taluk Committee or Sub-Divisional Committee and other Members. Administrative expenses of the Committee shall be defrayed out of the District Legal Aid Fund. The following functions have been entrusted with the Taluk Legal Services Committee[36], (a) Co-ordinate the activities of legal services in Taluk, (b) organise Lok-Adalat within Taluk and (c) Perform such other functions as the District Authority, may assign.

ORGANISATION OF THE LOK-ADALAT

A separate Chapter is inserted in the Act to deal with the organization, cognisance, power of the Lok-Adalat and the effect of settlement arising before Lok Adalats[37]. The Act empower every State Authority, Supreme Court Legal Services Committee, High Court Legal Services committees, District Legal Services Authorities and Taluk Legal Services Committees to organise Lok-Adalats at such intervals and places as they think fit[38]. It empowered the Authority or Committees to organize Lok-Adalats, to select the members for the Lok-Adalat consisting of retired or serving judges[39]. However, the power to prescribe the qualifications of the judges vest with the Central Authority in respect of Lok-Adalats organised by the Supreme Court Legal Services Committee and with State Government for other Lok-Adalats held in the State at State level, High Court Level, District level and Taluka Level[40].

The State Authority of West Bengal also prescribed the qualifications of the members of Lok-Adalat[41]. It prescribes for the constitution of Lok-Adalat consisting of three Members, in which one should be either a sitting or a retired judge and the other two Members from the legal profession, social workers, persons interested in legal services schemes, representative of NGOs and members of legal clinic. While the Regulation prescribing for the appointment of a sitting judge to the Lok-Adalat it is silent about the reference of cases from the Court of such a judge. The issue is, whether a Court in which the adversarial proceeding is continuing, will act as a conciliator in Lok-Adalat in such cases? Whether it will not prejudice the party, if the party fails to settle the disputes in front of such a judge when he is trying to persuade such parties to settle the dispute? Suppose if a party does not agree with the proposal of the judge, even after his continuing efforts; Will it not affect the sanctity of the judicial proceeding? Does the value neutral characteristic of a judge subsist on such occasion? In my view the best available option is to make the law in such a way that when a sitting judge act as conciliator in Lok-Adalat, the cases belonging to his Court shall not be referred to such Lok-Adalat. However, in West Bengal and in some other States, though the law prescribes for the appointment of both sitting judge as well as retired judge as conciliator' it is common practice to appoint retired judges. Now it become customary to appoint retired judges. However, a clear directive is required at this end. The Act provides wide jurisdiction to Lok-Adalat to determine and to arrive at a compromise or settlement in respect of any case, irrespective of whether it is pending before any Court or it is falling within the jurisdiction of any Court, though not brought before such Court, for which the Lok-Adalat is organized. However, the proviso rightly debars the Lok-Adalat to take cognizance of such cases, which is not compoundable under the Law. Initially, in the 1987 Act, this proviso was not there and as a result the Act empowered the Lok-Adalat to take cognizance even in grievous offences, for which Lok-Adalat cannot be the proper forum and accordingly the Legislature has amended the provision in 1994[42].

The Act empowered Lok-Adalat to take cognisance of both types of cases (a) which are pending in the Court, and (b) which are at pre-litigation Stage. Three ways have been prescribed for referring pending cases[43]. First when parties to the suit/case agree to refer the matter to the Lok-Adalat. Secondly, when one of the parties makes application for reference of the suit and Court is prima facie satisfied that there is chance of settlement and, thirdly if the Court is satisfied that the matter is an appropriate one to be taken cognisance of by the Lok-Adalat[44].

In pre-litigation cases, the authority concerned, who is organizing the Lok-Adalat can refer the matter to the Lok-Adalat, provided they are satisfied that the matter needs to be determined by Lok-Adalat. However, no matter can be referred to Lok-Adalat without providing opportunity to the other party of being heard[45]. If no compromise is arrived at in the Lok-Adalat the record of the case shall be returned to the concerned Court for disposal of the case in accordance with the law and in the pre-litigation cases, parties are advised to seek remedy in the Court of Law[46].

POWERS OF LOK-ADALAT

The Lok-Adalat enjoys vast powers to carry out the noble goal of the Act. The Lok-Adalat is conferred with the same powers as are vested for Civil Court under the Code of Civil Procedure, 1908 for the purpose of (a) summoning and enforcing the attendance of any witness and examining him on oath, (b) the discovery and production of any documents, (c) the reception of evidence on affidavits, (d) the requisition of any public documents on records or copy of such record or document from any Court or office, and (e) other matters also which may be prescribed later on[47]. To bring flexibility in the procedure of its functioning, as per the requirement, the Act empowered the Lok-Adalat to specify its own procedure of functioning. The Act also specifically laid down that all proceedings before the Lok-Adalat shall be deemed to be judicial proceedings under Sections 193, 219 and 228 of I.P.C. and every Lok-Adalat shall be deemed to be a Civil Court for the purpose of Section 195 and Chapter XXVI of the Code of Criminal Procedure, 1973[48]. The most important provision of the Act is the binding nature of the order passed by the Lok Adalat on the basis of compromise entered between the parties. It prescribed that every award given by the Lok-Adalat is deemed to be a decree of a Civil Court or order of any other Court. It debars appeal from the order of the Lok-Adalat[49].

All the States have enacted Rules under the Act relating to Lok-Adalat and Legal Aid. In West Bengal too the Rules have been made by the name The West Bengal Legal Services Rules 1994[50] and was supplemented by The West Bengal State Legal Authority Regulation, 1998[51]. The Rules provide guidelines for the formation of High Court Legal Services Committee, District Legal Services Authority, as well as Sub-Divisional Legal Services Committee[52]. The Rule also provides for the qualifications and other requirements for the panel of judges of Lok-Adalat and the members of different Authorities and Committees. To materialize the guidelines of the Act and for organizing legal literacy programmes, the Regulation specifies the organisation of the Legal Literacy Programme by the State Authority or by any other Authority or Committee and to establish Conciliation Committees at various centres in the State in view of providing- permanent or quasi-permanent infrastructure for resolving legal disputes between the parties, whether their cases are pending in the Court or are in the offing[53].

FORMATION OF PERMANENT LOK-ADALAT VIS-À-VIS 2002 AMENDMENT OF THE LEGAL SERVICES AUTHORITIES ACT

The 2002 Amendment of the Legal Services Authority Act bring a new dimension in the formation, organization and functioning of Lok-Adalat. It created the institution of permanent Lok-Adalat specifically to resolve the dispute concerning public utilities services[54]. The objective and reason for the amendment, which was shown in the Bill was to remedy the situation when the parties do not settle the disputes and the Lok-Adalat did not have power to decide on merit. The following objective and reason was shown.

> "The major draw back in the existing scheme of organization of Lok-Adalat under Chapter VI of the said Act is that the system of Lok-Adalats is mainly based on compromise or settlement between the parties. If the parties do not arrive at any compromise or settlement, the case is either returned to the Court of law or parties are advised to seek remedy in the Court of law. This causes unnecessary delay in the dispensation of justice. If Lok-Adalats are given powers to decide the cases on merit if the parties fail to arrive at any compromise or settlement, this problem can be tackled to a great extent. Further, the cases which arise in relation to Public Utility Services such as Mahanagar Telephone Nigam Limited, Delhi Vidyut Board, etc., need to be settled urgently so that people get justice without delay even at pre-litigation stage and thus most of the petty cases which ought not to go to the regular Courts, would be settled at the pre-litigation stage itself which would result in reducing the work load of the regular Courts to a great extent. It is, therefore, proposed to amend the Legal Services Authorities Act, 1987 to set up Permanent Lok-Adalats for providing compulsory pre-litigation mechanism for conciliation and settlement of cases relating to public utilities services".

The aforesaid reasons have sound logic behind it. However, once this system is implemented fully, the basic nature of Lok-Adalat, as a conciliatory body and the control of the process, which lies with parties, will change. It will become a para-adjudicatory process with certain characteristics of former Lok-Adalat. The Amendment Act created a separate Chapter vide Chapter VIA with the heading 'Pre-Litigation Conciliation and Settlement'. The term 'Permanent Lok-Adalat' has been defined as the Lok-Adalat established under Sec. 22B. This definition clearly made the distinction between this special category of Lok-Adalat and the other permanent Lok-Adalat, which were established earlier by different authorities for resolution of disputes continuously[55]. Thus by virtue of this Amendment now, two main categories of Lok-Adalats came into existence along with one permanent and continuous Lok-Adalat having the previous characteristic. The Act empowered the Central Authority and State Authority to constitute one or more permanent Lok-Adalats for Public Utility Services[56]. It also prescribed that such Lok-Adalats shall be consisting of three persons, one of them should be the judicial officer of the rank of District Judge or Additional District Judge or has held judicial office higher in the rank than that of District Judge and other two persons shall be nominated by the Government concerned[57]. The precautionary limit of the Lok-Adalat has been fixed up to ten lakhs. However, the government can extend this limit by notification. The amended Act prescribed an elaborate process for it's functioning. It empowered the permanent Lok-Adalat to receive complaint concerning the dispute for which the permanent Lok-Adalat was constituted. It also empowers to ask the parties concerned to submit complaint or written statements and on need, can allow the parties to file additional statements or other evidences. In addition, the Court will allow to file replies or additional statements. On completion of these processes the Court will start conciliation proceeding in an attempt to reach amicable settlement between the parties. If the parties agree on the terms, the

Lok-Adalat can pass orders as per terms of the agreement[58]. The Act rightly debars the parties from initiating any other proceeding or case relating to the same dispute in any other Court, if the matter appeared before the permanent Lok-Adalat[59]. Though the Lok-Adalats have power to ask for evidence or to take evidence on oath, it was not so in practice and the majority of cases were referred through Courts in the former Lok-Adalat system. In such Lok-Adalats informality in the proceedings are the basic characteristics. However, the new amendment has brought changes into the entire proceedings. The proceedings are similar to the Courts excepting the amount of formality. In order to make the institution free from technicalities and less formal, the amendment rightly prescribed that the institution of permanent Lok-Adalat shall not be bound by Code of Civil Procedure, 1908 and The Indian Evidence Act, 1872[60]. Indeed, it specifically prescribed that the institution of permanent Lok-Adalat shall be guided by the principle of natural justice, objectivity, fair play, equity and other principles of justice.[61] The most vital change made by the Act is to empower the Lok-Adalat to pass the order on merit, if parties failed to settle their disputes during the conciliation proceedings[62]. The Act imposes finality on the order made by such permanent Lok-Adalats. No appeal shall lie from such award either on compromise or on merit and can be executed by Civil Court[63].

Thus the new amendment not only empower the Lok-Adalat to pass order if parties failed to settle their disputes during conciliation proceedings but also put seal of finality on such awards. However, one can argue about the scheme of amendment. So far, providing finality on the awards, if settled through conciliation is concerned, it is no doubt a proper proposition and was effectively being utilized till date. But the finality on the award made on merit is a debatable issue. The law is clear in its views but whether it is justified is a matter of argument. Almost all Tribunal proceedings and judicial proceedings have certain provisions for appeal. Even the arbitral award, which is passed by the arbitrator appointed by the parties concerned, get the opportunity of appeal on certain occasions. Though the Lok-Adalat is a different form of institution, not only alternative to the adversarial proceedings but also alternative to the other alternative proceedings, but when a Tribunal has passed an order on merit some remedial measure should be required to be made if the Tribunal acts wrongly or interprets the law improperly.

CODE OF CIVIL PROCEDURE VIS-A-VIS LOK ADALAT

After the enactment of the Civil Procedure Code in 1908, the Code recognized the right of the parties to enter into a compromise and withdraw the suit on that basis. Order XXIII Rule 3 enables the parties either to abandon the claim or request the Court to record the compromise between the parties[64]. The Code made it clear that no appeal can be field from a compromise decree[65]. The provision was further strengthened in 1977 by insertion of Rule 3A which debars appeal even on the ground that compromise was unlawful[65] However, rightly some restrictions have been imposed upon such a compromise in the representative suit[67]. Under Order XIV Rule 6[68], an agreement may be entered into by the parties in writing upon a decision on an agreed question of facts or law as stated by them, the result would follow as specified in the agreement. The Court accordingly, is empowered to proceed and try such issues and pronounce judgment on that basis[69]. We have Order XXXII-A[70] under the Code of Civil Procedure, which imposes the duty on the Court under Rule 3 to endeavour and to assist the parties in arriving at the settlement in respect of the subject matter of the suit or proceedings relating to matters concerned with family disputes. These disputes can be relating to matrimonial relief or declaration of the legitimacy of any person in relation to guardianship of a person or the custody of the minor, for maintenance, validity of adoption, validity and legality of will and succession etc. Indeed, under sub-rule (2) of Rule 3 of Order XXXII-A, the Court is entitled to adjourn the matter so that such adjournment helps for a settlement between the family members[71].

The 1999 amendment of the C.P.C brings a new life in the movement of Lok-Adalat. Section 89 of CPC, which has been enforced recently, lays down that where it appears to the Court that there exists certain elements of settlement, which may be acceptable to the parties, the court shall formulate the terms of settlement and give them to the parties for their comments. On receiving the response from the parties, the Court may formulate the possible settlement and refer either to (i) arbitration, (ii) conciliation. (iii) Judicial settlement, including the settlement through Lok Adalat or (iv) Mediation. Sub-Sec. (2) of the Section 89 provides that when a dispute is referred to arbitration or conciliation, the provision of Arbitration and Conciliation Act, 1996 will apply. When the Court refers the matter to Lok-Adalat, the Legal Services Authority Act, 1987 will apply. Only in the case of mediation the court itself shall effect compromise and follow such procedure as may be prescribed by the rules. Though Sec. 89 prescribed different modes of alternative mechanism, but being the best available alternative mechanism in the form of Lok-Adalat, as far as the cost and time is concerned, we can hope that the provision will make a revolutionary change in the movement of the Lok-Adalat and a large number of masses can utilise the institution for resolution of their disputes. Secondly, the institution of Lok Adalat itself strengthens from this provision because earlier the institution did not have the power to mandate any consumer to appear before the forum. Now these difficulties being remedied by the provisions because it makes it mandatory for the parties to appear before the forum and try to settle their disputes.

CONCLUSION

When there was an urgent need felt for providing legal backing to the institution of Lok Adalat, the enactment of Legal Services Authorities Act was a welcome approach. Even though several short falls have been seen in the Act and were remedied by 1994 Amendment, which constituted High Court Legal Services Committee, S.C. Legal Services Committee along with several other changes. By the scheme of the Act it looks adequate for the functioning of the Lok-Adalat. However, in practice, to be effective, there are still certain issues have to be settled by the Act. One vital issue, on which the Act is silent, is the appearances of the parties. Although the statute provides power to Lok-Adalat to bring the witness by summoning but it does not have a power to mandate the parties to appear before the Forum. Even the Court, which refers the matter before the Forum, does not have power to mandate the parties to appear before the institution of Lok-Adalat at the time of hearing till the 1999 amendment of C.P.C. and the insertion of Sec 89. Even Sec. 89 is silent as to the consequence when the parties concerned do not appear before Lok Adalat.

Attendance of different parties depends upon different internal and external circumstances[72]. Some times parties themselves are willing to comprise or if the parties are given facility to sit together, the matter may get settled[73]. However, due to pressure from interested corners, although agreed before the Court to send the matter to Lok Adalat, they subsequently themselves do not turn up before the Lok Adalat because of such external influences. The Lok-Adalat has no right or power to pass the order without the agreement of the parties except in the case of permanent Lok-Adalat, which is going to be established by the virtue of Amendment Act, 2002. Will it be proper to allow the parties to waste the precious time of the Lok-Adalat? Do they continue be allow to play with the institution? Are the parties not having an obligation to appear before the Lok-Adalat when the cases have been referred? Will the Lok-Adalat sit as a spectator when parties do not appear before the forum voluntarily? Are the parties having absolute right whether to appear or not to appear before the Lok-Adalat? These are the numerous questions, which require explanations and remedial measures. In my view, the parties can claim the right reasonably, while settling disputes, as whether to settle the disputes or not. However, parties cannot claim liberty from appearance before the institution of Lok-Adalat and when the matter has been referred before the institution to explore the possibilities of settlement. So at least the party for whom the Lok Adalat is arranged is required to be present before the institution.

Therefore, it is essential that at least some provision would be inserted to bring the parties before the Lok Adalat and to evolve consequences for non-appearance. In order to remedy the situation two forms of steps can be taken. First, the Lok-Adalat can be empowered to proceed further if the parties failed to appear. Such proceedings of the Lok-Adalat can be hearing ex-parte on the same day or in a subsequent Lok-Adalat. The Lok-Adalat in such a situation can function in a similar way as the Civil Court functioning under Order IX of the Code of Civil Procedure. Secondly, the Civil Court, which referred the matter before Lok-Adalat can proceed further on the non-appearance of the parties, treating such non-appearance as failure on the part of parties to appear before the Court at the time of hearing. The author is of the view that the second proposition is much more viable than the first one[74]. The researcher suggests an amendment in section 20 of the Legal Services Authorities Act, 1987, to remedy the situation. A proposed sub-section 6A after the Sub section (6) of Section 20 can provide some remedy in such situation.[75]

> "Sec. 20 (6A) Where the parties fail to appear before Lok-Adalat at the time of hearing. *Where no award by the Lok-Adalat on the ground that no compromise or settlement could be arrived at, because of the non-appearance of the plaintiff, or the defendant, or both the parties, the Lok-Adalat record in writing the fact of such non-appearance of such party and shall return the record of the case to the Court, from which the reference has been received under sub-section (1), and such Court shall proceed further in accordance with the provisions of Order IX of the Code of Civil Procedure, 1908, treating such non-appearance as failure of the party to appear when the suit is called for hearing".*

The Second issue, which requires emphasis, is the legal awareness programme and training of the Para-legal personnel, because if the goal of providing justice is required to be achieved, such legal literacy and training can play vital role as to make people aware about their rights. The Legal Services Authorities Act, 1987 as well as Rules made there under emphasises on the literacy programme and legal awareness but no constructive procedure has been provided by the Statute or Rules made thereunder. However, Haryana State Legal Services Authority has taken a positive step in this direction and has constituted the Institution of Director for Legal Literacy and Training of Para-legal personnel. Rule 11(2) of the Haryana State Legal Services Authority Rules, 1995- provided that the Director of Legal Literacy and Training of Paralegals should be a University Professor of Law, serving or retired, of at least five years standing. Thus it has attempted to involve academicians for legal awareness and Training. This is a unique feature of Haryana Rules and other States can utilize the experience in a similar way.

The Amendment Act, 2002 will bring a revolutionary change in the movement of Lok-Adalat. A large number of cases will be taken care of by the Permanent Lok-Adalat. However, there is some apprehension of elimination of the former characteristic of Lok-Adalat of being a purely conciliatory institution. So a specific attempt is required to be made to regularly monitor and organise Lok-Adalat of former characteristics. Secondly, some remedial measures should be included in the Statute against the order of the Permanent Lok-Adalat, if passed on merit. A clue can be found in the Law Commission working paper on arbitration. There, Law Commission suggested for two-tier appeal system to decrease the period for disposal of cases. The first appeal can be filed before the Division Bench of High Court and on the issue of law, Petition of appeal can also be filed before Supreme Court. If similar provision can be made in respect of orders of the Permanent Lok-Adalat then also the period of completion of proceeding can be decreased significantly. The other aspect, which requires attention, is the appointment of the member of Lok-Adalat in general and the judicial officer in particular. The statute provides for appointment of either a sitting judge or a retired judge. In respect of a sitting judge, if appointed, a clause must require to incorporate in the statute that while a sitting judge act as a conciliator at Lok-Adalat no cases from his own Court shall be referred to such Lok-Adalat. Though in West Bengal as well as in most of the States it is an usual practice to appoint retired judges, the law is required to be clear in its views and expression.

The Statute creates institutions. Institutions functions on the participation of People. So far all-round development of the Institution is concerned, an active participation by all the people associated with Lok-Adalat is required, otherwise the goal to provide access to justice to all cannot be achieved.

REFERENCES

1. N.R. Madhava Menon, *Justice Sans Lawyer: Some India Experiments*, India Bar Review, 446 (Vol-2 1985).
2. Act 39 of 1987, It got the assent of the President on 11th October 1987.
3. Although the Act was passed in 1987, the provision of Act except Chapter - III, were enforced with effect from 9.11.95 by the Central Government Notification no. S.O. 893 (E) dated 9.11.95.
4. Nyaya Deep, *A resume of Legal Services Authority Act 1987*, 35 (Jan 1999).
5. See Unamended Sec 19 (3), *Legal Services Authorities Act*, 1987, hereinafter the Act.
6. Sec. 19 (5) being inserted in place of Sec 19(3), which debar the jurisdiction of Lok-Adalat in non-compoundable offences.
7. Sec. 3, The Legal Services Authorities Act, 1987, hereinafter The Act.
8. Sec. 3A, The Act.
9. Sec. 6, The Act.
10. Sec. 8A, The Act.
11. Sec. 9, The Act.
12. Sec. 11A, The Act.
13. Sec. 27 The Act.
14. Rule 6, National Legal Services Authority Rules. 1995, hereinafter, NLSA Rules, 1995.
15. Rule 3, NLSA Rules, 1995.
16. Sec. 3(7), the Act.
17. Sec. 5, the Act
18. Sec. 4, the Act
19. Sec. 15. the Act.
20. The Regulation was notified on 26.7.1996, Vide Notification No G.S.R. 336(E), pub in Gazette of India, Ext, Pt II, Sec 3(i), dated 26-7-1996, w.e.f 26.7.1996. Regulation five prescribed the power and functioning of the Committee.
21. Regulation 5(a) of The Supreme Court Legal Services Committee Regulations'1996. Sec 6, the act.
22. Sec. 6, The Act.
23. Sec. 6(3), The Act.
24. Sec. 6(4) & 6(5), The Act.
25. Sec. 6(7), The Act.
26. Sec. 7, The Act.
27. Rule 4, West Bengal Legal Services Authority Rules' 1994.
28. Sec. 8, The Act.
29. Sec. 16, The Act.
30. Sec. 8A, The Act.

31. In the original Act of 1987, the provision for formation of High Court Legal Services Committee was not there but subsequently Sec 8A was inserted in the Act in order to provide legal aid as well as to organise Lok-Adalat at High Court level.

32. Sec. 9, the Act.

33. Sec. 9(7), the Act.

34. Sec. 10(1), the Act.

35. Sec. 17, the Act.

36. Sec. 11B, the Act.

37. Chapter VI, which consist of four sections from 19 to 22.

38. Sec. 19(1), the Act.

39. Sec. 19(2), the Act.

40. Sec. 19(3) & 19(4), The Act.

41. Regulation 52, West Bengal State Legal Services Authority Regulation, 1998.

42. Sec. 19(5), The Act.

43. Sec. 20, The Act.

44. Sec. 20(1), The Act.

45. Sec. 20 (2), The Act.

46. Sec. 20(5) & 20(6), The Act.

47. Sec. 22, The Act.

48. Sec. 22, The Act.

49. Sec. 21, The Act.

50. Published in Calcutta Gazette on 19th April, 1994.

51. Published in Calcutta Gazette on 27th July, 1998.

52. Chapter II of the Regulation deals with the High Court Legal Services Committee, Chapter III of the regulation deals with the District Legal Services Authority, and Chapter IV deals with Sub-Divisional Legal Services Committee.

53. Regulation 65 (1) and 65(3), West Bengal State Legal Services Authority Regulation, 1998.

54. The Legal Services Authorities Amendment Act, 2002 received the assent of the President on the 11th day of June, 2002 and was published in The Gazette of India on June 12, 2002.

55. There are several permanent and continuous Lok-Adalats functioning in different Courts under the auspices of different authorities having power to organize Lok-Adalats. One such Lok-Adalats was operating earlier in Calcutta, in the City Civil Court. But the Act has created a separate category of Lok-Adalat for resolution of disputes relating to Public Utilities Service.

56. The term 'Public Utility Service' has been defined in sub. sec. (b) of Sec. 22A, which includes Transport Service, Postal, Telegraph or Telephone services, or Electricity, Water supply, Public Conservancy or Sanitation, Hospital or Dispensary, or Insurance services.

57. Sec. 22B (2), The Act.

58. See Sub-Secs. 3,4,5,6,7 of Sec. 22C, the Act.

59. Sec. 22C (2). It says, 'After an application is made under sub-sec. (i) to the permanent Lok-Adalat, no party to that application shall invoke jurisdiction of any Court in the same dispute.

60. Sec. 22D, of the Act. *The permanent Lok-Adalat shall, while conducting conciliation proceedings or deciding a dispute on merit under the Act, be guided by the principles of natural justice, objectivity, fair play, equity and other principles of justice, and shall not be bound by the Code of Civil Procedure, 1908 and the Indian Evidence Act, 1872.*

61. id

62. Sec. 22C (8) of the Act.

63. Sec. 22E of the Act.

64. Order XXIII Rule 3: Compromise of Suit: *Where it is proved to the satisfaction of the Court that a suit has been adjusted wholly or in part by any lawful agreement or compromise, in writing signed by the parties, or where the defendant satisfies the plaintiff in respect of he whole or any part of the subject-matter of the suit, the Court shall order such agreement, compromise or satisfaction to be recorded, and shall pass a decree in accordance therewith so far as it relates to the partes to the suit, whether or not the subject-matter of the agreement, compromise or satisfaction is the same as the subject-matter of the suit.*

    Provided that where it is alleged by one party and denied by the other that an adjustment or satisfaction has been arrived at, the Court shall decide the question; but no adjournment shall be granted for the purpose of deciding the question, unless the Court, for reasons to be recorded, thinks fit to grant such adjournment.

    See *K. Venkata Seshiah* V. *Kanduru Ramasubbamma,* 1991 (3) SCC 338. *Gurpreet Singh* V. *Chatur Bhuj Goel,* AIR 1988 SC 400.

65. Under Section 96(3) of the CPC read with Order XLI, no appeal lies against a compromise decree: See *Manik Chandra Nandy* V. *Deb Das,* AIR 1986 SC 446, *Banwari Lal* V. *Smt. Chando Devi,* AIR 1983 SC 1139, *Dr. Mahesh Chandra Sharma* V. *Smt. Rajkumari Sharma,* AIR 1996 SC 869.

66. Order XXIII Rule 3 A, Bar to Suit: *No suit shall lie to set aside a decree on the ground that the compromise on which the decree is based was not lawful.*

67. Order XXIII Rule 3B, Code of Civil Procedure, 1908.

68. Order XIV Rule 6: Question of facts or law may by agreement be stated in form of issues: *Where the parties to a suit are agreed as to the question of fact or of law to be decided between them, they may state the same in form of an issue, and entered into an agreement in writing that, upon the finding of the Court in the affirmative or the negative of such issue.*

69. Order XIV Rule 7, Code of Civil Procedure, 1908.

70. Order XXXII-A Rule 3: Duty of Court to make efforts for settlement: *(1) In every suit or proceedings to which this order applies, an endeavour shall be made by the court in the first instance, where it is possible to do so consistent with the nature and circumstance of the case, to assist the parties in arriving at the settlement in respect of the subject - matter of the suit,*

71. Justice S.B.Sinha, *Alternative Dispute Resolution with special reference to Civil Procedure (Amendment) Act, 1999,* 8, Souvenir published by LASWEB (2001)

72. Most of the occasion Lawyer's taken sceptical approach for Lok-Adalat for the reasons best known to them. However, it is general view as well as my analysis that due to fear of economic loss out of profession practice make them to be aloof from the process except in certain category of cases where chances of their economic loss is minimal.

73. *The author himself experienced, while was practicing in District Court that most of the Seniors instruct their client not to appear before the Lok-Adalat. On one occasion when one matter was referred to Lok-Adalat (U/s. 125 C. P. C.) the husband was willing to settle in the forum, to save himself from the burden of placing evidence, resulting in false charge and counter charge between husband and wife, the concerned Senior Advocate strictly instructed his client not to appear before the Lok-Adalat.*

74. The researcher is of the view that the responsibility of proceeding further should be left on the Civil Court. Firstly, because the parties against whom the order would be passed have certain remedy under Order IX by which he can filed petition for revival of the case, if his non-appearance was on some reasonable ground. Secondly, in such situation record of the case is always available before Civil Court. Thirdly, for evidence and other technical proceeding which required for vacating ex-partee, the Civil Court is appropriate forum. Fourthly, the Civil Court referred the matter for resolution through amicable means but not imposing decree. The other function should be left to Civil Court.

75. Order IX of the Code of Civil Procedure provides the guidelines to proceed on the occasion of non-appearance of the parties. As a consequence of non-appearance of the parties Court can proceed ex-parte or can dismiss

the plaint if the plaintiff doesn't appear at the time of hearing. Similar consequences can remedy the situation when the parlies willingly do not appear.

While in normal day to day proceeding of the Court, the Court may hear ex-parte on the same of when the case was fixed for hearing and party dóes not appeared or to fixed a date for ex-parte hearing. Thus in normal Court proceeding, the Court has two options. Firstly, to heard ex-parte instantaneously and decide the matter. Secondly, to fixed a date for ex-parte hearing. However, in the case of matter return from Lok-Adalat, Court can not proceed on the same day but have to fixed for ex-parte hearing. If the party by appearing on such date shows reasonable ground, Court can act reasonably and can impose cost on the other side. It is on the Court to decide.

CHAPTER 6

ROLE OF JUDICIARY IN STRENGTHENING LOK-ADALAT

INTRODUCTION

In no other system except perhaps in the United States of America, the judges and the judicial branch of the Government occupy as prominent and powerful a position as in the Indian system. Indeed, the importance of the Courts, particularly the Supreme Court and its judges has, if anything, increased over the decades[1]. Right from its inception, the apex Court in India has influenced the national policy making agenda in significant proportions[2]. The judiciary, specifically Apex Court, has not only indulged in judicial legislation but has even exercised the constituent power unknown anywhere in the World and the seemingly transcending all, received notions of separation of power[3]. In a large number of issues, while deciding the cases, the judiciary marched a long way in order to materialize the Constitutional goal and the protection of human rights. Among those, one was the goal of providing Legal Aid where judiciary propounded new legal aid jurisprudence so that the opportunity of securing justice are not denied to any citizen by reason of economic and other disability, of which Lok-Adalat is a strategic means.

Judiciary played vital role in not only providing legal aid but also institutionalising the concept of Lok-Adalat, which evolved as an instrument for providing legal aid. The institution of judiciary not only influenced the enactment of Legal Services Authority Act, 1987 but was also determined so that the Act can be implemented all over the country with its true spirit[4]. The judiciary even directed the Government to provide funds to NGOs in order to encourage people participation through legal awareness, so that the Legal Aid programme can succeed[5]. It went on further directing the Government and Governmental organizations to hold permanent Lok-Adalat in their concerned departments to settle the grievance of the citizens speedily and cost effectively[6].

JUDICIARY: A PATH PROVIDER FOR LOK-ADALAT AS LEGAL-AID STRATEGY

In the land mark judgement of the *Hussainara Khatoon* case[7], Justice Bhagwati spelt out the right to Legal Aid in criminal proceedings from the language of Article 21 and held that this is a Constitutional right of every accused person who is unable to engage a lawyer and secure legal services on account of reasons such as poverty, indigence or in-communicable situation and the State is under the mandate to provide a lawyer to an accused person, if the circumstances of the case and the needs of justice so received, provided of course, the accused person does not object to the provision of such lawyer. After two years of the judgement, the Court again reiterated similar views in the *Khetri* case[8]. The Supreme Court said, "It is difficult to understand how this state of affairs could be permitted to continue despite the decision of this Court in *Hussainara Khatoon's* case. This Court has pointed out that the right to free Legal Services is clearly an essential ingredient of reasonable, fair and just procedure for a person accused in an offence and it must be held implicit in the guarantee of Article 21 and the State is under the Constitutional mandate to provide a lawyer to an accused person if the circumstances of the case and the needs of justice so require. It is unfortunate that though this Court declared the right to legal aid as a fundamental right of an accused person, by a process of judicial construction of Article 21, most of the States have not taken note of this decision'. The Court directed the State Government to provide free legal services to the accused who is unable to provide lawyers on the ground of poverty and indigence. The Court also directed the Magistrate and Session Judges to inform the accused about the availability of the Legal Aid.

Again in 1986 the Supreme Court enhanced the ambit of the Legal Aid to the Appellate Court[9]. The Court asked, 'whether the fundamental right could lawfully be denied to the appellants if they did not apply for free legal aid? Is the exercise of this fundamental right conditioned upon the accused applying for free legal assistance so that if he does not make an application for free legal assistance the trial may lawfully proceed without adequate legal representation being offered to him?' Supreme Court while setting aside the conviction order said, "The result was that the appellants remained un-represented by a lawyer and the trial ultimately resulted in their conviction. This was clearly a violation of the fundamental right of the appellants under Article 21 and the trial must accordingly be held to be vitiated on account of total Constitutional infirmity, and the conviction and sentence recorded against the appellants must be set aside[10].

The most vital challenge before the judiciary was to provide access to justice to a large number of people of the country. Judiciary tried its best to provide access to justice to the downtrodden people. The significant statement made by former chief justice Dr A.S.Anand with regard to the process of access to justice through the means of social action litigation is noteworthy. To quote[11], *"While the judiciary was striving a balance between dignity of the individual and the unity of the nation, it found itself faced with a serious challenge concerning access to justice. It was noticed that the weaker section of the Indian humanity had been deprived of justice for long long years: they had no access to justice on account of their poverty, ignorance and illiteracy. They were not aware of the rights and benefits conferred upon them by the Constitution and other benefcial legislations. On account of their socially and economically disadvantaged position they lacked the capacity to assert their rights. Access to justice to protect their fundamentals rights was almost illusory for such sections of Indian Humanity. The judiciary rose to meet the challenge and regarded it as its duty to come to the rescue of the underprivileged to help them to reap the benefits of economic and social entitlement".*

Though social action litigation provided means to hopeless people to access to justice and to protect their rights through such instrument, even then the goal of access to justice is an unfulfilled reality. Large numbers of people do not have access to justice primarily because of the high cost of the administration of the justice system. In such a aggravated situation and on the role of judiciary, justice Dr A.S.Anand said[12], *"the high cost of litigation is a challenge, which judiciary has made attempts to meet though without any spectacular success. Even after decades of independence the poor, backward and weaker sections of the society feel that they do not have equal opportunities for securing justice because of their socio-economic conditions. The judiciary evolved schemes for providing legal aid to the poor. A Committee for Implementation of Legal Aid Scheme (CILAS) was set up by the judiciary to further the Directive Principles and assure 'equal protection of law' to the citizen"*

The judgment in *Hussainara Khatoon* case[13] was pronounced in 1979 and in 1980 Committee for Implementation of Legal Aid Scheme (CILAS) was constituted with Justice Bhagwati who was appointed as the Chairman of the Committee. The CILAS started holding Lok-Adalat as a legal aid strategy. The working of the CILAS and all the aforesaid judgements made Legislature bound to pass Legal Services Authorities Act, 1987. However, the Act came into force with effect from 9.11.1995. Thus the judicial efforts not only evolved the institution of Lok-Adalat but also made Legislature bound to provide legal backing to the institution of Lok-Adalat.

JUDICIARY AS WATCH DOG FOR PROPER IMPLEMENTATION OF LOK- ADALAT SCHEMES

Though the Legal Services Authorities Act, 1987 was passed and enforced through Central notification, the Part III of the Act was not enforced by most of the States. Part III of the Act provides directives for the formation of State Authority, District Authority, High Court Committee and Taluka level Committee. Again, when most of the States have not implemented the law, which in result jeopardized the object of the Act to provide Legal Services at grass root level and holding Lok-Adalat as a mechanism for providing legal services, judiciary has to appear for materializing the aim and object of the Act. In *Supreme Court Legal Aid Committee* V. *Union of India*[14] the Supreme Court directed all the States and Union Territories, which have not framed the

Rules so far, to frame Rules u/s. 28 and notify the same within a period of two months. It also directed the States or Union Territory for constitution of High Court Legal Services Committees and other Committees within two months and a compliance report was asked for by February 3, 1998. However, most of the States did not initially comply with the order and the matter again came up for hearing on 10th February, 1998. The Court threatened to initiate contempt proceedings against the Chief Secretary of the concerned State. However, by extending some time, the court again directed the Union Territory and State Government to comply with the direction saying, 'We give in the mean while, time till 30.4.1998, to all the defaulting States/Union Territory Administration to comply full direction".

Thus, judiciary not only played a vital role in the enactment of the Act but also in the enforcement of the Act. The Judiciary not even stop here, it went further to constitute a permanent Lok-Adalat in different Governmental agencies, concerning the public utilities services. Delhi High Court in *Abul Hassan and N.L.S.A. V. Delhi Vidyut Board and others*[15] highlighted the aim of the LSA Act and said "One of the aims of the Act is to organise Lok-Adalats to secure that the operation of the legal system promotes justice on the basis of equal opportunity. The Act gives statutory recognition to the resolution of disputes by compromise and settlement by the Lok-Adalat. The concept has been gathered from the system of Panchayat, which has root in the history, and culture of this country. It has a native flavor known to the people". Court further highlighted the need for the Lok-Adalat and said that the need of the hour is practically beckoning for setting up Lok-Adalat on permanent and continuous basis. What we do today will shape our tomorrow. The choice is between an overburdened Court system being crushed under its own weight and the alternative dispute resolving machinery including an impressive dispensation of justice by Lok-Adalat. Court further said that for facilitating expeditious disposal of all kinds of cases, permanent Lok-Adalat must be set up in DVB, MCD, NDMC, DDA, MTNL, GIG and various departments of Government for resolving the disputes between the citizens and Government of India and the Government of India and its employees. Court directed all such Governmental Agencies to establish permanent Lok-Adalats.

Now the 2002 Amendment of Legal Service Authority Act, which mandate for constitution of permanent Lok-Adalat for resolving disputes in public utility service, is nothing but materialization of the thought expressed by the Delhi High Court in 1999.

LEGAL AID, LEGAL LITERACY, NGO AND JUDICIARY

Since the inception of the Lok-Adalat, as a Legal Aid strategy, the NGO played critical role in mobilizing people of all segments, specifically the down trodden people. Appreciating the functioning of the voluntary organization, justice Bhagwati said[16] "If we want to secure people participation and involvement in legal aid programme, we think the best way of securing is to operate through voluntary organization and social action groups. These organizations are working among the deprived and vulnerable sections of the community at the grass root level and they learn what are the problems and difficulties encountered by the neglected section of Indian humanity. They have their fingers on the pulse of the people and they know from their own experience as to what are the unmet legal needs of the people and what measures are necessary to be taken for the purpose of ending such exploitation and injustice and reaching social or distributive justice to them."

Even before the enactment of the Legal Service Authority Act, 1987, the issue was raised before the Supreme Court as to whether voluntary organisations or social action groups engaged in legal aid programme should be supported by the State Government financially. Such issues which are normally considered in the purview of the executive, the Court transcends the boundary and direct the Government to provide funds to such NGOs[17].

Supreme Court speaking through justice Bhagwati held, '*We therefore definitely of the view that voluntary organizations and social action groups must be encouraged and supported by the State in operating the Legal Aid programmes. It is now widely acknowledged through out the country that the Legal Aid programme, which is needed for reaching social justice to the people, cannot afford to remain confined to the traditional or litigation oriented legal aid programme. But it must, taking into account the socio-economic conditions prevailing in the country, adopt a more dynamic positive steps and take within its sweep what we call strategic legal aid programmes, consisting of promotion of legal literacy, organisation of legal aid camps, encouragement of PIL and holding Lok-Adalat for bringing about the settlement of disputes, whether pending in the Court or outside"*[18].

The judiciary not only paves the ways for the moral encouragement of the NGOs but also arrange for their economical needs. The bold attempt of the judiciary will provide new energy in the Lok-Adalat movement vis-a-vis NGOs participation in the movement.

LOK-ADALAT IN THE EYES OF JUDICIARY

Few cases appeared before the higher judiciary relating to Lok Adalat. In almost all cases judiciary discouraged appeal or revision against the compromise order passed by the Lok Adalat. However, a decade ago the Gujarat High Court set aside the decree passed by the Civil Judge on the compromise entered before Lok Adalat. The contention of the appellant was that they did not agree on compromise as are being imposed on them. If so, the High Court was justified in setting aside the order[19]. However, caution is essential so that litigant with bad intention could not take alike pleas. In *Punjab National Bank* V. *Laxmi Chand Rai & others*[20], the Madhya Pradesh High Court dismissed the appeal filed against the decree passed by the Lok Adalat. In this case during the negotiation before Lok Adalat, the official of the appellant bank agreed on the award consisting of full dues amount as well as pendente lite interest and the period of instalment left on the Lok Adalat to decide. The argument of the appellant was that they never agreed on the instalment and the rate of pendentilite interest is bad and unacceptable. The Court highlighted the aim and object of the Act and the provision of Sec. 21 of the Act, which debars appeal along with sec. 96(3) of C.P.C., which also debar any appeal from compromise decree. Court said that the Code of Civil Procedure intends that once a consent decree is passed by Court, finality is attached to it. Such finality cannot be permitted to be destroyed, particularly under Legal Services Authorities Act, as it would amount to defeat the very aim and object of the Act.

In *Kishan Rao* v. *Bidar District Legal Services Authority*[21] the issue was raised as to whether the Lok Adalat can pass a decree when all the parties to the suit did not appear before Lok Adalat or any notice has been issued to them. A compromise was entered between the plaintiff and defendant 2 & 4 and accordingly the Lok Adalat passed the decree. Whether the Lok Adalat was right while passing the decree is the issue? Sec. 20(3) of the Act empower the Lok-Adalat to proceed to dispose of the suit, proceeding, dispute or matter arrived at a compromise or settlement between the parties. Court interpreted the provision and said that the term "parties" used in the Section indicates all the parties in the suit. Court declared the decree illegal, null and void and remanded the case for trial.

In another case[22] the issue raised as to whether Court can refer the matter to the Lok Adalat if one party does not agree on such reference. The language of section 20 is clear which not only empowers the Court to refer the case, when one party file application for reference, but also the Court can *suo-moto* refer the case to the Lok Adalat if Court satisfied that there are chances or possibilities of settlement. However, the proviso mandates the Court to provide opportunities to the other parties to place their views. The Court appreciated the view of referring the matter to the Lok-Adalat by saying; "The purpose of such reference is to explore the possibility of conciliation with the mediation of an independent agency which has the expertise in that behalf and statutory backing for the decision. In the matter like the present one, it is bounded duty of the Court to first explore the possibility of settlement. Such an approach alone would serve the legislative, intent of creating Lok Adalats and for providing them statutory backing for their decision. Any other view would not only frustrate the legislative intent but also result in affecting the authority of the Courts to the extent that it enables the Court to require the parties to submit to the jurisdiction of Lok-Adalat, in cases where the Courts are satisfied that the case is an appropriate case to be referred to the Lok-Adalat".

However, the Court forgets that the power of reference is for settlement of dispute and when one party had refused for reference and had even come for appeal, on the face of it, looks that the case is not a fit one to be settled before Lok Adalat. Thus in my opinion, for the sake of sending cases to Lok-Adalat one can not pressurize the party to refer the case, where the Court knows that the matter will again come back.

CONCLUSION

The Indian judiciary through its activist role when attempted to reform almost all sectors and to evolve new jurisprudence for their materialization, the sector of Legal Aid vis-a-vis Lok Adalat is no exception to it. From the inception of Lok Adalat movement, the judiciary played a significant role. It not only made its effect on the enactment of Legal Services Authority Act but also reflected on the proper implementation of the Act. When the Executive fails to implement the statute in most of the States, the judiciary appeared as a messiah and made it enforceable in such places. It also played a role of policy maker by directing the State to provide funds to different NGOs for such purposes.

Now when the Lok Adalat is functioning as an effective dispute resolution mechanism, the judiciary is working as a watch-dog on the process so that no one can abuse the process. It is also rectifying the fault through judicial pronouncements. The 2002 amendment of the Act is nothing but the materialization of the verdict of the judiciary. So now it is in the process of expanding the scope of Lok Adalat.

Thus the judiciary not only acted as the policy maker but also as executors. However, very few cases appear before higher judiciary, we have to see further for assessing its role in future. While directing for formation of organization, like permanent Lok-Adalat, which the Legislature makes parallel to all almost adversary processes, except few differentials in the procedure, judiciary is required to take caution. However, the judiciary attempted to provide modern additional means for resolution of disputes but the legislature has moulded it in a different tune. Now we have to see further, for its effective functioning. Again the responsibility came on the shoulder of judiciary to safeguard the institution from losing its basic characteristics and evolving newly developed processes to make it more effective.

REFERENCES

1. Mool Chand Sharma, *Justice P.N.Bhagwati, Court Constitution and Human Right,* 1, (1995), Universal Book Traders.
2. George H. Gadbois, *"The Supreme Court of India: As a political institution"* in Rajeev Dhavan, R. Sudarshan & Salman Khurshid, *Judge and Judiciary power,* (1985) P-251 referred in id,
3. Upendra Baxi, *The Indian Supreme Court and politics,* (1980), referred in Supra-111.
4. *In Supreme Court Legal Service Committee* V. *U.O.I.* AIR 1998 SC 2940, *The Court directed all the states those had not framed rules till that time, to frame rules and implement the Law constructively.*
5. See *Centre for Legal Research & Other* V. *State of Kerala.* AIR 1986 SC 2195.
6. *Abdul Hassan and N.L.S.A.* V. *Delhi Vidyut Board and others,* AIR 1999 DEL 88.
7. *Hussainara Khatoon* V. *State of Bihar.* AIR 1979 SC 1369;
8. *Khatri & Others* V. *State of Bihar,* AIR 1981 SC 928;
9. Sukh Das & Others V. Union Territory of Arunachal Pradesh, AIR 1986 SC 991.
10. id.
11. Justice Dr A.S. Anand, *Fifty years of Indian Judiciary - Its achievements & failures,* 19, Nyaya Deep, April-June 2000.
12. id 22.
13. *Hussainara Khatoon* V. *State of Bihar.* AIR 1979 SC 1369.
14. 1998 (5) SCC 762.
15. AIR 1999 DEL 88.
16. *Centre of Legal Research and another* V. *State of Kerala.* AIR 1986 SC 2195.
17. id.
18. Id;
19. *Union Bank of India* V. *Narendra Plastic.* AIR 1991 Guj 67.
20. AIR 2000 MP 30.
21. AIR 2001 Karnatka 407.
22. *Puspa Suresh Bhutada & other* V. *Subhash Bansilal Maheswari & Other.* AIR 2002 Bom 126.

CHAPTER 7

LOK-ADALAT IN INDIA STUDY OF THE OVERALL PERFORMANCE OF THE INSTITUTION

INTRODUCTION

In India, the institution of Lok-Adalat is gaining popularity quite steadily since its inception in March 1982, when the first Lok-Adalat was held at village 'Una' in Junagarh, Gujarat, as an experiment. The first Lok-Adalat was successfully held. As it was the first experience, the significant words used by Justice Desai while inaugurating the Lok-Adalat is note worthy. The learned judge said, *'it is a noble experiment in the direction of amicably resolving legal disputes between parties. If it succeeded it might be repeated, if not, it be forgotten'*. Fortunately, for the State of Gujarat, as well as for the Country, this experiment instead of failing, became more and more successful and deep-rooted in the system of administration of justice. The institution achieved excellent results at every level, whether Central or State or at the District level. In the state of Gujarat alone, where the first Lok-Adalat was held in 1982, 114 Lok-Adalats were held within a span of four years. During that period, till May 1986, total 32,032 cases were taken up by the Lok-Adalat for the purpose of conciliation out of which 19,353 cases were disposed of and advice was given in 1942 cases[1].

The institution of Lok-Adalat is growing continuously at the national level. A large number of cases were settled by utilizing the instrument of Lok-Adalat. Study reveals that till 1996, a total 13061 Lok-Adalats were held in the country. A total number of 57,38,423 cases settled in these Lok-Adalats, in which the number of MACC cases alone stood at 2,78,801 and a total amount of Rs. 861,27,79,423/- was paid as compensation in MACC cases. The amount paid as compensation is itself the testimony of the performance of the institution. The number of Lok-Adalats organized as well as the number of cases settled thereupon, has increased considerably in the subsequent years. The following statement of, the then Chief Justice of India Dr. A.S. Anand, itself highlights the aspiration, expectation and satisfaction expressed by judiciary on the functioning of the institution of Lok-Adalat. To quote[2],

> *"the holding of Lok-Adalats for settlement of disputes- Including pending court cases- has proved quite effective. Up to 31st December' 1998, 33,347 Lok-Adalats were held around the country where over 84,91,759 cases (nearly 8.5 million cases) were settled by consent of the disputing parties. Between 1.1.99 and 31.12.99, 9364 Lok-Adalats were held in various States and 10,96,378 cases (more than one million) were settled. These 'Courts of the people' are mainly manned by retired justices of the High Courts, District Judges along with some prominent individuals in the public life (social workers) and judicial officers past and present. Every award of the Lok-Adalat is deemed to be a civil decree. One of the greatest advantages of the settlements by Lok-Adalat is that the award of the Lok-Adalat is treated as a binding decree of a Court and is not subject to any further appeal in any forum. Thus it brings the litigation to an end completely".*

Till the end of 1999 a total number of 49415 Lok-Adalats were organized throughout the Country. In these Lok-Adalats a total number of 97,20,289 cases were brought to an end through this condiatory mechanism. The number of settlements of MACC cases alone stood at 5,09,171. Moreover, the award of compensation in tune of Rs. 23,06,07,32,170/- is the testimony of the tremendous success of the institution in providing participatory justice. Apart from settlement of disputes through the institution of Lok-Adalat a large number of persons benefited through legal aid scheme. The legal aid and advice in Law Courts have been provided to 24,45,078 persons, till 31st Dec' 1999 by different Authorities through out the country. However, the progress of the institution is not similar in all the States, for which analysis of few a States is essential to understand the progress of the institution in the different States.

LOK-ADALAT IN THE STATE OF GUJARAT

Gujarat, the initiator of the institution, is marching ahead than the other States so far. While, at the beginning of the year 1996, when in the half of the States of the country, the institution of Lok-Adalat was a newborn child, 921 Lok-Adalats were held in the state of Gujarat alone. The number of Lok-Adalats organized in Gujarat increased significantly and had reached 10,165 by the end of 1999 and became the highest number of Lok-Adalats organizing State. The success of functioning of the institution in the state of Gujarat can be seen from the fact that the Gujarat Government successfully held 500th Lok-Adalat long back in August 25th 1991, under the guidance of Chief Justice of India and patron CILAS. 2187 cases were placed before this Lok-Adalat out of which 2044 cases were finally settled. The success of 500th Lok-Adalat lies in the fact that it could successfully settle 93.5% cases referred to it by the Courts[3]. Till November 1992, 571 Lok-Adalats were held in Gujarat. The Lok-Adalats in Gujarat till that time were able to settle 83,640 cases amicably, out of which 18,000 cases were of MACC. The Lok-Adalat paid an amount of Rs 42,80,000/- as compensation to the claimants[4]. The number of cases settled increased further and till March 1996, a total number of 921 Lok-Adalats were held in Gujarat in which 1,37,667 cases were settled. The number of MACC cases settled were 25,848 and an amount of Rs. 72,41,00,000/- was awarded as compensation. The number of Lok-Adalat organised and settlements reached thereupon increased significantly thereafter. Studies revealed that till the end of 1999,10165 Lok-Adalats were held in Gujarat in which 6,90,687 cases were settled out of which 53,327 cases were relating to MACC. An amount of Rs. 225,99,75,343/- was paid as compensation in such MACC cases alone.

The institution got further impetus in the year 2000, when the highest number of cases were settled in a year. During the year 2000, 4530 Lok-Adalats were held in the State in which 5,13,787 cases were settled. For MACT cases 237 Lok-Adalats were organised in the State during the year in which 12,874 cases were settled and an amount of Rs. 77.24 crores was awarded as compensation to the claimant. The Table 7.1 below will exhibit the performance of the institution in last few years.

Table - 7.1[5]
Lok Adalt in Gujarat

Particulars	Until 1997	1998	1999	2000	2001	Until 1st Sep'02	Grand Total
1	2	3	4	5	6	7	8
L.A. Held	1470	2529	6580	4530	5290	4404	24763
Cases Dealt With	251388	315157	245900	553796	239349	104297	1709889

1	2	3	4	5	6	7	8
Cases Disposed of	198140	296713	211179	513787	206425	86462	1512706
MACT L.A. Held	484	254	273	237	172	178	1598
MACC Cases Dealt With.	44643	12801	14270	15287	8341	5028	100370
MACC Cases Settled.	32874	10488	10952	12874	6895	3927	78010
Compensation In Crores.	113.2	67.66	552	77.24	51.68	39.7	404.68

While the number of Lok-Adalats held reached at 1470 in the year 1997, 2529 Lok-Adalats were organised in the year 1998. Similarly, while until 1997, 198140 cases were settled in the Lok-Adalats, the institution in the year 1998 succeeded in settling 2,96,713 cases. A large number of Motor Accident Claim cases were also settled in Lok-Adalats. During 1998, 10488 MACT cases were settled in which 67.66 Crores were awarded as compensation. Thus, the aforesaid figure exhibit that the institution had seen a boom after clothing it with legal instrument in the form of Legal Services Authorities Act, 1987. Though the highest number of cases were settled during the year' 2000 but the number of settlements decreased substantially in the year 2001 in spite of organising 5250 Lok-Adalats. 2,06,425 cases were settled during the year. Similarly the figure of 2002 indicates a decrease in the number of settlements. Until 1st September, 2002, 4404 Lok-Adalats were held in which 86462 cases were settled.

Studies revealed that during 1998 to 2002, 23293 Lok-Adalats were held in the State in which 13,14,566 cases were settled. Until October' 2002, 1.7 lakhs MACT cases were settled in the State in which 404 Crores had been paid to the claimants.

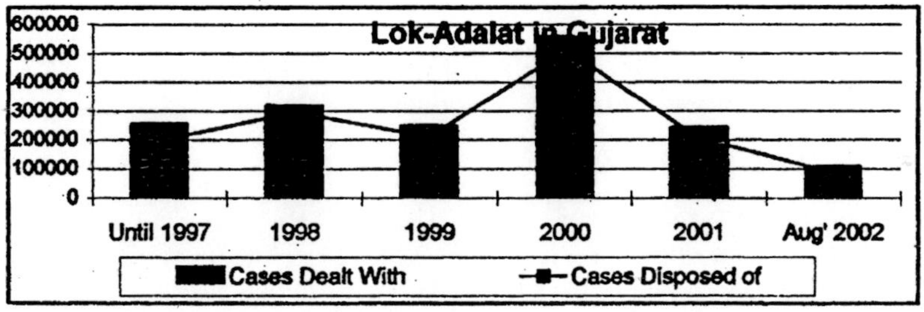

It is evident from the above graph that the performance of the institution has decreased during 2001 and 2002. However, the number of settlements in the State is much more than several other States. Apart from this, the performance of the State Legal service Authority was remarkable after the earthquake to provide quick, easy and inexpensive access to justice to the victims. During 26th Jan'2001 to 31st August 2001, 44040 applications were received in the different Earthquake Cells established in the State in which 30796 cases were disposed off before 31st August'2001.

The State Legal Services Authority started Permanent Legal Services Clinic on 4th July 1999. The Clinic was functioning round the clock to provide access to justice to the large number of people. During 4th July' 1999 to 1st September' 2002, 32257 cases were received in Permanent Legal Aid Clinic including Women Cell, which is functioning under the Clinic. Among those applications only 1876 applications were pending till 1st Sep'2002. The State Authority successfully organised 18000 Gram Sabha in different parts of the State in order to make the people literate about the Lok-Adalat and legal aid programmes. 103 Para Legal training camps were organised in which 2700 Para-Lawyers and people from NGOs were trained. During 1998 to 2001, 70721 Legal Literacy Camp were organised throughout the States to make the masses aware about the legal aid movement and Lok-Adalat.

Thus, the State Authority not only succeeded in implementing Lok-Adalat scheme in the State but also organised a large number of legal literacy camps, Gram Sabhas, publication of Magazines, literature etc. However, the decrease in the number of settlements in the State is a matter of concern for all.

LOK-ADALAT IN THE STATE OF UTTAR PRADESH

Though the highest number of Lok-Adalats organized, is in the State of Gujarat, the highest number of people enriched from the fruit of the institution of Lok-Adalat was in the State of Uttar Pradesh. Till March 1996, the State of Uttar Pradesh was leading, in both, organizing Lok-Adalat and settling disputes in such Lok-Adalats. But at the end of 1999 the State of Gujarat became the highest Lok-Adalat organizer. However, Uttar Pradesh still leads in the settlement of disputes by settling a sky-scraping figure of cases numbered at 36,06,531, till 31st Dec 1999, while the other States were far behind this figure. The first Lok-Adalat in the State was organized in the year 1984 in order to settle civil criminal and revenue cases. During the short span of two years, till May 1986,170 Lok-Adalats were held in the State of Uttar Pradesh and a total number of 2,07,753 persons were benefited by the instrument of Lok-Adalat. The success of the institution in the State can be reckoned from the attempt of the Legal Aid Board of Uttar Pradesh and the success obtained from the programmes. The Board attempted to make District and the Taluk free from litigation and declare it 'litigation free zone'[6] The experiment to this effect was first of all carried out by District Legal Aid Advice Committee, Varanasi. It convened a meeting of 22-Gram Pradhans and appraised the scheme of litigation free zone. Gram Pradhans prepared a list of cases pending in different Courts. There were 82 cases in which the parties were invited on a fixed day. On that day, the Lok-Adalat was organised and the conciliators of the institution succeeded in getting 68 disputes compromised. Hence, by this experiment, 17 out of 22 villages were made litigation free. There were only 14 cases, which could not be compromised because they were of serious criminal nature[7]. In the State of Uttar Pradesh till the March 1996, a total number of 2333 Lok-Adalats were held, which was the highest figure of organisation of Lok-Adalat till that time, and in those Lok-Adalats 23,39,943 cases were settled, which is 40% of the total cases settled through the instrument of Lok-Adalat through out the Country. The State of Uttar Pradesh is still leading in settling the disputes from all other States and Union Territories. Till the end of 1999, 4184 Lok-Adalats were organised in the State in which 36,08,531 cases were settled, out of which 44999 cases were relating to MACC and an amount of Rs 2,41,19,16,270/- was awarded as compensation. Thus being the largest populated State of the Country, Uttar Pradesh has maintained to be the highest achiever in providing justice through the institution of Lok-Adalat.

LOK-ADALAT IN THE STATE OF ORISSA

The second largest number of cases by Lok-Adalat have been settled in the State of Orissa. The first Lok-Adalat in the State was organised at Cuttack on November 24, 1985 by the Orissa Legal Aid and Advice Board[8]. In the initial four years period, the State of Orissa succeeded in organising more than 400 Lok-Adalats. Till July 1989, 437 Lok-Adalats were organised in the State in which 1,16,345 cases were settled and an amount of Rs 80017891/- was awarded as compensation in motor accident compensation cases and under Workmen's Compensation Act[9]. At the end of March'1996, the State of Orissa became the second highest in the number of Lok-Adalats organised, by organising 2266 Lok-Adalats. In these Lok-Adalats a large number of cases were settled. The disputants in 621115 cases were benefited by the institution, as they were able to settle their disputes with the help of the conciliators. Among those more than 6 lakh cases, 8126 cases were relating to motor accident compensation claims in which an amount of Rs 274141803/- was awarded as compensation to the victims or their heirs. Thus the high magnitude itself highlights the importance of the institution and its successful functioning. The number of settlements further increased substantially and till the end of 1999, the institution of Lok-Adalat succeeded in bringing to compromise between the disputants in 1513757 cases. Thus the fruit of the institution had reached a large number of people of Orissa. 3485 Lok-Adalats were organised till the end of 1999, which provided justice to more than 15 lakhs of people in cost effective and time effective manner. Among such high magnitude of settlements, 14756 cases were relating to motor accident compensation claims and Rs 717519430 was awarded as compensation in those MACC cases.

LOK-ADALAT IN THE STATE OF RAJASTHAN

The third highest number of Lok-Adalats were organized in the State of Rajasthan. The first Lok-Adalat in the State of Rajasthan was organized on 30th Nov' 1985 and in this first Lok-Adalat, 532 cases were settled. The number of Lok-Adalats organized and the cases settled thereupon increased significantly in the subsequent period. In one month, till Dec 1985, 6 Lok-Adalats were held and 6637 cases were settled in these Lok-Adalats. Study reveals that during the year 1986, 154 Lok-Adalats were held in which 2,02,579 cases were settled amicably. This includes 1982 MACC cases and 1875 cases pertaining to industrial and labour disputes. Besides, many matrimonial suits were also decided. The success of the Lok-Adalats is visible from the facts that a large amount, Rs 45197808/- had been paid to the claimants as compensation in motor accident claims[10]. The institution of Lok-Adalat increased substantially from 1996 onwards. While till March'1996 only 304 Lok-Adalats were held in the State and was far behind from some of the leading States, the State of Rajasthan became the third highest Lok-Adalat organiser in the year 1999 by organising 4300 Lok-Adalats in the State. However, in spite of organising a small number of Lok-Adalats till March1996, the State of Rajasthan gained the second highest result through the instrument of Lok-Adalat till that period! The Lok-Adalat in the State was able to settle 8,38,573 cases till March 1996, which is higher than all the states except Uttar Pradesh where 23,39,943 cases were settled. A total amount of Rs. 757637629/- was paid as compensation till March 1996. Until 1999, advantages of Lok-Adalats utilised in 10,36,618 cases and disputes in such cases came to an end. Among these large number of cases, the number of motor accident claims were alone 33,353 and an amount of Rs. 1427137978 have been paid as compensation. In the year 2000 alone 8215 Lok-Adalats were held in the State in which 199416 cases were settled and an amount of Rs. 292247517 has been awarded as compensation in MACC cases. Apart from the organisation of Lok-Adalats a large number of legal literacy camps were organised in the State. In the year 1999, 2396 and in the year 2000, 2676 legal literacy camps were organised in the State. In the year 2001, till September, different authorities in the State organised 6842 Lok-Adalats in which 119928 cases were settled and an amount of Rs 149172284 awarded as compensation[11]. The State Authority in the State observed 9th November 2001 as Legal Services Day at the call of NALSA. The different authorities in the State organised legal literacy camps, Lok-Adalats and other programmes in almost all Districts. On this single day, a total number of 1897 cases were settled in different Lok-Adalats. However, it is revealed from the study that the number of cases settled in the Lok-Adalat is decreasing in recent years. In the year 1999, white the number of settlements was recorded at 354383, the number decreased to 199416 in the year 2000 and again the performance of Lok-Adalat, till September 2001, indicates the declining phenomenon, as till September, only 119928 cases were settled[12].

LOK-ADALAT IN THE STATE OF MADHYA PRADESH

While, the third highest number of Lok-Adalats were organised in the State of Rajasthan, the third highest number of cases were settled in the State of Madhya Pradesh. In Madhya Pradesh, 708 Lok-Adalats were held till March'1996 and the number was increased substantially in subsequent years. Till the end of 1999, the State of Madhya Pradesh successfully held 3327 Lok-Adalats. The disputant belonging to 703935 cases were benefited from the institution till March 1996 and till the end of 1999 such numbers reached to 1057139. A large number of motor accident claims were also settled in these Lok-Adalats, numbering at 14004, in the year 1996 and 40928 in the year 1999 and an amount of Rs. 315771299/- and Rs. 903756500/- were awarded in such motor accident compensation claim cases till the year 1996 and 1999 respectively.

It is also crystal clear from the study of Madhya Pradesh and other States as well as Table 7.2 that the number of settlements of MACC cases is not even more than 5%, which establishes the fact that the institution has succeeded in settling 95% disputes in different categories. The above Table 7.2, clearly exhibits the performance of the institution in the previously mentioned States as well as in other States of the Country.

LOK-ADALAT IN OTHER STATES

In several other states also the institution of Lok-Adalat successfully settled millions of cases. Therefore, if we consider the overall experience of the institution of Lok-Adalat in the country, it has functioned effectively and an out standing performance is recorded in some parts of the country. In the State of Karnataka 3576 Lok-Adalats were organised till the end of 1999 in which 486940 cases were settled.

In Karnataka itself, 64819 motor accident compensation cases were settled during the same period. The amount of compensation awarded by the Lok-Adalat will show the magnitude of the institution. An amount of Rs. 172,89,22,408/- (one hundred and seventy two crores eighty nine lakhs twenty two thousand four hundred and eight) was awarded as compensation to the victims or their heirs in motor accident compensation cases. In the State of Maharastra also, the institution of Lok-Adalat made a remarkable achievement. A large number of people were able to secure cheap and fast justice and benefited out of this institution. While till 1996, 1519 Lok-Adalats were held in the State, the number reached to 3949 in the year 1999. Similarly, while 93606 cases were settled till 1996, the disputants belonging to 177114 cases were benefited from Lok-Adalat, until 1999. A large number of motor accident claims were also settled in the Lok-Adalats. White, until 1996, 17342 insurance claim cases! were settled, the number reached 34630 at the end of 1999 and more than Rs. 301 crores was awarded as compensation.

In the similar direction, Haryana, effectively implemented the Lok-Adalat scheme. Even till 1996, 607 Lok-Adalats were organised in the State in which 200657 cases were settled including 7882 motor accident compensation cases and an amount of Rs. 328405064/- was awarded as compensation. Such a number of Lok-Adalats as well as settlements reached, increased significantly thereafter. The number of Lok-Adalats organised, reached 1126 in the year 1999 and disputants belonging to 285190 cases utilized this conciliatory mechanism for the resolution of their disputes and more than 60 crores was awarded in 13485 motor accident compensation claim cases. In the similar direction, a large number of cases were also settled in the State of Bihar. 110418 cases were settled by Lok-Adalats in the State of Bihar, till the end of 1999 in which 1187 cases were settled relating to MACC and an amount of Rs. 10,19,67,512 was awarded to the claimants.

However, there are a large number of States where the institution is still a new born child and much more is required to be done to activate the institution in such regions. So that the people of such regions can utilize the fruit of the institution and the Constitutional goal of access to justice constructively become meaningful to them. In West Bengal a small number of cases were settled till 1998 but it significantly increased in the year 1999. However, comparatively some contemporary and even smaller states have also successfully implemented the scheme and settled more than that of West Bengal. White in West Bengal a total number of 10616 cases were settled till the end of 1999, the number of settlements recorded in Assam and Delhi were 34299 and 77744 respectively. In Himachal Pradesh also a large number of cases were settled. Until 1999, 48,052 cases were settled in which MACC cases alone were 1562 and an amount of Rs. 161667228/- was awarded as compensation.

There are also a large number of States, which have not used the institution effectively, or the institution failed to achieve a remarkable goal. In the State of Arunachal Pradesh, only two Lok-Adalats were held till 1999 in which twenty three cases were settled. All of them were relating to motor accident compensation claims. In Goa only 28 Lok-Adalats were held till 1996 but the number of Lok-Adalats organised significantly reached 102 in the year 1999. Similarly, while 2669 cases were settled until 1996, the disputants belonging to 3024 cases were benefited from the institution till the end of 1999. A large number of such cases were belonging to motor accident compensation claims. Out of 3024 settlements, 2689 cases were related to MACC and Rs 135740760/ was awarded as compensation to the claimants. However, some States though having potentiality to make the institution more successful failed to achieve the target. Until March 1996 only a small number of cases were settled. As in West Bengal, only 2400 cases were settled until such period, in 39 Lok-Adalats. Comparatively, in Kerala, until March 1996, 29804 cases were settled in 45 Lok-Adalats. The reason of comparison of both States is that both the States have effectively implemented the Panchayat system and the traditional Panchayat systems have provided clues for the institution of Lok-Adalat. Some other States also failed to implement the scheme, which is evident from the above given data. Even in some places, only a few Lok-Adalats were held. As in Manipur, only 9 Lok-Adalats were held in which 1808 cases were settled. Similarly, in Andaman & Nicobar, Tripura, Chandigarh, Dadar & Nagar Haveli, Daman & Diu, and in Lakshadweep, 7, 29, 21, 2, 2 and one Lok-Adalats were held respectively until the end of 1999.

Thus, at national level the institution has shown a mixed performance. In some places it has effectively implemented the scheme and was succeeded in providing justice speedily and in-expensively to millions of people. On the other hand, in some places it has not succeeded so far as it required to be.

Table 7.2
Data of Disposal of Cases by Lok-Adalat in India

Sl No.	Name of State	No. of Lok-Adalat		Total no. of cases settled		No. of MACT Cases settled		Compensation Paid in MACC Cases (Rs.)	
		1996	1999	1996	1999	1996	1999	1996	1996
1	Andhra Pradesh	540	6835	225070	3,30.261	25212	48.444	763346638	2,10,10,52,643
2	Arunachal Pradesh	–	2	–	23	–	23	–	N-A
3	Assam	70	233	7300	34,299	2850	4,713	87533356	12,57,00,565
4	Bihar	42	361	53360	1,10,418	288	1J87	130112480	10,19,67,512
5	Goa	28	102	2669	3,024	1771	2.689	69768751	13,57,40,760
6	Gujrat	921	10165	137667	6,90,687	25848	53327	724100000	2,25,99,75,343
7	Haryana	607	1126	200657	2,85,190	7882	13.485	328405064	60,74,41,450
8	Himachal Pradesh	228	645	23830	48,052	2575	1362	34779893	16,16,67,228
9	Jammu & Kashmir	4	198	215	7,532	215	1.629	19137000	23,08,29,304
10	Karnatka	1828	3576	336223	4,86,940	40280	64.819	760203031	1,72,89,22,408
11	Kerala	45	1352	29804	43,182	21329	22.807	408883207	58,59,24,588
12	Madhya Pradesh	708	3327	703935	10,57,139	14004	40.928	315771299	9037,56,500
13	Maharashtra	1519	3949	93606	1,77,114	17342	34.630	766285114	3,01,96,52,394
14	Manipur	7	9	1483	1,808	248	347	12378500	1,52,26,500
15	Meghalaya	7	32	525	1960	246	294	9719500	3,51,19,500
16	Mizoram	5	52	325	215	172	210	4399000	44,14,080
17	Nagaland	–	–	–	–	–	–	–	–
18	Orissa	2266	3485	621115	15,13,757	8126	14.763	274141803	71,75,19,430
19	Punjab	189	1044	46484	72,222	6525	11,998	123266862	90,38,58,755
20	Rajasthan	304	4300	838573	10,36,618	21234	33353	757637629	1,42,71,37,978
21	Sikkim	3	28	10	348	–	13	–	51,85,000
22	Tamil Nadu	1289	3976	44787	94,182	44600	83.935	1342055036	3,60,35,04,036
23	Tripura	7	29	842	1.654	130	130	7413630	1,23,56,946
24	Uttar Pradesh	2333	4184	2339943	36,08,531	25215	44.999	993246274	2,41,19,16,270
24	West BengaJ	39	86	2400	10,616	2400	9353	59147700	50,29,37,907
26	Andaman & Nicobar	–	7	–	94	–	–	–	–
27	Chandigarh	11	21	10667	20.445	3%	1127	26223200	9,14,68,700
28	Dadar & Nagar Hav	–	2	–	81	–	24	–	21,74,000
29	Daman & Diu	–	2	–	68	–	14	–	–
30	Delhi	37	173	15121	77,744	8105	12.750	672691988	1235.85.694
31	Lakshadweep	–	1	–	65	–	5	–	4,35,000
32	Pondicherry	24	113	1812	6,020	1807	5,224	39232468	14,12,61,436
33	Supreme Court Legal Services Committees	–	–	–	–	–	–	–	–
	TOTAL	13061	49,415	5738423	9720289	278801	509171	8612779423	23060732170

CONCLUSION

The institution of Lok-Adalat has shown an outstanding performance in the country. It's able to resolve millions of cases through out the Country by conciliatory mechanism. However, the institution has not developed uniformly in all the places, which is clear from the above study. In some places, the performance of the institution was extremely good but in some places, it is still a newborn institution. It is also evident that in some places, while the institution was new in the year 1996, it performed extremely well in the subsequent years. One such example is the State of West Bengal. Nevertheless, it is not a matter of satisfaction. Much more is essential to be done to make the institution more effective.

In some States, it is found that the number of settlements decreased in the last couple of years. As in Rajasthan, the number of settlements substantially decreased in the year 2000. The State of Rajasthan considered as one of the most successful implementer of the programme of Lok-Adalat, there also the number of settlements is decreasing. While in the year 1999 a total number of 354383 cases were settled, the number substantially decreased to 199416 in the year 2000. Even in Gujarat, the settlements substantially decreased in the year 2001 and a similar phenomenon is prevalent in the year 2002. In the year 2001, 206425 cases were settled compared to the corresponding figure of 513787 of the year 2000. Indeed, the settlement of the year 2000 of the State of Gujarat is around 30 times more than the entire settlements reached in West Bengal.

As of the State of Gujarat and Rajasthan, in West Bengal too the number of settlements decreased slightly in the year 2000 & 2001. Thus in order to understand the reasons for declining of the popularity of the institution of Lok-Adalat in a few States, an in depth study is required on each State's functioning. In the next chapter, the researcher is tracing causes for success and failure of the institution functioning in all Districts of West Bengal.

REFERENCES

1 Sunil Deshta, *Lok-Adalat in India, Genesis and functioning*, (1995) P. 117.

2 Justice A.S. Anand, Inaugural address by Hon'ble justice at UNCITRAL-ICCA Judicial Colloquium, On Sunday, 5th March' 2000. See, 11, Nyaya Deep, Jan-Mar 2000.

3 Supra 1, See also Legal Aid News Letter, Vol XI, Part 2&3, July-Dec, 1991, P. 3.

4 Legal Aid News Letter, Vol-XII, Part 1, April-June 1992, P19, Legal Aid News Letter, Vol-XII, Part 2, July-Sep 1992, P 36.

5 See Nyaya Path, Year 3, September (2002)

6 Legal Aid News Letter, Vol DC, Pert 1-4, May 1969- Feb. 1990, P.16.

7 id. See ate Supra 1.125-126.

8 Supra 1, 129.

9 id 130.

10 id. at 131.

11 The current statistics obtained from the Souvenir published by Rajasthan State Legal Services Authority.

12 id.

CHAPTER 8

STUDY OF THE FUNCTIONING OF LOK-ADALAT IN WEST BENGAL

INTRODUCTION

The institution of Lok-Adalat was introduced in West Bengal much later than other States. In fact till 1996, the State of West Bengal was considered as a newcomer in the field of Lok-Adalat movement. A small number of Lok-Adalats were held in the State till such period. Indeed till March 1996, while in most of the other states, a large number of Lok-Adalats were held in which millions of people benefited form the institution, in West Bengal only 39 Lok-Adalats were held under the auspices of State Legal Aid and Advice Board, in which only 2400 disputants got the fruit of the institution through conciliatory mechanism. The initiation of the institution of Lok-Adalat is done by motor accident compensation claim cases. In fact, until March 1996, all the cases settled in West Bengal were relating to motor accident compensation claims and an amount of Rs. 59147700/- was awarded as compensation to the victims or their heirs. However, one NGO organised several Lok-Adalats in the State in which a large number of cases belonging to other categories were also settled[1]. The first Lok-Adalat was organised by LASWEB on 14th & 15th Dec'1991 in which 58 cases were settled and an amount of Rs 1 Crore 9 Lakhs was awarded. Among those 58 cases, 15 were relating to commercial suits, 33 were insurance claim cases, 4 were matrimonial cases and 6 were electricity cases[2].

In West Bengal, the NGOs played a vital role in popularising the institution of Lok-Adalat. A large number of cases were settled in the Lok-Adalats but in comparison to other contemporary States, the State of West Bengal is far behind. On the one hand, while a small number of Lok-Adalats were held until 1996, on the other hand improvement has not been seen in the state even in the year 1997 & 1998. However, after the enforcement of the Legal Services Act, 1987, attempt was made to activate the institution so that the rural people can avail justice, cost effectively and time effectively. In order to activate the institution, the different District Authorities were constituted under the Act on 15th July, 1998. However, all the District Authorities did not immediately start functioning effectively but most of them got activated in the beginning of 1999. As a result, an extremely good performance has been recorded in the year 1999. Indeed, ten fold increase in the number of settlements have been seen during the year.

In order to provide justice at the grass root level through the instrument of Lok-Adalat, Sub-Divisional Legal Services Committees were constituted under each district, for their Sub-Divisions, on 18th April, 2000. However, almost all sub-Divisional Legal Services Committees exist on paper only as Sub-Divisional Committees are not activated for the purpose of Lok-Adalat in most or the places. Even, the number of settlements in the State slightly decreased in the year 2000 & 2001, instead of increasing. Thus, the institution of Lok-Adalat in the state has seen an extremely good up-ward movement, in the year 1999, as well as a tiny downward movement in the year 2000 & 2001. However, a slight increase has been recorded in the year 2002. Nevertheless, this is not a common feature of all the districts. Indeed, in some districts the number of settlements are increasing effectively. It has also been seen in the State that while in most of the States the percentage of MACC cases varies from 5% to 20%, the percentage of MACC in West Bengal is around 73% and a small number of other cases were also settled. In these circumstances, the question arises as to whether the MACC cases are only appropriate form of disputes for conciliatory mechanism as adopted in Lok-Adalat? Or whether some other forms of disputes, which is normally considered proper for conciliatory mechanism on jurisprudential aspect, are also proper forms of disputes for Lok-Adalat? If so, why Lok-Adalats fail to provide justice to the large number of disputants in other categories of cases? However, previously mentioned monolithic characteristic of the institution is not similar in all districts. Even, in some districts, the number of settlements of MACC cases is below than the other categories of cases.

Thus, in order to properly appreciate the achievement of the institution in the State and to understand the root causes of its success as well as the causes for the declining phenomenon of the institution, I have divided this Chapter into three parts.

In the first part, I have tried to find out the root cause of the success of the institution as well as the failure of the institution by analysing the functioning of institution in different districts followed by the over all performance at State level.

In the second part, I have critically analysed the functioning of the institution in the State, and

In the third part, I have discussed the responses of different people on the questionnaire about the functioning of the institution of Lok-Adalat in West Bengal.

PERFORMANCE OF LOK-ADALAT IN WEST BENGAL

The Lok-Adalat movement was started in West Bengal much later than other States. In fact, the first Lok-Adalat in the State was organised almost a decade after the first Lok-Adalat was held at Gujarat. However, efforts had been made by judiciary, NGOs, Law Teachers, para-lawyers and the other legal fraternity to popularise the institution. Their joint efforts materialized when they organised the first Lok-Adalat in the State, on 14th & 15th December'1991, under the auspices of one NGO namely LASWB[3]. This Lok-Adalat was organised at the High Court in which 272 cases were referred. The Lok-Adalat was able to bring an end to 58 disputes in which 15 cases were commercial suits, 33 were insurance claim cases, 4 were matrimonial cases and 6 were relating to electricity disputes. A long effort was made for organizing the Lok-Adalat. The law students played an important role by making research on each case referred before Lok-Adalat. Hundreds of people from Bar, Social Welfare Organisations, Law Teachers, Law students and the co-ordination from the members of judiciary made the Lok-Adalat a great success with their joint efforts. The second Lok-Adalat was organised again by LASWEB on 21st & 22nd, August, 1992 in which 316 cases were referred consisting of 199 commercial suits, 60 insurance claims and 57 matrimonial cases out of which, 15 commercial cases, 33 insurance claim cases and 11 matrimonial cases were settled and an amount of Rs 1.26 Crore was awarded. The third Lok-Adalat was organised on 11th & 12th December, 1993 in which 34 disputes were settled. The first Lok-Adalat in the District was organised on 13th & 14th March'1993 at Siliguri in which a large number of cases were referred. Justice A.M. Ahmadi inaugurated the Lok-Adalat. The lawyers, para lawyers, professors, social welfare organisations as well as judiciary actively participated with great enthusiasm in the Lok-Adalat to make it a great success[4]. Thus, before the enforcement of the Legal Services Authorities Act, 1987 and Rules made there under, the Lok-Adalats were organised on the one hand by State Legal Aid and Advice Board, on the other hand by LASWEB.

However, until March'1996 only 39 Lok-Adalats were organised by Legal Aid and Advice Board in which 2400 cases belonging to motor accident compensation claims were settled. In those Lok-Adalats, an amount of Rs 59147700/- was awarded as compensation to the victims or their heirs. Though, 2400 cases itself is not a low figure, as each case settled out of mutual compromise is a success of the institution and will help in bringing the disputant nearer to each other. It can make the breaking family unite. It can improve the relation between the Bank and the borrower. However, compared to the other States, where thousands of cases were settled on a single day, the functioning of the institution was minimal and was still a newborn institution. The situation was not even improved in the year 1997 & 1998. In both the years, 12 Lok-Adalats were held. Study reveals that 571 cases were settled in the 12 Lok-Adalats held during the year 1997. Among those 571 cases, 564 cases were relating to motor accident compensation claim cases and an amount of Rs 30553573/- was awarded as compensation. The number of settlements of cases even decreased during the year 1998 and only

301 cases were settled in which 279 cases were related to motor accident compensation claims. An amount of Rs 9605269/-was awarded as compensation in MACC cases. Thus, it is apparent from previously mentioned data that the Lok-Adalat had effectively performed only in settling MACC cases until 1998.

The institution of Lok-Adalat was itself a new institution until mid' 90s. Therefore, the Lok-Adalat was not so effective under the old scheme in West Bengal in spite of several efforts made by the legal fraternity. However, the enactment of the Legal Services Authorities Act, 1987 provided a new vista to the institution of Lok-Adalat. Though, the Legal Services Authorities Act was enforced in the year 1995, the West Bengal Government passed The West Bengal State Legal Services Authority Rules[5] in the year 1994. In furtherance of, The West Bengal State Legal Services Regulation, 1998 was notified on 27th July'1998[6]. Thus, after the notification of the Regulation, the different district legal services authorities were constituted and the Lok-Adalat started functioning with a new enthusiasm with all its statutory backings.

The first Lok-Adalat under the auspices of West Bengal State Legal Services Authority was organised on 22nd Nov'1998 in the District Nadia. Despite the fact that before this Lok-Adalat, the institution was functioning under the old scheme, but this was the first Lok-Adalat of the State having statutory backing. The institution of Lok-Adalat started a new march, with new enthusiasm from this Lok-Adalat in order to provide justice quickly without any cost. In the first Lok-Adalat, 74 cases were settled in which MACC alone were 66 and an amount of Rs 30,43,000/- was awarded as compensation. Apart from 66 MACC cases, 6 maintenance cases and 2 matrimonial cases were also settled in the Lok-Adalat. Thus, a large number of people were benefited from the institution in a single day. The march of providing equal justice through Lok-Adalats under the new scheme, which started during the end of Nov'1998, has not looked back and the fruit of the institution reached a large number of masses until now.

The development of the institution in the post 1996 period can be established by the fact that while until Mar'96 only 39 Lok-Adalats were held in the State, 1153 Benches of Lok-Adalats were constituted up to the end of 2002. Thousands of cases were settled in these Lok-Adalats. 20893 cases were settled in the Lok-Adalats out of which 15164 cases were relating to motor accident compensation claims. The magnitude of the performance can be seen from the amount of compensation awarded in MACC cases. Until 2002, an amount of Rs 351,42,51,186/- (Rupees three hundred and fifty one crores forty two lacks fifty one thousand one hundred and eighty six) was awarded. Therefore, the institution has shown an outstanding performance in MACC cases in the State.

The graph below will clearly show the high percentage of settlement of MACC cases, which alone is around 73% of the total cases, settled in the State up to the year 2002. However, a large number of other cases also settled in the Lok-Adalat until 2002, which includes 492 Money Suits, 311 Title Suits, 1075 Bank Suits, 605 Criminal Cases, 404 cases relating to maintenance U/S 125 CrPC, 822 Matrimonial Disputes, 123 execution cases, 1240 pre-litigation cases, 186 Writs and 471 other categories of cases.

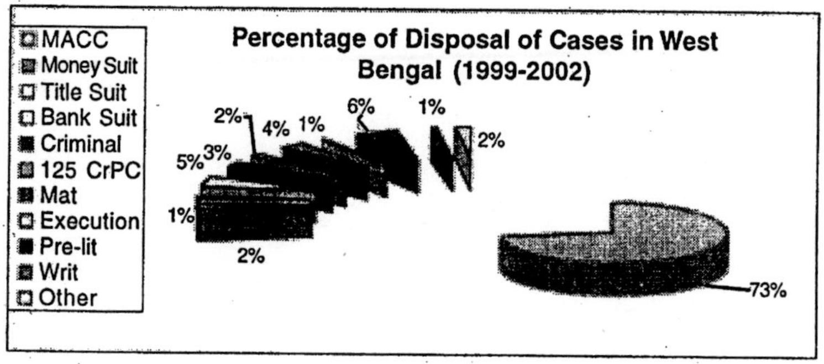

Thus, while out of the total settlement of 20893 cases 73% cases belonged to MACC; other varieties of cases were also settled in Lok-Adalats. Among those other cases, 2% cases were relating to money suit, 1% were relating to Title Suit, 5% relating to Bank Loan cases, 3% relating to criminal cases, 2% relating to maintenance cases, 4% relating to matrimonial disputes, 1% relating to execution cases, 6% relating to pre-litigation cases, 1% relating to writ petition and 2% cases were relating to other different categories of disputes.

While until March'1996, only 2400 cases were settled at Lok-Adalats and during the year 1998, only 301 cases were settled, the number of settlements reached 4512 in the year 1999. It is revealed from the study that during the year, 9434 cases were placed before the Lok-Adalats in which the aforesaid 4512 cases were settled. Among such cases, the MACC alone was 3500 and thus 77.5% cases settled during the year were relating to motor accident compensation claims. Apart from MACC cases, 192 money suits, 129 Title Suits, 280 Bank Loan cases, 42 criminal cases, 84 maintenance cases U/S 125 CrPC, 165 matrimonial cases, 25 execution cases, 10 pre-litigation cases and 7 other categories of cases settled in the Lok-Adalat. A slight increase in the number of reference of cases to the Lok-Adalat has been recorded during the year 2000 & 2001. While in the year 1999, 9434 cases were referred before the Lok-Adalat; the number reached 9616 in the year 2000 and was further increased to 9748 in the year 2001. Nevertheless, the institution of Lok-Adalat got a large popularity during the year 1999, which are exhibited in the figures about the increasing of settlement during the year. It was expected that in the subsequent years the institution would be able to provide justice, speedily and without any cost, to much more citizens with conciliatory mechanism. However, study reveals that the number of settlements slightly decreased in the year 2000 and was further decreased in the year 2001. While the number of settlements during the year 1999 was 4512, the number decreased to 4387 in the year 2000 and further decreased to 4025 during the year 2001. Indeed, in the year 2002 while the number of reference decreased to 9045, the number of settlements were increased up to 4697.

The MACC cases again takes a lead during the year 2000. While a total number of 4387 cases were settled during the year 2000, the MACC alone was 3095. Thus, 70.54% cases settled during the year were relating to motor accident compensation claims. However, the benefit of the institution reached to the other categories of cases also. A large number of such different categories of cases were settled in the Lok-Adalat. Apart from MACC cases during the year 2000, 148 Money Suits, 43 Title Suits, 302 Bank Loan Cases, 67 Criminal Cases, 148 maintenance cases U/S 125 CrPC, 224 matrimonial cases, 35 execution cases, 179 pre-litigation cases and 124 other categories of cases were also settled in the Lok-Adalat.

Similarly, in the year 2001, while 4025 cases were settled during the year, MACC alone were 2420. However, 80 Money suits, 62 Title suits, 343 Bank loan cases, 203 criminal cases, 138 Maintenance cases U/S 125 CrPC, 200 Matrimonial cases, 53 execution cases, 329 pre-litigation cases, 111 writ petitions and 87 other categories of cases were also settled.

Data of Disposal of Cases by Lok-Adalat In West Bengal
Table: 8.1

	Lok-Adalat	Put-Up	Settled	MACC	Money Suit	Title Suit	Bank Suit	Criminal Suit	125 CrPC	Mat	Execution	Pre-lit	Writ	Other	Awarded Money
Till 1996	39		2400	2400											59147700
1997	12		571	564										7	30553573
1998	12		301	279										22	9605269
1999	285	9434	4512	3500	192	129	280	42	84	165	25	10	0	85	275394488
2000	315	9616	4387	3095	148	43	302	67	148	224	35	179	22	124	2706886393
2001	279	9748	4025	2420	80	62	342	203	138	200	53	329	111	87	189988906
2002	211	9045	4697	2906	72	77	151	293	34	233	10	722	53	146	242674857
GrandTotal	1153	37843	20893	15164	492	311	1075	605	404	822	123	1240	186	471	3514251186

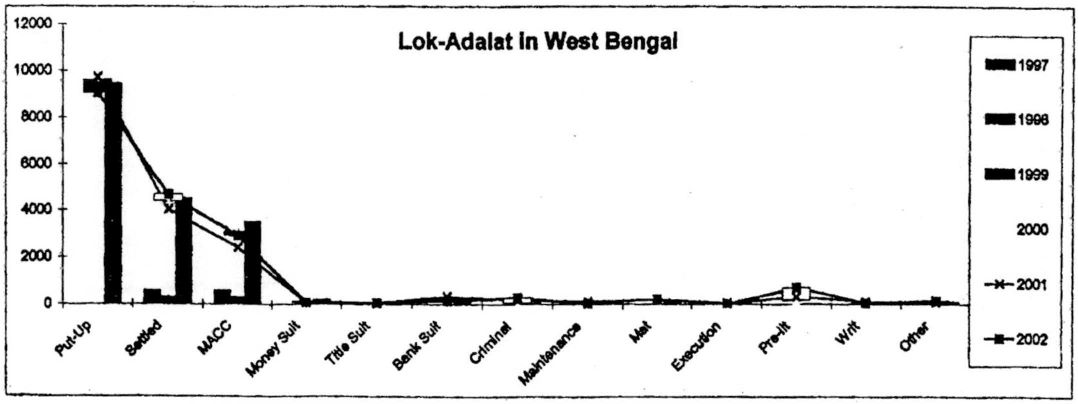

The aforesaid data as well as the graph exhibits the phenomenal growth of the institution from 1997 to 1999 and the slight decrease in the year 2000 & 2001. In the year 2002, 2906 MACC cases, 72 Money Suits, 77 Title Suits, 151 Bank Suits, 293 Criminal Suits, 34 Maintenance cases, 233 Matrimonial cases, 10 Execution cases, 722 pre-litigation cases, 53 writ petition and 146 other categories of cases were settled. It is evident that the institution Lok-Adalat while on one hand settled a large number of MACC cases, on the other hand it also succeeded in bringing into compromise other different categories of cases. However, the number of different categories of cases is not comparable with MACC cases as the percentage of the other cases is extremely low. If we look at the national scenario, the average percentage of the MACC cases are around 5.23%, while the over all percentage of MACC cases in different States is in between 2% to 15%, except the State of Tamil Nadu and Pondicherry. In West Bengal, such a percentage is around 73%. Thus, in practice, though the institution settled different forms of cases, it has taken a monolithic approach. The other thing which has been established so far from the data is that the institution, though performed extremely well in the year 1999, failed to increase the number of settlements in the subsequent years. Even, the number of settlements decreased in the year 2000 & 2001. Indeed, the slight increase was made in the year 2002.

However, the situation is not similar in all the districts. In some districts the number of settlements are increasing regularly, at the same time, the downward movement has been seen in some other Districts. In some Districts, while MACC has been given top priority, in some other Districts the highest numbers of settlements reached, are Bank Loan cases or even in matrimonial cases.

In order of analyse the institution properly, an in-depth study of the functioning of each district as well as High Court is made hereunder.

LOK-ADALAT AT HIGH COURT, CALCUTTA

The High Court Legal Services Committee was constituted with 11 members including the members from Bar, Bench and the Social Activists in order to settle the disputes amicably through the instrument of Lok-Adalat. Until June 2002, only sixteen Lok-Adalats were held at the High Court under the auspices of High Court Legal Services Committee. In these 16 Lok-Adalats a large number of cases were settled. While in these Lok-Adalats 1055 cases were referred for settlement of disputes through conciliatory efforts, the Lok-Adalats were able to bring disputes to an end in 375 cases.

Lok Adalat at High Court Calcutta
Table 8.2

	MACC	Writ	Bank Loan	Civil Cases	Pre-lit	Total	Compensation
1st Lok-Adalat	45	0	2	0	0	47	6903573
2nd Lok-Adalat	31	0	2	0	0	33	56,89,000
3rd Lok-Adalat	11	0	0	0	0	11	2410000
4th Lok-Adalat	26	24	0	1	0	51	
5th Lok-Adalat	18	5	0	1	0	24	
6th Lok-Adalat	4	0	4	1	0	9	
7th Lok-Adalat	3	0	0	0	0	3	6,84,000
8th Lok-Adalat	3	2	0	0	0	5	4,50,000
9th Lok-Adalat	1	12	0	0	0	13	80,000
10th Lok-Adalat	0	11	1	0	0	12	
11th Lok-Adalat	4	14	1	0	0	19	2,00,000
12th Lok-Adalat	4	2	1	0	0	7	9,54,000
13th Lok-Adalat	1	63	0	3	1	68	2,98,000
14th Lok-Adalat	0	33	1	0	2	36	
15th Lok-Adalat	1	4	1	0	1	7	
16th Lok-Adalat	1	30	0	0	0	31	1,00,000
Grand Total	**153**	**200**	**13**	**6**	**4**	**375**	

In the beginning, mainly MACC cases were settled in the Lok-Adalats but the ambit spread over in subsequent Lok-Adalats and now a large number of writ cases have also been settled in the High Court. Even the writ cases are ahead, by settling 200 cases in these Lok-Adalats, than the MACC cases, whose number of settlements recorded at 153. An amount of Rs 21519445/- was awarded as compensation in these Lok-Adalats. A small number of civil, pre-litigation and other cases were also settled in these Lok-Adalats.

The first Lok-Adalat in the High Court was organised on 18th September'1999. In the first Lok-Adalat, a large number of motor accident claims cases were settled. In this Lok-Adalat, 47 cases were settled, in which motor accident claim cases alone were 45 and two were Bank cases. The second Lok-Adalat was organised on 19th February, 2000 with four Benches. Altogether 106 cases were placed before the four Benches, in which 10 cases were relating to matrimonial disputes, 18 Bank cases and remaining 88 cases were motor accident compensation claims. 33 MACC cases were settled in the second Lok-Adalat along with 2 Bank cases and an amount of 56,89,000/- was awarded as compensation in MACC cases. Not a single matrimonial case was settled not because parties were not able to settle their disputes before the forum but because none of the parties appeared before the forum. Similarly, in other cases also a large number of parties did not appear. The graph below exhibits the functioning of the institution at High Court level.

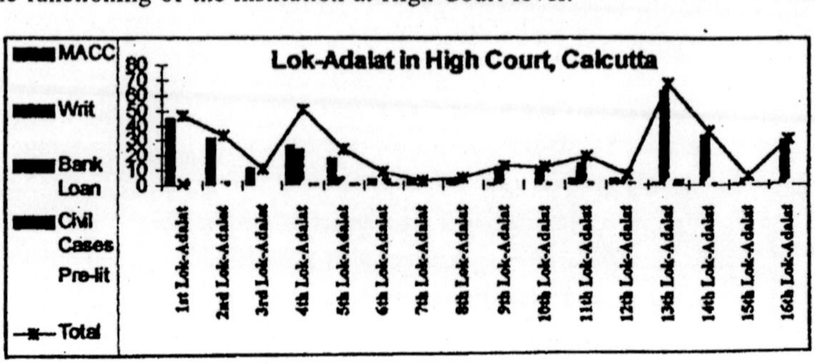

The third Lok-Adalat was organised on 8th April, 2000 with three Benches. 74 cases were placed before the three benches of Lok-Adalat, consisting of 10 Matrimonial cases, 9 Bank cases, 1 writ and the remaining 54 motor accident compensation cases. However, only 11 MACC cases were settled in which an amount of Rs. 2410000/- was awarded. The reason for non-settlement of cases is not that the parties concerned appeared before the Lok-Adalat and declined to settle the disputes but a large number of them did not turn up before Lok-Adalat and in matrimonial cases none of the parties appeared before the forum of Lok-Adalat. Similarly in the fourth Lok-Adalat 51 cases were settled including 26 MACC, 24 writs and 1 civil case and in the fifth Lok-Adalat 18 MACC cases, 5 writs, and 1 civil case settled. However, the number of settlements decreased substantially in the 6th Lok-Adalat and only 9 cases were settled consisting of 4 MACC cases, 4 Bank loan cases and 1 civil case. The number of settlements further decreased in the 7th Lok-Adalat, which was held on 17th May, 2001. Study reveals that only 25 cases were placed before this Lok-Adalat in which 5 cases were relating to Bank disputes, 16 MACC cases and 4 writ petitions. Only three cases relating to motor accident compensation claims were settled and an amount of Rs. 6.84 lacs was awarded to the claimants. Study further reveals that the situation did not even improve in the 8th Lok-Adalat, which was held on 16th June'2001. In this Lok-Adalat only 33 cases were referred before Lok-Adalat, in which 10 cases were relating to MACC, 10 Bank matters and remaining were writ petitions, mostly against the electricity companies. Out of 33 cases 5 cases were settled in which three cases were relating to motor accident compensation claim cases and two writ petitions relating to connection and supply of electricity. The 9th and 10th Lok-Adalats also could not make improvement. In the 9th Lok-Adalat, which was held on 7th July, 2001, only 60 cases were referred, out of which 13 cases were settled, in which one case was relating to motor accident compensation claim and other 12 were writ cases. Similarly, in the 10th Lok-Adalat, 45 cases were referred for resolution of disputes, out of which 12 cases were settled, in which 1 was a Bank case and the rest 11 cases were against the CESC/WBSEB. In all the cases both the parties agreed to give electric connection or resume connection.

Study reveals that the number of reference of cases as well as settlements increased slightly in the 11th Lok-Adalat, which was held on 25th August, 2001 with three Benches. The performance of Lok-Adalat got wide publicity and the news media covered the Lok-Adalat. In this Lok-Adalat 112 cases were submitted before the Lok-Adalat in which 57 cases were relating to recovery of Bank loans, 41 were writ petitions against the electricity provider pertaining to disputes of electric connections or installation of electric meters and 14 were Motor Accident Claim Appeals. Out of this, 19 cases were settled in which 1 Bank loan case, 4 MACC cases and 14 writs concerning the electricity provider. Thus from this Lok-Adalat the electricity disputes became hot cakes for the institution of Lok-Adalat. In the 12th Lok-Adalat also, which was held on 15th September, 2001, 2 writs relating to electricity dispute were settled. In this Lok-Adalat, total 48 cases were referred, in which 7 cases were settled, including 4 MACC and 1 civil case. An amount of Rs. 13,75,0007/- was awarded in MACC cases and civil cases. The number of cases considerably increased in the 13th Lok-Adalat dated 13th October'2001. In this Lok-Adalat, 3 Benches were constituted in which 144 cases were referred, out of which 68 cases were settled. Among those 68 cases, the number of the Civil cases was 3, 63 writ petitions, 1 MACC and 1 was interestingly pre-litigation. The pre-litigation case was relating to dispute between father and son concerning maintenance. However, after enhancement of number of settlements in the 13th Lok-Adalat, the figure again decreased considerably in the 14th & 15th Lok-Adalats. While in the 14th Lok-Adalat a total number of 139 cases were referred, out of which 36 cases were settled. In the 15th Lok-Adalat, 157 cases were referred, out of which 6 cases were settled.

The number of settlements slightly increased in the 16th Lok-Adalat, which was held on 18th May, 2002. In this Lok-Adalat, a total number of 85 cases were referred in which writ petitions alone were 78. Out of which 31 cases were settled and the percentage of settlements recorded was 36.47%. However, out of 31 cases settled, 27 cases were pertaining to electricity disputes, three were concerning retirement benefits and one MACC cases.

The institution has continuously seen an upward and down ward movement at High Court level. However, the institution was not able to provide the fruit of this conciliatory mechanism to a large number of people at the High Court level and still much more is required to be done in this regard. On several occasions, it has seen that, though the cases are referred before Lok-Adalat, the parties concerned do not bother to appear before the forum. Hence, some instrumentality is required to be evolved at this end. Lok-Adalat also failed to settle disputes excepting couple of categories of cases and a continuing effort became essential to improve the situation.

LOK-ADALAT IN KOLKATA DISTRICT

The Lok-Adalats in Kolkata District are organised by District Legal Services Authority, Kolkata. The District Authority was constituted by the Governor in consultation with the Chief Justice of Calcutta High Court, by virtue of power conferred by Sec. 9(2) B of the LSA Act, 1987, on 15th day of July 1998[7]. It took one year for DLSA to organise the first Lok-Adalat, which was held on 27th June'1999 in the premises of City Civil Court, Kolkata. Though before the enforcement of the LSA Act there were some Lok-Adalats held in the Districts of Kolkata, but it was the first Lok-Adalat after the enforcement of the Act.

Initially only MACC cases were placed before Lok-Adalat but soon other cases, like matrimonial cases, maintenance cases, money suits, pre-litigation cases, Title suit etc, were also presented before Lok-Adalat. In the first Lok-Adalat, 76 MACC cases were placed, out of which 59 cases were settled and an amount of Rs. 40,61,000/- was paid as compensation. In the second Lok-Adalat, which was held on 28th August'1999, 59 cases relating to MACC were placed, out of which 42 cases were settled and an amount of Rs. 27,46,000/- was decreed as compensation.

In the third Lok-Adalat also, only MACC cases were referred before the Lok-Adalat. Total 32 such cases were referred before such Lok-Adalat out of which 8 cases were settled and an amount of Rs. 6,40,000/- was awarded as compensation. However, from the fourth Lok-Adalat onwards the other categories of cases were also successfully attempted to be conciliated. In this Lok-Adalat also 27 MACC cases were referred, out of which 12 were settled. Apart from MACC, 18 Matrimonial cases and 15 Maintenance cases were also referred before Lok-Adalat out which one Matrimonial case and 2 Maintenance were settled.

Till the completion of the year 2002, the total number of Lok-Adalats held were 31, in which 866 cases were placed before the Lok-Adalat out of which 378 cases were settled, in which a large number of cases were motor accident compensation claim (MACC) cases. A total number of 424 MACC cases were placed before the Lok-Adalat out of which 294 cases were settled and an amount of Rs. 2,09,52,150 was paid as compensation. The data and graph given under, points to a disturbing trend.

It is apparent from the data that the number of other cases, which were placed before the Lok-Adalats, till June 2002 were, 33 pre-litigation cases, 123 maintenance cases, 147 matrimonial cases, 2 execution cases, 17 civil cases and 9 money suits in which 22 pre-litigation cases were disposed of, 37 maintenance cases, 23 matrimonial cases and 1 execution cases were settled. Thus while the over all percentage of settlement is 43%, the percentage of settlement of MACC cases, matrimonial cases, maintenance cases, execution cases and pre-litigation cases are 55%, 16%, 30%, 50%, and 67% respectively. However, not a single title suit or money suit was settled during the last four years period.

Lok Adalat in Kolkata District
Table 8.3

Period	Lok-Adalat Held	MACC Cases Placed	MACC Cases Settled	Compensation Paid	% of Settle-ment	Other Cases Placed	Other Cases Settled	% of Settle-ment	Total Cases placed	Total Cases settled	% of Settle-ment
Jan'99-June'99	1	76	59	40,61,000	77%	0	0	0	76	59	77%
July'99-Dec' 99	4	59	42	27,46,000	71%	136	49	36%	195	91	46%
Jan'00-June'00	6	128	77	43,63,500	60%	64	18	28%	192	95	50%
July'00-Dec' 00	5	62	28	21,52,500	45%	71	27	38%	133	55	40%
Jan'01-June'01	6	63	18	22,22,000	29%	78	18	23%	141	36	26%
July'01-Dec'01	4	21	11	11,19,000	52%	61	13	21%	82	24	29%
Jan'02-June'02	3					22	5	22%	22	5	22%

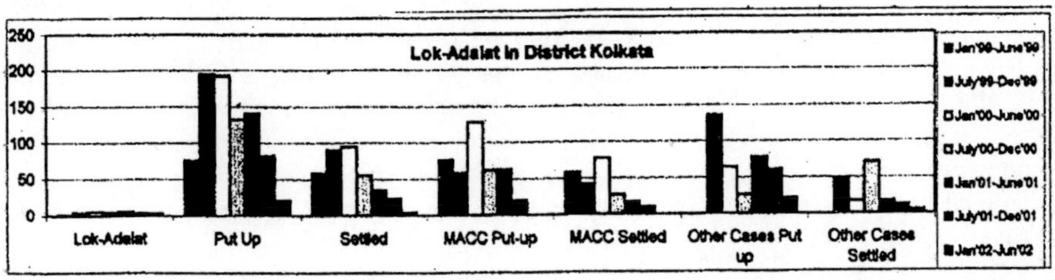

The most vital draw back relating to the functioning of Lok-Adalat in the Kolkata is that the numbers of cases being referred to Lok-Adalats as well as the number of settlements reached in such Lok-Adalats are decreasing continuously since the first Lok-Adalat held. Number of Lok-Adalats organised in the District has also decreased. White during the first half year of 2000 and 2001 the number of Lok-Adalats organised in the District was 6, the number came down to 3 during first half-year of 2002. The highest number of settlements in a single Lok-Adalat was achieved in the first Lok-Adalat, in which 59 cases were settled, out of 76 cases referred before Lok-Adalat.

It is revealed from the study that while the number of settlements of cases were 195 during second half of the 1999, the number decreased to 192 in the first half of 2000 and were further decreased to 55 in the second half or 2000. It is further revealed that the number decreased further to 36 in the first half of 2001 and to 24 in the second half of 2001. White the number decreased continuously, now it has decreased further during the first half-yearly period of 2002 and only 5 cases were settled. Not a single MACC case was settled in this Lok-Adalat. However, in the second half of year 2002, 13 cases were settled in which 10 cases were relating to MACC and 3 were of other categories of cases. The under shown graph will show the ratio of filing of different cases and their disposal through the instrument of Lok-Adalat, till June 2002 at Kolkata District.

CASES PLACED

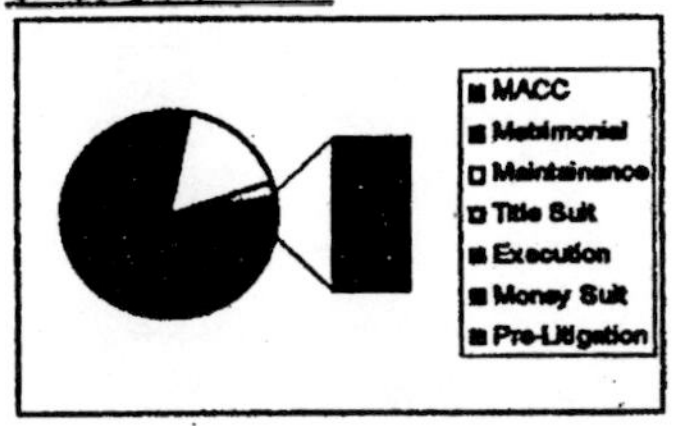

CASES SETTLED

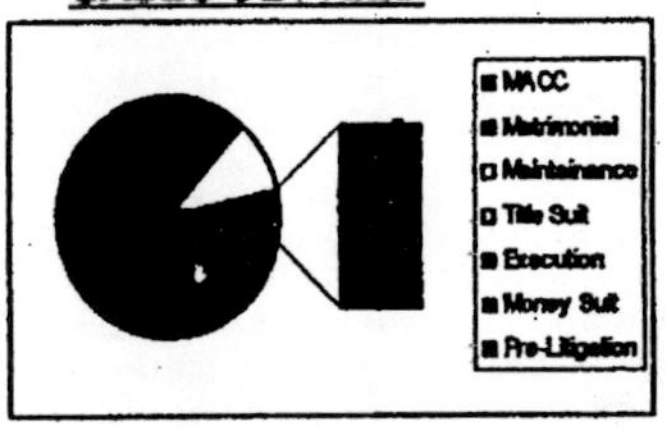

MACC cases also decreased tremendously along with other categories of cases. While in the first Lok-Adalat the entire lot of cases were relating to MACC, in the 1st half of 2002, not a single MACC case was settled. The number of settlements of MACC cases increased initially and the number reached 77 during the first half of 2000, from the figure of 59, but it again decreased to 28 in first half of 2001 and to 11 during second half of 2001. Similarly, other cases also performed in the same way. Initially, the number of settlements were increased from 49 to 71 during the second half of the 2000 but it decreased enormously and reached 18 in the first half of 2001 and to 13 in the second half of 2001. In the 1st half yearly of 2002, it reached at a ground level of 5 cases and in 2nd half yearly to 13. Thus from the functioning of the District Calcutta it can be said that the institution of Lok-Adalat is losing popularity among the disputants.

LOK-ADALAT IN DISTRICT SOUTH 24 PARGANAS

The Lok-Adalat in the District is organised under the auspices of District Legal Services Authority, 24 Pgs (south). The District Authority was constituted by notification dated 15-07-98 consisting of 16 members[8]. Under the DLSA of 24 Parganas (South), five Sub-Divisional Legal Services Committees were constituted by notification, dated 18th April' 2000[9], namely, Alipore Sub-Divisional Legal Services Committee, Baruipur Sub-Divisional Legal Services Committee, Canning Sub-Divisional Legal Services Committee, Diamond Harbour Sub-Divisional Legal Services Committee and Kakdwip Sub-Divisional Legal Services Committee. All of these Sub-Divisional Legal Services Committees are not properly functioning mainly due to lack of infrastructure and finance. Only the Baruipore Sub-Divisional Legal Services Committee was active to the extent of providing few legal aids but so far the Lok-Adalat is concerned that these Committees have not contributed any thing constructive. Not a single Lok-Adalat in the District is being held out side the District Head Quarter, which is in Alipore. However, the functioning of the District Authority is comparatively better than the several other District Authorities, so far as the functioning of Lok-Adalat is concerned. This District Authority can be considered as one of the most successful implementer of the Lok-Adalat scheme where continuously a large number of cases are being settled.

Though the District Authority was constituted in the mid 1998, the first Lok-Adalat in the District was held on 13-2-1999 in which 155 cases were placed before three Benches of the Lok-Adalat However, only a few cases were settled in this Lok-Adalat. Only 16 cases were settled, out of which 13 were related to the Title Suit/ Mortgage Suit and 3 were MACC cases Till June 2002, 31 Lok-Adalats were held in which 67 Benches were constituted and 3013 cases were put up in these Lok-Adalats out of which 1804 cases were settled including 1762 cases relating to MACC. The amount as compensation paid by itself, highlight the magnitude of the performance of the institution in the District. During these periods an amount of Rs. 19,45,08,596/- (Nineteen Crores Forty Five Lakhs Eight Thousand five hundred and ninety six) was paid as compensation. The data given under will exhibit the performance of Lok-Adalat in the district during the last three and half years period.

For the proper understanding the performance of Lok-Adalat during last four years period, to know whether the number of settlements are increasing or decreasing, I have divided the data on a half yearly basis. In the first half of the year 1999 a total number of 366 cases were referred before the Lok-Adalat in the District, out of which 89 cases were settled in which 34 cases were relating to civil dispute, 3 were relating to matrimonial disputes and 52 were relating to MACC cases and an amount of Rs 77,36,000/- was awarded as compensation.

Lok Adalat in 24 Pargamas (South)
Table 8.4

Period	Total Cases Referred	Total Cases Settled	%of Settle-ment	MACC Settled	Title Suit & Money Suit	Matri-monial Cases	Compensation Paid
Feb'99 to June' 99	366	89	24.31	52	34	03	77,36,000
July '99 to Dec 99	146	64	43.83	61	00	03	48,94,000
Jan' 2000 to June'00	434	251	57.83	250	00	01	2,42,78,000
July' 00 to Dec'00	290	223	76.89	223	00	00	2,75,30,000
Jan' 01 to June' 01	535	324	60.56	324	00	00	3,21,61,000
July' 01 to Dec'01	488	357	73.15	356	01	00	3,39,49,096
Jan' 02 to June02	754	496	65.78	496	00	00	6,39,60,500
July'02 to Dec'02	542	365	67.34	365	00	00	108904000
TOTAL	3555	2169		2127	35	7	109,312,953

It is apparent from above data that during the second half of the year, the number of cases being referred to Lok-Adalat decreased and only 146 cases were referred, out of which 64 cases were settled, in which 61 cases belong to MACC and 3 cases were relating to matrimonial disputes. However, the number of cases referred to the Lok-Adalat has increased thereafter, except in the second half of the year. While the number of reference to the Lok-Adalat was 436 in the year 2000, the number reached at 535 in 2001 and 754 in 2002 and the total number of settlements were 251, 324 and 496 respectively in the year 2000, 2001 and 2002 and an amount of Rs. 2,42,78,000/-(Two crore forty two lakhs seventy eight thousand), Rs. 3,21,61,000/- (Three crore twenty one lakhs sixty one thousand) and Rs. 6,39,60,500/- (Six crore thirty nine lakhs sixty thousand five hundred) was awarded on compromise as compensation respectively.

It is exhibit from the aforesaid figure that a large number of cases were being settled in Lok-Adalats but most of them were relating to MACC and only 7 cases were relating to mat suits and 35 cases of civil nature were settled in these Lok-Adalats. The graph given below will exhibit the high magnitude of settlements of MACC cases, which is alone 98% of the total settlements.

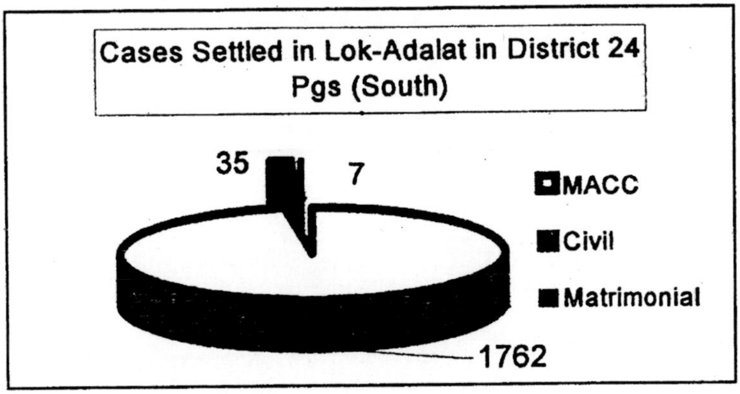

The overall percentage of settlements is 59.87%. The average settlement of disputes in per Lok-Adalat is 58, which can be considered as a satisfactory number when compared with the other Districts but the main draw back is that the entire system of Lok-Adalat in the District became monolithic and now the process has survived on MACC cases alone.

The percentage of settlements differs from year to year. The lowest percentage of settlements was during the first half of the year1999 where it was 24.31% and the highest settlement percentage was seen during the second half yearly of 2000, where it was 76.89%. Though initially some different forms of cases were referred to Lok-Adalats and some settlements were reached, out of such cases, but now, only MACC cases are referred to Lok-Adalat. Thus, the process, as far as District of 24 Pgs (South) is concerned, is becoming monolithic, which is itself not a healthy symptom for the institution of Lok-Adalat. The graph below will show the movement of the settlements of cases in Lok-Adalat either in the upward direction or in the downward direction during the aforesaid half yearly period.

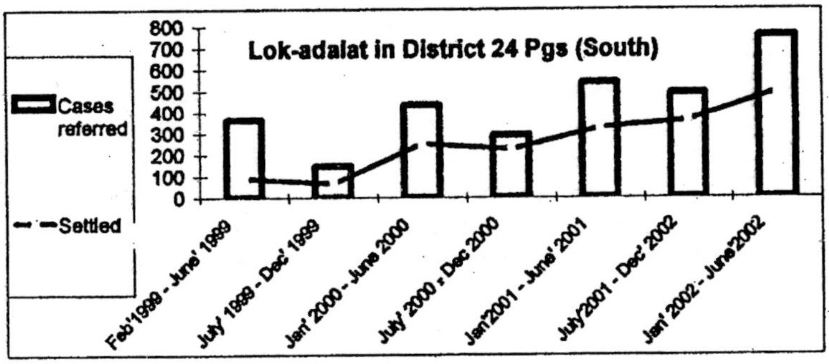

The up-ward movement of Lok-Adalat is evident from the graph. The reason behind the success of MACC cases in the District is the active participation of Advocates. One of the reasons of the unsuccessful performance of the institution in other categories of cases is the inactive participation of the Advocates. The vital draw back in the movement of Lok-Adalat in the District is the non-functioning of the Taluka Level Committees or Sub Divisional Committees. Even though the infrastructure is not adequate in the Taluka, it cannot be the sole reason for ineffective functioning. The foundation of the Lok-Adalat was made without any statutory backing and the infrastructure was also not adequate, but even in those periods, the institution functioned effectively in most of the States and Districts. Thus infrastructure cannot be the excuse for non-functioning of the different Authorities and Committees.

LOK-ADALAT IN DISTRICT UTTAR DINAIPUR

District Legal Services Authority organises the Lok-Adalat in the District. Government of West Bengal constituted the District Authority of Uttar Dinajpur on 15.07.98 consisting of 14 members[10]. Two Sub-Divisional (Taluk) Legal Services Committees were also constituted by State Legal Services Authority for the Sub-Division of Raiganj & Islampur[11]. However, among those two Sub-divisional Committees only Islampur has organised Lok-Adalat in the District and rest of the Lok-Adalats were organised at the District Head quarter. The cases referred to Lok-Adalat were small in number in the initial period. However, the numbers increased each year. In the year 1999 while the total 133 cases were referred before the Lok-Adalat, out of which 105 cases were settled, the number of references to Lok-Adalat reached 236 in 2000 and 352 in the year 2001 in which 94 and 252 cases were settled respectively during 2000 and 2001. The number of references were further increased to 427 in the year 2002 out of which 285 cases were settled. While the percentage of settlements during the year 1999 was 78.94%, the percentage during 2000, 2001 and 2002 were 39.83%, 71.59% and 66.74% respectively. Though till 2001, the highest number of cases referred as well as settled were relating to MACC but in the year 2002, Criminal cases marched ahead than the MACC. 185 Criminal Cases were disposed of during 2002 and the total number of Criminal cases that were disposed of during last four years was 321. A large number of matrimonial cases, civil cases as well as other categories of cases were also settled.

The overall percentage of settlements fluctuated during these four years period. During 1999, while the percentage of settlements was 78.94%, the percentage of settlement during 2000 was 39.83% but again in 2001 it reached 71.59% and was further decreased to 66.74% in the year 2002, while the overall percentage was 67.82%. During 1999 an amount of Rs. 38,96,500/- was awarded as compensation and this amount of compensation reached Rs. 41,75,000/- in the year 2001. However, it decreased to merely 490000/- in the year 2002. An amount of 1,09,23,988/- was awarded as compensation during these four years. The most significant aspect of the Lok-Adalat in the District was the settlement of a large number of criminal cases. Even during the period of 2001 & 2002, the number of settlement of criminal cases were more than that of MACC. The Table 8.4 as well as the Graph below will establish the performance of Lok-Adalat.

During the 2001 period while MACC cases settled were 79, the number of settlement of criminal cases were 94 and in 2002, while only 5 MACC cases were settled, the number of criminal cases settled were 185. While a large number of MACC cases and criminal cases were settled in the District, a variety of other cases were also settled. During 1999, apart from the MACC cases and criminal cases, 2 civil suits, one Bank loan case, 1 maintenance case, 8 matrimonial disputes and 18 other category of cases also settled. Similarly in the year 2000, 7 money suits, 1 civil suit, 4 Bank loan cases, 11 maintenance cases U/S 125 CrPC, 31 matrimonial cases and 4 other categories of cases also were settled. In the year 2001, while the number of settlement of MACC cases and criminal cases were 79 & 94 respectively, the number of matrimonial cases were 36. Apart from these, 10 money suits, 9 civil suits, 12 maintenance cases, 9 pre-litigation cases and 3 other category of cases were also settled in these Lok-Adalats. In the year 2002, 5 MACC cases, 38 Civil suits, 185 Criminal cases, 26 Matrimonial cases, 5 Maintenance cases, 18 pre-litigation cases and 8 other Categories of cases were settled in Lok-Adalats. So far the Benches of the Lok-Adalat are concerned, every Bench of Lok-Adalat in the District settled 12 cases on the average. However, the number of settlements of cases per Bench is not as high as of other several Districts. The performance of Lok-Adalat in the District is not monolithic. It is the trend, now a days, in few Districts, that the types of cases becoming monolithic and only one or two types of cases are appearing before Lok-Adalats, but in the District of Uttar Dinajpur the civil, criminal, bank loan, matrimonial, maintenance and even pre-litigation cases are being settled.

Lok Adalat in Uttar Dinajpur
Table - 8.5

Period	Benches	Total Cases Put-up	Total Cases Settled	%of Settlement	MACC Settled	Civil Suit	Bank Loan Cases	Criminal Cases	Matrimonial Cases	Maintenance	Pre-Litigation Cases	Other Cases	Awarded Money
1999	12	133	105	78.95%	64	2	1	11	8	1	0	18	3896500
2000	11	236	132	55.93%	43	8	4	31	31	11	0	4	2362488
2001	15	352	252	71.59%	79	19	0	94	36	12	9	3	4175000
2002	12	427	285	66.74%	5	38	0	185	26	5	18	8	490000
Grand Total	50	1148	774	67.42%	191	67	5	321	101	29	27	33	10923988

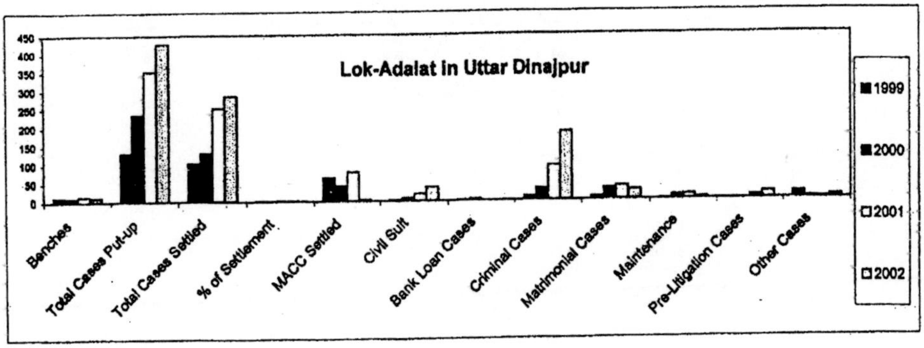

The graph clearly highlights that the number of cases are increasing every year. Though the number of MACC cases decreased during 2000 but again it increased in 2001 but it reached at mere 5 in the year 2002. Except such MACC cases all other form of cases were increased every year. The pre-litigation cases are newcomers in the field. Thus the performance of Lok-Adalat in the District is satisfactory so far the achievements of Lok-Adalats in the settling of different forms of cases are concerned. But the number of cases settled during the three-year period is not at all satisfactory, if we compare it with other Districts like North 24 Pgs or South 24 Pgs.

LOK-ADALAT IN DISTRICT BANKURA

The District Authority of Bankura was constituted on 15-7-98 consisting of 16 members and the District Judge of the District, appointed as ex-officio chairman of the Authority[12]. There were three Sub-Divisional committees constituted by State Legal Services Authority under the District Bankura namely Khatra Sub-Divisional Committee, Bankura Sub-Divisional Committee and Bishnupur Sub-Divisional Committee[13] consisting of nine members in each Committee. However, none of the Sub-Divisions are effectively activated for the purpose of Lok-Adalats. During the last three years from 1999 to 2002, a total number of 814 cases were put up before the Lok-Adalats, out of which 426 cases were settled and the percentage of settlements was 52%. The total number of cases referred during 1999 was 187 out of which 92 cases were settled and the percentage of settlements was 49.19%. However, the number of references of cases in Lok-Adalat, reached at 233 in 2000 and 250 during 2001 and the number of settlement reached at 94 and 129 respectively. Indeed, number of references as well as settlements decreased in the year 2002. While only 144 cases were referred before Lok-Adalats out of which 111 cases were settled. The higher percentage of settlements seen during 2002 where the percentage of settlement was 77.08%. The average number of settlements per Bench of Lok-Adalat in the District is around 9. Though various categories of cases were settled in the Lok-Adalat but the highest number of cases settled as well as referred before Lok-Adalats were MACC cases.

The Table 8.5 as well Graph below will show the performance of the institution of Lok-Adalat in the District during the last four years.

Lok Adalat in Uttar Bankura
Table - 8.6

Period	Benches	Total Cases Put-up	Total Cases Settled	%of Settlement	MACC Settled	Civil Suit	Bank Loan Cases	Criminal Cases	Matrimonial Cases	Maintenance	Pre-Litigation Cases	Other Cases	Awarded Money
1999	12	187	92	49.20%	65	19	5	0	1	2	0	0	5157841
2000	13	233	94	40.34%	68	10	4	1	6	4	0	1	3504200
2001	11	250	129	51.60%	100	10	6	0	7	1	5	0	4175000
2002	8	144	111	77.08%	103	3	2	0	3	0	0	0	6406154
Grand Total	44	814	426	52.33%	336	42	17	1	17	7	5	1	22326948

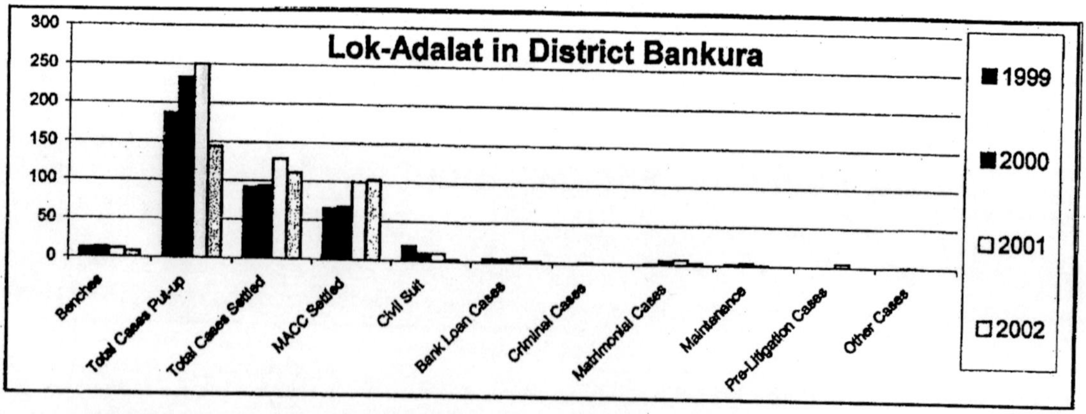

It is apparent from above data that while during 1999 the MACC cases settled were 65, the number reached 68 in 2000, 100 in 2001 and 103 in the year 2002. The total amount of Rs. 2,23,26,948/- was awarded during last four years period. Few civil and Mat cases also settled in the District.

The number of cases increased continuously in last three years in the District and the average percentage of settlements is 47%, which is comparatively higher than several other Districts. While during 2000, only 46 more cases appeared before the Lok-Adalat than the previous year, it was further decreased to 17 in the year 2001. The number of Matrimonial cases decreased during 2001 and 2002. Not a single Civil case was settled during the year 2002. In the year 1999, while the number of settlements of MACC cases were 65, 18 civil suits, 5 bank loan cases, one maintenance case, one matrimonial case and one execution case were also settled in the District. Similarly, in the year 2000, while 68 MACC cases were settled, the number or settlements or civil suit, bank loan cases, criminal cases, maintenance cases U/s 125 CrPC, matrimonial suit and other categories of cases were ten, four, one, four, six and one respectively. In the year 2001, the number of settlements of MACC cases increased significantly and reached 100. While the corresponding year figure was 68. Apart from MACC cases one money suit, nine title suits, six bank loan cases, one maintenance case, seven matrimonial suits were also settled in the district along with five pre-litigation cases. In the year 2002, 103 MACC, 3 Civil suits, 2 Bank loan cases and 3 matrimonial cases were settled. However, not a single Criminal case, Maintenance case, Pre-litigation case and other categories of cases settled.

In this District also, the MACC cases were most favourite ones for the institution of Lok-Adalat. However, a large variety of cases were settled in the District and people utilised the institution for resolution of their disputes by conciliatory means of Lok-Adalat, though such cases are small in number. There are a lot to be done in the district to make the institution more popular.

LOK-ADALAT IN DISTRICT BURDWAN

The Lok-Adalats in the District are organised by District Legal Services Authority, Burdwan. The formation of District Authority was done by State Government on 15th July 1998[14]. The District Authority is consisting of 16 members and the District Judge who is appointed as the ex-officio Chairman of the Authority. There are five Sub-Divisional (Taluk) Legal Services Committees constituted by State Legal Services Authority for the Sub-Divisions or Burdwan, namely Burdwan Sub-Divisional Legal Services Committee, Katwa Sub-Divisional Legal Services Committee, Asansol Sub-Divisional Legal Services Committee, Kalna Sub-Divisional Legal Services Committee and Durgapur Sub-Divisional Legal Services Committee[15]. Three Sub-Divisional Committees, namely Katwa, Asansol and Kalna actively participated in the Lok-Adalat movement and organised Lok-Adalats in their sub-Divisions. Though different categories of cases are being settled in the District but the number or settlements or other cases except MACC are negligible However, total 2 7 civil cases were settled in the district during 1999-2002. A total number of 1746 cases were placed before Lok-Adalats during four years period out of which 549 cases were settled and the overall percentage of settlements was 31.44%. The highest number of cases was referred in the Lok-Adalat during 1999, which stood at 598 out of which 177 cases were settled and the percentage of settlements was 29.59%. Such a number of references as well as settlements decreased during the subsequent years except the year 2000. While during 2000, the number of cases referred was 558, the number decreased to 277 in the year 2001. Even the number of settlements as well as the percentage of settlements decreased during 2001. While during 2000, the number of settlements stood at 184, it decreased to 74 in the year 2001. However, in the year 2002, 114 cases were settled. The percentage of settlement decreased to 26.71% in 2001, from 32.97% of 2000 but it further increased to 31.44% in the year 2002. The Table 8.6 given under, as well as the Graph will show the descending figure of cases in the District.

Lok Adalat in Burdwan
Table - 8.7

Period	Benches	Total Cases Put-up	Total Cases Settled	%of Settlement	MACC Settled	Civil Suit	Bank Loan Cases	Criminal Cases	Matrimonial Cases	Maintenance	Pre-Litigation Cases	Other Cases	Awarded Money
1999	19	598	177	29.60%	126	15	16	1	4	15	0	0	10205733
2000	19	558	184	32.97%	152	5	7	1	3	15	1	0	13376420
2001	13	277	74	26.71%	47	5	13	1	1	0	6	49	5009260
2002	11	313	114	36.42%	13	2	7	0	1	0	42	0	1539016
Grand Total	62	1746	549	31.44%	338	27	43	3	9	30	49	49	30130429

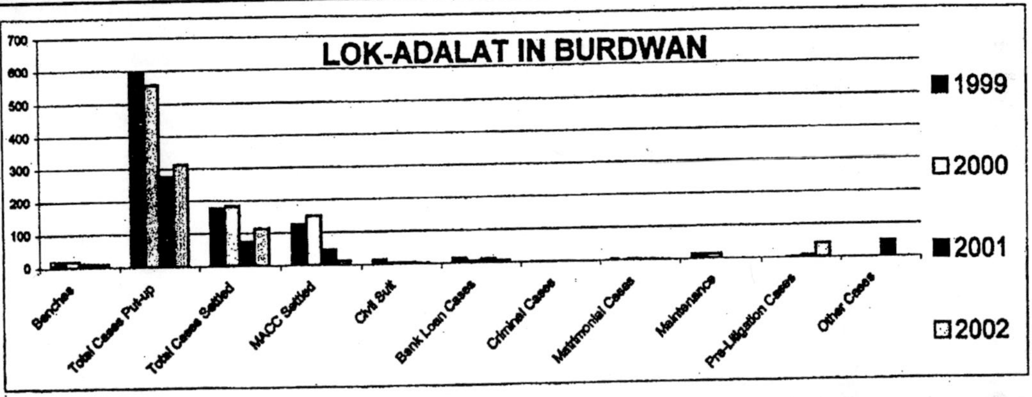

The numbers of settlements of MACC, civil cases as well as matrimonial cases were highest during 1999. However, the number of pre-litigation cases increased during 2001 While during 2000, only one pre-litigation case was disposed of, it reached 6 during 2001. The number of MACC cases settled, increased during 2000 but it again decreased during 2001 & 2002. While during 1999, a total number of 126 MACC cases were settled, the number reached 152 during 2000 but it again decreased to 47 during 2001 and 13 in the year 2002. In the year 1999, apart from MACC cases, 15 civil suits, 16 bank loan cáses, one criminal case, fifteen cases of maintenance and four matrimonial suits were also settled in the District. Similarly, in the year 2000, one money suit, four civil suits, seven bank loan cases, one criminal case, fifteen cases of maintenance under section 125 CrPC, three matrimonial suits and one pre-litigation cases were also settled. In the year 2001, the number of settlements of civil suits, bank loan cases, criminal case, maintenance cases and other categories of cases were five, thirteen and rest were one only respectively. During the year 2002, 13 MACC cases, 2 Civil suits, 7 Bank loan cases, one Matrimonial case and 42 Pre-litigation cases were settled. Thus it can be seen that a remarkable improvement is being made in Pre-litigation cases. During the four years period a total amount of Rs 3,01,30,429/- was paid as compensation in MACC cases in which an amount of Rs 1,02,05,733/- was paid during 1999 and an amount of Rs. 1,33,76,420/-, Rs. 50,09,260/- and Rs. 1539016/- during 2000, 2001 and 2002.

The number of cases decreased in respect of all forms of cases except the pre-litigation. It note worthy to mention here, that the District has a lot of potentiality but is not being materialized. There are five Sub-

Divisional Courts in the District. However, such Sub-Divisions are not being utilized or we can say that the access to justice through the means of Lok-Adalat has not been fulfilled in those Sub-Divisions. If one Lok-Adalat was organized in each Sub-Division in a quarter, then also the number of Lok-Adalats will be at 40 but during 1999 only 8 Lok-Adalats were held in the district and during 2000 it was 10 with 19 Benches.

LOK-ADALAT IN DISTRICT HOOGHLY

The District Legal Services Authority was constituted on 15th July'1998 by the State of West Bengal consisting of 16 members including the District Judge of the Hooghly District, who shall act as the Chairman of the Authority[16]. In order to further strengthen the institution of Lok-Adalat and to provide legal services including the organisation of Lok-Adalat at the Sub-Divisional level, so that the fruit of the institution can reached the people of sub-urban areas, State Legal Services Authority constituted four Sub-Divisional Legal Services Committees[17]. A large number of cases are settled by utilizing the instrument of Lok-Adalat in the District. During the period from 1999 to 2002 total 85 Benches of Lok-Adalats were constituted in which a total number of 3005 cases were referred for resolution of disputes through conciliatory mechanism. The Lok-Adalat was able to bring to an end 1187 disputes and thus 40.22% of cases were settled in these Lok-Adalats.

Though a large number of cases were settled in the District utilizing conciliatory mechanism yet the number of references of cases as well as settlement thereupon is decreasing continuously. The highest number of cases settled, as well as the highest percentage of settlements was achieved in the year 1999. During 1999, 695 cases were referred before the Lok-Adalat out of which 468 cases were settled and the percentage of settlements was recorded at 67.33%. The highest number of cases settled were relating to motor accident compensation claim cases. 283 of such cases were settled in which an amount of Rs 2,54,01,886/- was paid as compensation. The most important feature of the institution of Lok-Adalat in the District is the settlement of a high number of Bank Cases. Study reveals that in the year 1999 a total number of 152 Bank Cases were settled in the District.

Lok Adalat in Hooghly
Table - 8.8

Period	Benches	Total Cases Put-up	Total Cases Settled	% of Settlement	MACC Settled	Civil Suit	Bank Loan Cases	Criminal Cases	Matrimonial Cases	Maintenance	Pre-Litigation Cases	Other Cases	Awarded Money
1999	29	695	468	67.34%	283	30	152	1	1	1	0		25401886
2000	21	1055	279	26.45%	145	10	120	3	0	1	0	0	15111095
2001	20	704	240	34.09%	108	0	127	2	2	0	1	0	13633662
2002	15	551	188	34.12%	41	0	27	0	0	0	120		8013843
Grand Total	85	3005	1175	39.10%	577	40	426	6	3	2	121	0	62160486

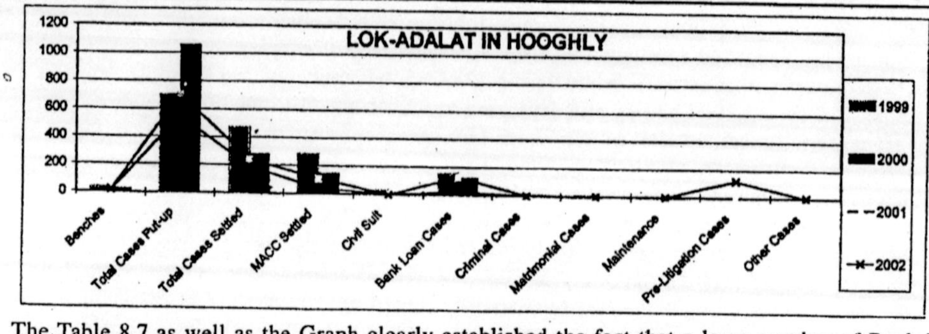

The Table 8.7 as well as the Graph clearly established the fact that a large number of Bank loan cases were settled in the District. During 1999, apart from these cases, one criminal case, one case U/S 125 CrPC and one matrimonial case were also settled in the District during the year. In the year 2000, the number of settlements decreased substantially. Only 279 cases were settled. However, a large number of cases were referred in the Lok-Adalat during the year numbered at 1055, which is around 40% above the previous year's reference. In spite of such high references, the number of settlements decreased. During this year, out of such 279 cases settled, 145 cases were relating to motor accident compensation claims and 130 were civil in nature. Among these 130 civil cases, 120 cases were relating to bank loans. Apart from this, one case U/S 125 CrPC, 1 matrimonial dispute and 2 criminal cases were settled in the District during the year 2000. During the year 2001, the number of settlements further decreased to 240 from the previous year figure of 279 cases However a large number of Bank loan cases were settled in the district during the year, even more than those of MACC cases. During the year, total 127 Bank Loan cases ended in compromise between Banks and the borrowers and 108 claimants benefited from the institution in motor accident compensation claim cases and an amount of Rs 1,36,33,662/- was awarded by the Lok-Adalats in the District Apart from the above cases 2 criminal cases, 2 matrimonial cases and one pre-litigation case were also settled in the District during the year Study reveals that 34.09% percentage of cases were settled in Lok-Adalats during the year. The number of settlements were further decreased in the year 2002. Only 188 cases were settled, in which 41 cases were relating to MACC, 27 were relating to Bank Loan disputes and 120 cases were pre-litigation cases.

Though during the four-years period, a large number of cases were settled in the District, but the phenomenon, which most concern the people associated with the institution, is the declining performance of the institution. Only in pre-litigation cases, a remarkable improvement has been made during the year 2002. If the performance continued in a similar way, then soon the institution will subsist in the books only. However, the District opens a path for the resolution of different forms of disputes. While in all Districts, MACC is the most successful kind of cases but in Hooghly, the Bank cases and pre-litigation cases are the most successful. Thus other Districts can also take clue from the institution and a large number of Bank cases and pre-litigation cases can also be settled by the instrument of Lok-Adalat.

LOK-ADALAT IN DISTRICT HOWRAH

The Lok-Adalat in Howrah District is organized under the auspices of Howrah District Legal Services Authority[18]. In order to strengthen the institution of Lok-Adalat and to provide access to justice to a large number of people living in the sub-urban area, the State Legal Services Authority constituted two Sub-Divisional Legal Services Committees under the District Authority[19]. While a large number of MACC cases were settled in the district during last four years period, where at the same time plenty of matrimonial disputes were also settled in the Lok-Adalats. During the last four years period, the total number of 1565 cases were referred before the Lok-Adalats in which 1020 cases were settled. Among those 1020 cases, the MACC cases were leading in the list by settling 547 cases and in 307 cases the matrimonial disputes were brought to an end. Apart from these cases, 99 civil cases, 19 criminal cases, 8 pre-litigation and 17 other cases were settled during the last three years period.

Study reveals that the highest number of cases settled was in the year 1999. During the year, 300 cases were settled in the Lok-Adalats, out of which 185 cases were relating to Motor Accident Compensation Claim cases. The second highest number of cases settled were relating to matrimonial disputes. 83 matrimonial disputes were settled in the District along with 19 Title Suits, 12 maintenance cases U/S 125 CrPC and one money suit.

Lok Adalat in Howrah

Table - 8.9

Period	Benches	Total Cases Put-up	Total Cases Settled	% of Settlement	MACC Settled	Civil Suit	Bank Loan Cases	Criminal Cases	Matrimonial Cases	Maintenance	Pre-Litigation Cases	Other Cases	Awarded Money
1999	19	466	300	64.38%	185	20	0	0	83	12	0	0	17580223
2000	18	343	229	66.96%	160	14	0	0	55	0	0	0	10746000
2001	11	334	241	72.16%	123	24	0	3	72	9	1	9	7914200
2002	9	423	250	59.10%	79	41	0	16	97	2	7	8	6760000
Grand Total	57	1565	1020	65.18%	547	99	0	19	307	23	8	17	43000423

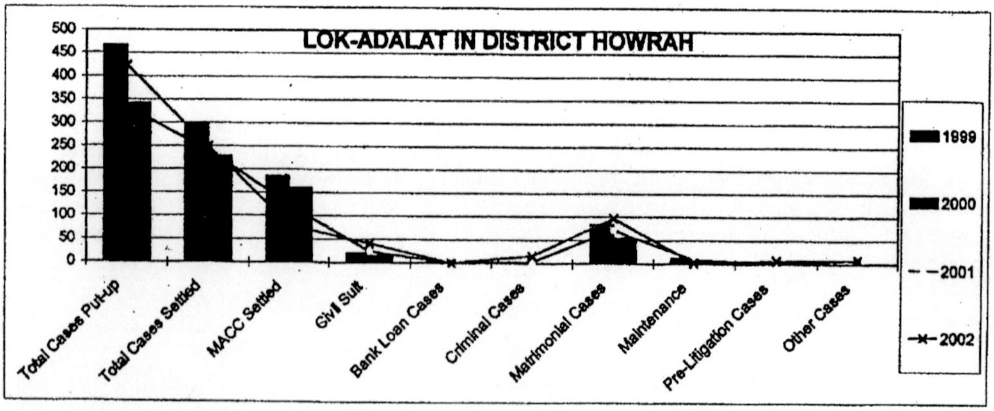

The Table 8.8 and the Graph clearly shows the functioning of the institution in District. The important aspect of the functioning of the institution is that, it not only is able to settle a large number of matrimonial disputes but also plenty of maintenance cases.

However, the number of settlements were decreased during the subsequent years. In the year 2000 the number of settlements decreased to 229 from the previous year's figure of 300. During this period, 160 claimants of MACC cases were benefited from the institution, otherwise their cases would have been litigated for years. A significant number of matrimonial disputes were also settled in these Lok-Adalats. Study reveals that during the year, the Lok-Adalats succeeded in bringing to an end, 55 matrimonial disputes and 14 civil suits, apart from the MACC cases.

It is also revealed from the study that in the year 2001 the number of settlements increased slightly to 241 from 229 cases of the previous year but the number is still below than that of 1999, which is exhibited by the graph. During this year significantly, 123 cases were settled relating to motor accident compensation cases along with 72 cases relating to family disputes. Apart from these settlements, the institution succeeded in bringing compromise in 9 maintenance cases, 24 civil cases, 3 criminal cases, one pre-litigation case and 9 other categories of cases. The institution of Lok-Adalat has awarded an amount of Rs 7914200/- during the year. In the year 2002, 423 cases were placed before Lok-Adalats, out of which 250 cases were settled. Among those settlements, the number of settlements of MACC cases were 547, Civil Suits 41 along with 16 Criminal cases, 97 Matrimonial cases, 2 Maintenance cases, 7 Pre-litigation cases and 80 other categories of cases.

However, the decrease in the number of disposals by the institution of Lok-Adalat is a matter of despair. One significant achievement of the institution is the large number of settlements of matrimonial disputes, which clearly exhibits the fact that the matrimonial disputes are also one of such kinds of disputes for which the institution of Lok-Adalat is the right destination. It is important also because on theoretical perspective, the conciliatory mechanism is the best suited one in such disputes where continuing relation between the parties subsists. Instead of that in most of the Districts a small number of matrimonial disputes were settled. To this end. the institution of Lok-Adalat in the District corroborated the, theoretical analysis and can provide guidance to other Districts.

LOK-ADALAT IN DISTRICT MALDA

The Lok-Adalat in the District of Malda is organized under the auspices of Malda District Legal Services Authority. The District Authority was constituted on 15th July, 1998 consisting of 15 members including the District Judge who was appointed as the Chairman of the Authority[21]. A large number of people in the District benefited from the institution of Lok-Adalat in the last four years and significantly a large number of pre-litigation cases were settled in these Lok-Adalats. During the last four-years period, 3042 cases were referred before the institution of Lok-Adalat, out of which 1135 cases were successfully settled in these Lok-Adalats. Among those 1135 settled cases, MACC alone were 379 and significantly 219 pre-litigation cases were settled along with 92 civil cases, 126 criminal cases, 33 matrimonial cases, 98 Maintenance cases and 187 other categories of cases.

The number of cases are increasing continuously in the District from the year 1999. In the year 1999, 353 cases were referred to the Lok-Adalats out of which 190 cases were settled. Among those 190 cases, MACC alone were 132 in which an amount of Rs 48,00,000/- was awarded as compensation. Apart from MACC cases, 26 civil cases, one Bank loan case, 8 maintenance cases, 23 matrimonial cases and one execution case were settled in the Lok-Adalat during the year. The number of settlements increased substantially during the year 2000. During this year 799 cases were referred before the Lok-Adalat and the disputes belonging to 332 cases were settled. Though the highest number of cases settled were relating to MACC cases but significantly a large number of pre-litigation cases were also settled utilizing the instrument of Lok-Adalat.

Lok Adalat in Malda
Table - 8.10

Period	Benches	Total Cases Put-up	Total Cases Settled	% of Settlement	MACC Settled	Civil Suit	Bank Loan Cases	Criminal Cases	Matrimonial Cases	Maintenance	Pre-Litigation Cases	Other Cases	Awarded Money
1999	14	353	190	53.82%	132	26	1	0	23	8	0	0	4800000
2000	17	799	332	41.55%	111	18	0	13	1	42	82	65	4392000
2001	25	1200	364	30.33%	110	35	0	48	2	42	69	58	4930300
2002	14	690	249	36.09%	26	13	0	65	7	6	68	64	1801000
Grand Total	70	3042	1135	37.31%	379	92	1	126	33	98	219	187	15923300

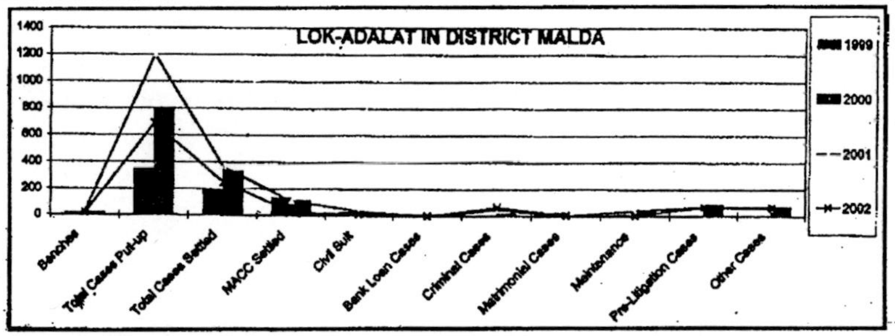

During the year 2000, while 111 MACC cases were settled, the number of settlements of pre-litigation cases were 82. Similarly a large number of maintenance cases and execution cases were also settled in the Lok-Adalat. 7 maintenance cases along with 35 execution cases were settled in the Lok-Adalat along with 17-money suits, one civil suit, 13 criminal cases, one matrimonial dispute and 65 other categories of cases. During the year 2000, 13 Lok-Adalats were held and the average percentage per Lok-Adalat was standing at around 25 cases while the per Lok-Adalat references were around 61 cases.

Study reveals that the number of settlements further increased in the year 2001. During the year 2001, the number of settlements increased to 364, while the corresponding years figure was 332. It is further revealed that 1200 cases were referred to the Lok-Adalat during the year and the percentage of settlements for the year was 30.33%. Among those 364 cases settled, the MACC alone was 110 and an amount of Rs 4930300/- was awarded by the Lok-Adalat. Significant numbers of pre-litigation cases were also settled in the District during the year. 69 pre-litigation cases were settled in the Lok-Adalats along with 34 money suits, one civil suit, 48 criminal cases, 11 maintenance cases U/S 125 CrPC, 31 execution cases, 2 matrimonial cases, and 58 other categories of cases were settled in those Lok-Adalats during the year 2001. However, during 2002, the number of references as well as settlements decreased. 690 cases were referred before Lok-Adalats, out of which 249 cases were settled. Merely 26 MACC cases were settled along with 13 Civil suits, one Bank loan case, 65 Criminal cases. 7 Matrimonial disputes, 6 Maintenance cases, 68 pre-litigation cases and 64 other categories of cases.

It is an established fact that Lok-Adalat in the Malda District was able to settle a large variety of cases, which we found missing in most of the Districts The most significant aspect of the functioning of the institution in the District is the settlement of a large number of pre-litigation cases. One of the reasons for low performance of Lok-Adalat, even in such a category of cases, which theoretically considered, most appropriate forms of dispute for conciliatory mechanism, is that the cases, when appeared before the conciliatory body, the relationship between the parties were totally broken[22]. In these circumstances it is more appropriate that the matter must go to the conciliator in the initial stage. This might be one of the reasons for the settlement of a large number of pre-litigation cases in the District and the other Districts can take inspiration from these experiments of the Malda District.

LOK-ADALAT IN DISTRICT MIDNAPUR

The Midnapur District Legal Services Authority is organising the Lok-Adalat at the District. The District Authority was constituted on the same day along with the different District Authorities, on 15th July, 1998, consisting of 16 members[23]. In order to make the institution of Lok-Adalat as well as legal aid and legal awareness programmes more effective and more accessible, the State Legal Service Authority constituted six Sub-Divisional Legal Services Committees under the District Authority, namely Tamluk Sub-Divisional Legal Services Committee, Contai Sub-Divisional Legal Services Committee, Jhargram Sub-Divisional Legal Services Committee, Kharagpur Sub-Divisional Legal Services Committee, Ghatal sub-Divisional Legal Services Committee and Midnapur Sub-Divisional Legal Services Committee[41]. However, though six Sub-Divisional Committees were constituted but none of the Committees are functioning for the purpose of Lok-Adalat. The institution of Lok-Adalat was able to bring into compromise a large number of cases during the last four years. A total number of 1774 cases were referred before the Lok-Adalat during 1999 to 2002, out of which the disputants belonging to 815 cases were benefited from the institution by settling their disputes amicably Study reveals that among those 815 settlements, 588 cases were relating to motor accident compensation claim, which is 72% of the total settlements Apart from MACC cases a large number of civil cases were also settled in the Lok-Adalats. During such period, 62 civil cases, 22 Bank loan cases, 3 criminal cases, 18 matrimonial cases, 89 pre-litigation cases and 33 other category of cases were settled in different Lok-Adalats in the District. Though a large number of cases were settled in the District, the performance of the institution is not similar in the last four years. In the year 1999, while the number of settlements were 232 and increased to 273 in the year 2000, it decreased substantially in the year 2001 & 2002. The institution of Lok-Adalat was able to settle only 154 cases during the year 2001 and 156 cases in the year 2002. Study reveals that during the year 1999 a total number of 359 cases were referred before the Lok-Adalats out of which, Lok-Adalats were able to bring the dispute to an end in 232 cases. Thus, the institution of Lok-Adalat was able to bring into compromise in 64.62% cases. However, the monolithic form of cases were settled in the Lok-Adalat. All the 232 cases were belonging to motor accident compensation claim cases and an amount of Rs 1,62,29,000/- was awarded as compensation to the helpless claimants.

Lok Adalat in Midnapur

Table - 8.11

Period	Benches	Total Cases Put-up	Total Cases Settled	% of Settlement	MACC Settled	Civil Suit	Bank Loan Cases	Criminal Cases	Matrimonial Cases	Maintenance	Pre-Litigation Cases	Other Cases	Awarded Money
1999	13	359	232	64.62%	232	0	0	0	0	0	0	0	16229000
2000	21	739	273	36.94%	170	58	17	0	0	0	0	28	22067550
2001	11	456	154	33.77%	114	4	5	3	0	18	5	5	7783650
2002	5	223	156	69.96%	72	0	0	0	0	0	84	0	N.A
Grand Total	50	1777	815	45.86%	588	62	22	3	0	18	89	33	46080200

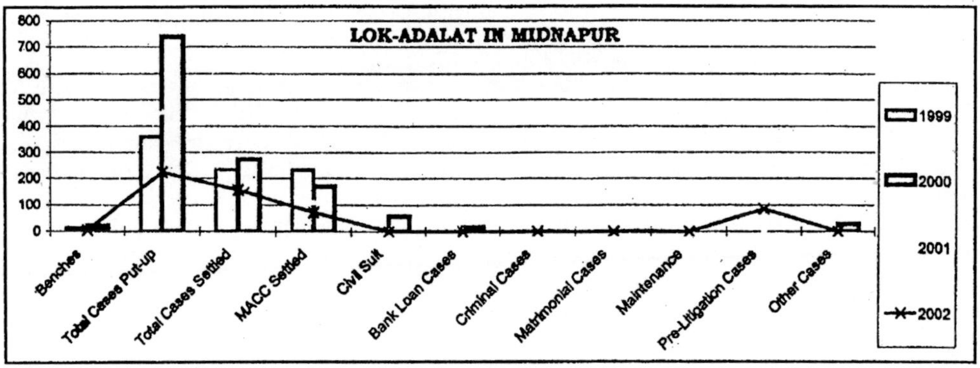

Study reveals that in the year 2000, the number of references as well as settlements increased significantly. While in the year 1999 only 359 cases were referred before Lok-Adalat, the number increased to 739 in the year 2000 and 273 cases were disposed of by the Lok-Adalats as per the terms of the settlement of the parties. The most significant achievement of the institution during the year was that it was able to settle a significant number of different categories of cases apart from MACC cases. During the year. 170 claimants in the motor accident claim cases were benefited and they settled their disputes amicably with conciliatory efforts taken in the Lok-Adalats. Study further reveals that apart from MACC cases 58 civil cases, 17 Bank cases and 28 other categories of cases were also settled in these Lok-Adalats.

Indeed, it is apparent from the above data that the number of settlements decreased in the year 2001 & 2002 and the institution has seen a downward movement during the years. In the year 2001, only 456 cases were referred before Lok-Adalat out of which only 154 cases were brought into compromise Among those 154 cases. MACC were alone 114 and the amount of compensation paid was Rs. 7783650/- Apart from such MACC cases, 4 civil suits. 5 Bank Suits, 3 criminal cases, 5 cases for maintenance along with 13 cases of execution, 5 pre-litigation cases and 5 other categories of cases were settled in the Lok-Adalat utilizing this conciliatory mechanism. In the year 2002, 223 cases were referred before Lok-Adalats out of which 156 cases were settled and the percentage of settlement was 69.96%. Among those 156 cases settled, 72 cases were MACC and 84 cases were pre-litigation cases.

Thus while the initiation of Lok-Adalat was made by MACC cases, subsequently the benefit was also reached in different categories of cases as well. However, the most important aspect, which is a matter of despair for the institution, is the declining phenomenon. The number of references as well as disposals substantially decreased in the year 2001 & 2002. To this end special effort is required to make the institution more accessible to a large number of people so that justice can be delivered speedily and without cost.

LOK-ADALAT IN DISTRICT PURULIA

The Lok-Adalat in the District has been organized by Purulia District Legal Services Authority. The District Authority was constituted on 15.7.1998 consisting of 16 members including the District Judge of the District who acts as Chairman or the Authority[24]. Further the State Legal Services Authority constitutes two Sub-Divisional Legal Services Committees, in order to provide access to justice to a large number of people at the grass root level, namely Raghunathpur Sub-Divisional Legal Services Committee and Purulia sub-divisional Legal Services Committee[25]. The basic characteristic of the Lok-Adalat in the District is, which makes it different from other Districts, is that the different categories of cases being initiated in the District, from the beginning. However, the performance of the District is not at all satisfactory, because the number of cases referred as well as settled is decreasing continuously. The Lok-Adalat in the District was able to make available the fruit of the institution to the disputants, in 565 cases during the four years period from 1999 to 2002. The said 565 cases were settled out of total reference of 1020 cases. Thus 55.39% of the cases were settled in the

District through the institution, an amount of Rs. 2,04,81,136 was paid as compensation to the claimants in the MACC cases.

The study reveals that the highest number of cases were settled in the year 1999, which were 204 cases out of 376 references. But the highest percentage of settlements was recorded in the year 2000. While the percentage of settlements in the year 2000 was 76.88%, the percentage of settlements in the year 1999, 2001 and 2002 were 54.25%, 50% and 45.09% respectively. It is revealed by the study that while during 1999 the total number of cases settled were 204, the number of cases settled in the year 2000. decreased to 143. It further decreased to 117 in the year 2001. and to 101 in the year 2002. The number of cases referred before Lok-Adalats were also decreased substantially. While in the year 1999 a total number of 376 cases were referred to the Lok-Adalat in the District, the number decreased to 186 in the year 2000. However, this figure slightly developed to 234 in the year 2001. The study further shows that though the highest number of cases settled in the Lok-Adalat in the District were relating to MACC but a substantial number of other cases were also settled in the District from the beginning. In the year 1999, while 152 MACC cases were settled, the number of settlements of money suits, civil cases, maintenance cases, matrimonial cases, pre- litigation cases and other categories of cases were thirty, eight, nine, one and remaining both were two respectively.

Lok Adalat in Purulia
Table - 8.12

Period	Benches	Total Cases Put-up	Total Cases Settled	% of Settlement	MACC Settled	Civil Suit	Bank Loan Cases	Criminal Cases	Matrimonial Cases	Maintenance	Pre-Litigation Cases	Other Cases	Awarded Money
1999	12	376	204	54.26%	152	38	0	0	1	9	2	2	11264728
2000	11	186	143	76.88%	94	19	0	8	2	15	0	5	6312908
2001	11	234	117	50.00%	55	13	0	37	1	9	0	3	3892500
2002	7	224	101	45.09%	65	17	0	13	2	1	0	3	5011000
Grand Total	41	1020	565	55.39%	366	87	0	58	6	34	2	13	26481136

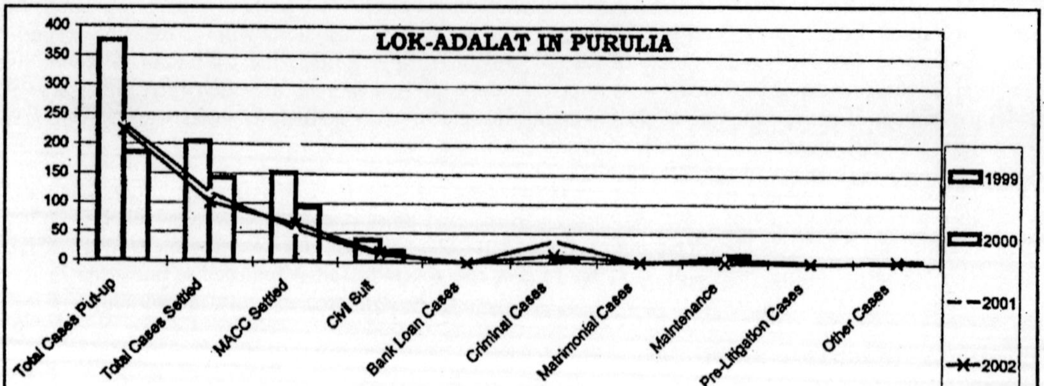

The table 8.11 as well as the Graph shows that while the number of settlements or MACC cases were 94, nine money suits, ten civil suits, eight criminal cases, fifteen maintenance cases, two matrimonial disputes and five other categories of cases were also settled in the Lok-Adalats in the District during the year 2000. Like wise in the year 2001, 55 MACC cases, 7 money suits, 6 civil suits, 37 criminal cases, 9 cases for maintenance under section 125 CrPC, one matrimonial dispute and 3 other categories of cases were settled. In the year 2002, 65 MACC cases, 17 Civil suits, 13 Criminal cases, 2 Matrimonial cases, 1 Maintenance case and 3 other categories of cases were settled.

The declining phenomenon of the institution imposed a question on its functioning in the District. Only the put-up part of the graph and the criminal cases part show a certain increase. Other wise, in all spheres, the institution is losing faith in the District. Immediate remedial measures are required in order to bring back the faith of the disputants and other segments of the legal fraternity, so that the institution can provide justice to a larger number of people.

LOK-ADALAT IN DISTRICT NADIA

The Lok-Adalat in District Nadia is organised under the auspices of Nadia District Legal Services Authority. The Government of West Bengal constituted the Nadia District Legal Services Authority for popularising legal aid programme and for organising Lok-Adalats in order to provide time effective and cost effective justice to the large number of disputants through the process of conciliation[26]. In furtherance of formation of District Authority, four Sub-Divisional Legal Services Committees were formed by the State Legal Services Authority, namely, Krishnanagar Sub-Divisional Legal Services Committee. Tahata Sub-Divisional Legal services Committee, Kalyani Sub-Divisional Legal Services Committee and Ranaghat Sub-Divisional Legal Services Committee[27]. The Sub-Divisional Committees of Krishnanagar and Kalyani organised a few Lok-Adalats in their Sub-Divisions. However, most of the Lok-Adalats were organised in the District Headquarters'.

The District of Nadia had the privilege of organising first the Lok-Adalat in the State of West Bengal after the enforcement of the Legal Services Authorities Act. The first Lok-Adalat in the District was organised on 22nd Novenber'1998, in which 66 MACC cases were settled and an amount of Rs. 30,43,000/- was awarded as compensation Apart from MACC cases, 6 maintenance cases and two matrimonial disputes also were settled in the Lok-Adalat. It is revealed from the study that during the four years period from 1999 to 2002, a total number of 2472 cases were placed before Lok-Adalats, out of which 685 cases were settled, consisting of 251 MACC cases, 5 civil cases, 127 bank cases, 23 Criminal cases, 12 pre-litigation cases, 158 matrimonial cases and 109 maintenance cases. An amount of Rs 1,91,97,500/- was awarded in Lok-Adalats in the District.

It is revealed from the study the number of cases settled in the Lok-Adalat is decreasing continuously. It is further revealed that the percentage of settlement of cases in the Lok-Adalat also decreased during the last four years. Initially in the year 1999 a total number of 380 cases were placed before the Lok-Adalats. However, this number reached to 927 in the year 2000 but again it decreased to 606 in the year 2001 and to 559 in the year 2002. In a similar direction the number of settlements of cases also increased slightly in the year 2000 but decreased subsequently. While in the year 1999, the number of settlements of cases stood at 176, the number reached at 200 in the year 2000 but again it decreased substantially to 164 in the year 2001 and to 145 in the year 2002, which is lower than the 1999 mark.

Lok Adalat in Nadia
Table - 8.13

Period	Benches	Total Cases Put-up	Total Cases Settled	% of Settlement	MACC Settled	Civil Suit	Bank Loan Cases	Criminal Cases	Matrimonial Cases	Maintenance	Pre-Litigation Cases	Other Cases	Awarded Money
1999	12	380	176	46.32%	139	0	16	2	7	12	0	0	7159500
2000	21	927	200	21.57%	23	3	45	10	68	49	2	0	4763000
2001	19	606	164	27.06%	37	2	35	9	33	43	5	0	2057000
2002	16	559	145	25.94%	52	0	31	2	50	5	5	0	5218000
Grand Total	71	2472	685	27.71%	251	5	127	23	158	109	12	0	19197500

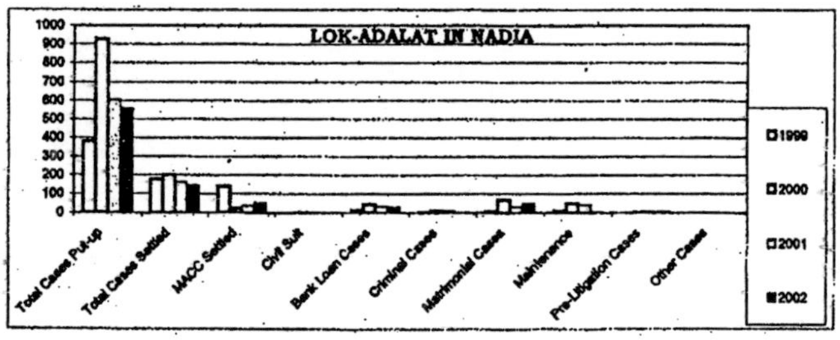

The Table 8.12 and Graph will establish the upward and downward movement of institution in the District. Study revealed that during the year 1999, the bulk of cases settled were relating to MACC. Out of 176 cases settled in the District, 139 cases were relating to MACC and only 16 civil cases, 19 matrimonial cases, which included 17 maintenance cases, were settled along with 2 criminal cases. However, this trend changed substantially in the year 2000 and a large number of matrimonial cases were also settled in the Lok-Adalat along with a large number of civil cases. Study reveals that during the year 2000 while total number of cases settled were 250, the number of settlements of matrimonial cases were alone 117 and 23 MACC cases, 3 civil cases, 45 cases relating to bank loan disputes, 10 criminal cases and 2 pre-litigation cases were settled in Lok-Adalat. Among the aforesaid 117 matrimonial disputes, 49 cases were relating to maintenance and the rest 68 were other forms of disputes.

Similarly, in the year 2001, 33 matrimonial cases. 43 maintenance cases, 37 MACC cases, 35 bank loan cases, two money suits, 9 criminal cases and 5 pre-litigation cases were settled. It is found that the highest percentage of settlements was recorded in the year 1999 where the percentage of settlements was 46.31%, but it decreased subsequently and reached at 26.98% in the year 2000, 27.06% in the year 2001 and to 25.94% in the year 2002. Study further reveals that in the year 2002, 52 MACC cases, 31 bank loan cases, 2 Criminal cases, 50 Matrimonial disputes, 5 Maintenance cases and 5 pre-litigation cases were settled.

The matter, which requires careful attention, is the declining phenomenon of the settlement of cases in the District. However, one thing which is appreciable in the District, is the large number of settlements of matrimonial cases. In most of the Districts the settlements of matrimonial cases are extremely low. However, immediate remedial measures are required to be taken for achieving the goal of providing justice to all, in a cost effective manner and a time effective manner.

LOK-ADALAT IN DISTRICT DAKSHIN DINAJPUR

The Lok-Adalat in the District is organised under the patronage of Dakshin Dinajpur District Legal Services Authority. The District Authority was constituted by the Government of West Bengal for the organisation of Lok-Adalat and for providing legal aid to the needy[28]. In furtherance of the formation of District Authority, two sub-Divisional Legal Services Committees were constituted by State Legal Services Authority, West Bengal for the District of Dakshin Dinajpur, namely, Gangarampur Sub-Divisional Legal Services Committee and Balurghat Sub-Divisional Legal Services Committee[29]. It is revealed from the study that during the last four years, a total number of 2457 cases were referred before Lok-Adalat in the District, out of which 862 cases were settled and the percentage of settlement was 35.08%. It is further revealed that the numbers of cases referred to Lok-Adalat, as well as settlements reached there upon are increasing continuously.

It is revealed from the study that while during 1999 a total number of 206 cases were referred to Lok-Adalat, the number increased to 337 in the year 2000 and it was further increased to 873 in the year 2001 and 1041 in the year 2002. Similarly the number of cases settled in the Lok-Adalat during the past four years has also increased. While in the year 1999 the number of settlements in the Lok-Adalat was 146, the number reached at 176 in the year 2000, and further increased to 201 in the year 2001 and 339 in the year 2002. During the last four years period an amount of Rs 1,20,41,361/- was awarded to the disputants through mutual consent. However, the MACC cases, which are considered as one of the best forms of dispute resolvable by the instrument of Lok-Adalat failed to survive in the same direction in the District. The Table 8.13 and the Graph will show the performance of Lok-Adalat in the District during last four years period.

Lok Adalat in Dakshin Dinajpur
Table - 8.14

Period	Benches	Total Cases Put-up	Total Cases Settled	% of Settlement	MACC Settled	Civil Suit	Bank Loan Cases	Criminal Cases	Matrimonial Cases	Maintenance	Pre-Litigation Cases	Other Cases	Awarded Money
1999	12	206	146	70.87%	77	6	14	1	16	22	8	2	2683890
2000	12	337	176	52.23%	49	2	12	0	13	7	90	3	5025190
2001	12	873	201	23.02%	0	2	0	9	9	16	174	0	1140075
2002	18	1041	339	32.56%	0	0	0	0	6	12	321	0	3192206
Grand Total	54	2457	862	35.08%	126	10	26	1	44	57	593	5	12041361

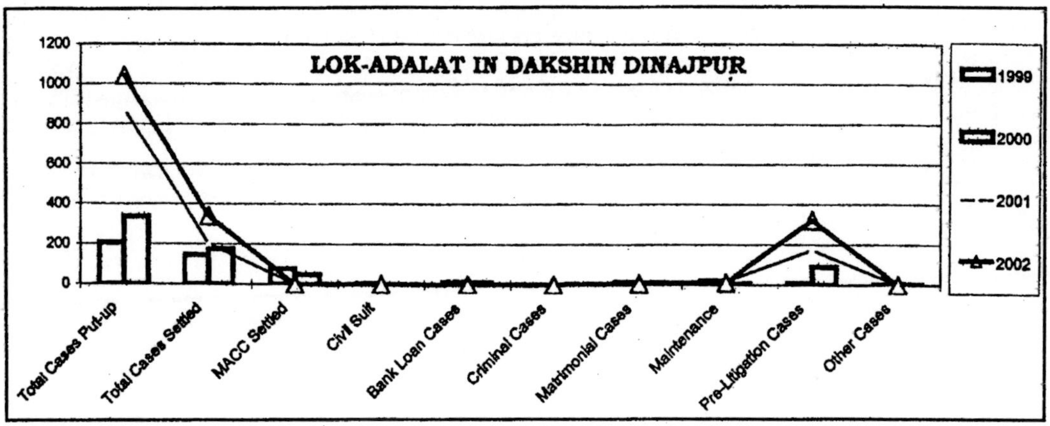

It is revealed from the study that while in the year 1999 a total number of 77 cases were settled in the Lok-Adalat, the number decreased to 49 in the year 2000. Not a single MACC case was settled in the Lok-Adalat in the District during the period of 2001 and 2002. The most significant achievement made by the institution of Lok-Adalat in the District is the disposal of pre-litigation cases. While during 1999, total 8 pre-litigation cases were disposed by the Lok-Adalat, the number increased to 90 in the year 2000 and further to 174 cases in 2001. Remarkably, in the year 2002, 321 pre-litigation cases were settled. The other few cases settled by the Lok-Adalat are relating to civil cases, matrimonial cases, criminal cases and other categories of cases. The number of civil cases, matrimonial cases, criminal cases and other categories of cases decreased each year consecutively. While 20 civil cases settled during 1999, the number decreased to 14 in the year 2000 and was further decreased to 2 in the year 2001 and not a single civil case was settled during 2002. Similarly while 16 matrimonial cases were settled during 1999, the number decreased to 13 in the year 2001 Similarly the number of other categories of cases also decreased.

It is established from the Table and Graph that the increase of cases before Lok-Adalat and the their settlements there upon are not in the same proportion. Proportionately the number of cases referred each year is much higher than the settlements. As a result the percentage of settlement of cases decreased substantially. While the percentage of settlement of cases in the year 1999 was 70.87%, the percentage decreased to 52.22% in the year 2000 and further decreased to 23.02% in the year 2001. Thus while the number of settlements increased in the District, the percentage of settlements decreased. The District maintained the high number of disposal of cases because of the pre-litigation cases. It is good so far that the disputes were attempted to be resolved through conciliation out side the atmosphere of adjudication process and a large number of such cases were settled, but at the same time, the cases which are pending in the Courts for a long time must be attempted for settlement. Secondly, the Sub-Divisional Legal Services Committees are not functioning properly and the organisation of Lok-Adalat is on the shoulder of District Authority. In these circumstances it became essential to make the Sub-Divisional Committee active. That is the only way to make cheaper and quicker justice available to the large number of masses at the grass root level.

LOK-ADALAT IN DISTRICT NORTH 24 PGS

The Lok-Adalats in the District are organised under the auspices of District Legal Services Authority, North 24 Pgs. The District Authority was constituted, consisting of 16 members, by the Government of West Bengal for providing legal aid to persons in need and for organisation of Lok-Adalat, in order to provide speedy and inexpensive justice at the doorsteps of the people[30]. Further, in order to make the institution available at grass root level and to popularise the legal aid scheme, four Sub-Divisional Legal Services Committees were formed in the District at Taluka level namely, Basirhat Sub-Divisional Legal services Committee, Barasat Sub-Divisional Legal Services Committee, Bongaon Sub-Divisional Legal Services Committee and Barrackpore Sub-Divisional Legal Services Committee[31]. Among these Sub-Divisional Committees, the Basirhat Sub-Division

Committee and Barasat Sub-Divisional Committee organised a few Lok-Adalats A large number of cases were settled in the District during the last four years, from 1999 to 2002. During these four years period, a total number of 4522 cases were referred before the Lok-Adalats, out of which 3712 cases were settled. The District can be considered as one of the pioneers in resolution of disputes by the instrument of Lok-Adalat.

Though, the number of references of cases to the Lok-Adalat as well as the settlement had decreased during 2001, it increased substantially in the year 2002. The Table 8.14 and Graph will provide a insight on the functioning of Lok-Adalat in the District during the last four years.

Lok Adalat in North 24 Parganas
Table - 8.15

Period	Benches	Total Cases Put-up	Total Cases Settled	% of Settlement	MACC Settled	Civil Suit	Bank Loan Cases	Criminal Cases	Matrimonial Cases	Maintenance Cases	Pre-Litigation Cases	Other Cases	Awarded Money
1999	18	1058	880	83.18%	855	9	0	4	0	12	0	0	78051979
2000	26	1182	929	78.60%	901	4	0	0	13	0	0	11	152638636
2001	14	733	590	80.49%	562	1	0	0	16	7	4	0	39267100
2002	15	1549	1313	84.76%	1305	0	0	0	6	0	2	0	75151750
Grand Total	73	4522	3712	82.09%	3623	14	0	4	35	19	6	11	345109465

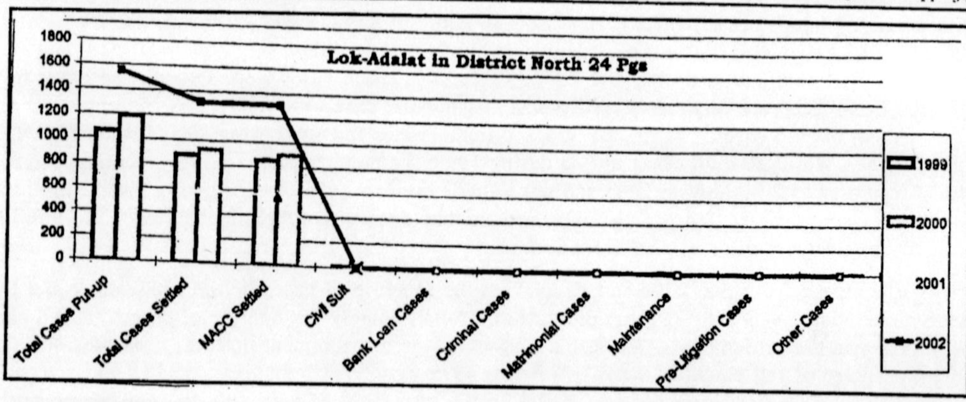

It is revealed from the above data that while during 1999 a total number of 1058 cases were referred before Lok-Adalat, the number decreased to 733 in the year 2001 after a slight increase in the year 2000. Indeed, it increased substantially to 1549 in the year 2002. Similarly, while the number of cases settled in 1999 was 880 it decreased to 590 in the year 2001 after a slight increase in the year 2000, but it again increased to 1313 in the year 2002. The other aspect of the function of Lok-Adalat in the District is its monopolistic approach. Out of total 3712 cases settled in the District, the number of MACC cases alone were 3623. The other cases settled in the District are 14 civil cases, 4 criminal cases, 35 matrimonial cases, 19 maintenance cases, 6 pre-litigation cases and 11 other categories of cases. While during 1999 the total number of cases settled were 880, the MACC alone stands at 855. Similarly in 2000 while the number of settlements were 929, MACC cases settled alone were 901. During the year 2001, while the total number of settlements were 590, the number of settlements of MACC cases alone were 562. Thus, alone 96.7% of the cases settled were MACC. Similarly in the year 2002, while the total number of cases settled were 1313, MACC alone were 1305.

The other significant characteristic of the functioning of Lok-Adalat in the District is the lofty percentage of settlements It is revealed through the study that the highest percentage of settlements were recorded in the year 2002 with a percentage of 84.76%. During the years 1999, 2000 and 2001 the percentage of settlements were 83.17%, 78.59% and 80.49% respectively. The number of cases among all categories of disputes are decreasing continuously except the MACC cases. The pre-litigation cases are the new entrants and for the first time, 4 pre-litigation cases were settled in the District during the year 2001. The matrimonial cases increased slightly to 16 in the year 2000, from the figure of 13 of the year 1999. However, only one civil case was settled in the year 2001, while the figure was 9, in the year 1999 and the criminal cases moved to zero level in the year 2000 from the figure of 4 in the year 1999.

Thus, the declining phenomenon persists in the District, though a large number of cases were settled during the last four years and a immediately certain remedial measure is required to be taken to make the institution of Lok-Adalat more popular among the public. Emphasis should be given on other cases also, so that the functioning of the institution cannot stand as monolithic.

LOK-ADALAT IN DISTRICT JALPAIGURI

The Lok-Adalat in the District is organised by Jalpaiguri District Legal Services Authority. The Government of West Bengal for popularising legal aid programme and organising Lok-Adalat constituted the District Authority so that access to justice cannot be denied to any one[32]. In order to attain the objective and to make the institution available to the people at grass root level, the State Legal services Authority formed two Sub-Divisional Legal Services Committees at Sub-Division level namely, Jalpaiguri Sub-Division Legal Services Committee and Alipurdour Sub-Divisional Legal Services Committee[33]. During the period of 1999 to 2002 a total number of 1195 cases were referred before Lok-Adalat out of which 758 cases were settled. While the number of cases referred before the Lok-Adalat is increasing continuously the number of cases settled in the Lok-Adalat is decreasing.

The number of cases referred before Lok-Adalat during 1999 was 319 and it increased to 348 in the year 2000 and further to 376 in the year 2001. It was decreased in the year 2002 where only 152 cases were referred. On the contrary, the number of cases settled in the Lok-Adalat decreased to 198 in the year 2000 from the figure of 315 of the year 1999 and it was further decreased to 173 in the year 2001 and 78 in the year 2002. Initially, an exceptionally high percentage of cases were settled but subsequently the percentage decreased substantially. The Table 8.15 and Graph will established the performance of Lok-Adalat in the District.

Lok Adalat in Jalpaiguri
Table - 8.16

Period	Benches	Total Cases Put-up	Total Cases Settled	%of Settlement	MACC Settled	Civil Suit	Bank Loan Cases	Criminal Cases	Matrimonial Cases	Maintenance Cases	Pre-Litigation Cases	Other Cases	Awarded Money
1999	20	319	315	98.75%	262	13	12	13	3	6	0	6	15320000
2000	21	348	192	55.17%	184	0	8	0	0	0	0	0	10874188
2001	16	376	173	46.01%	132	0	13	0	0	0	28	0	7709037
2002	8	152	78	51.32%	51	0	8	0	0	1	18	0	3566400
Grand Total	65	1195	758	63.43%	629	13	41	13	3	7	46	6	37469625

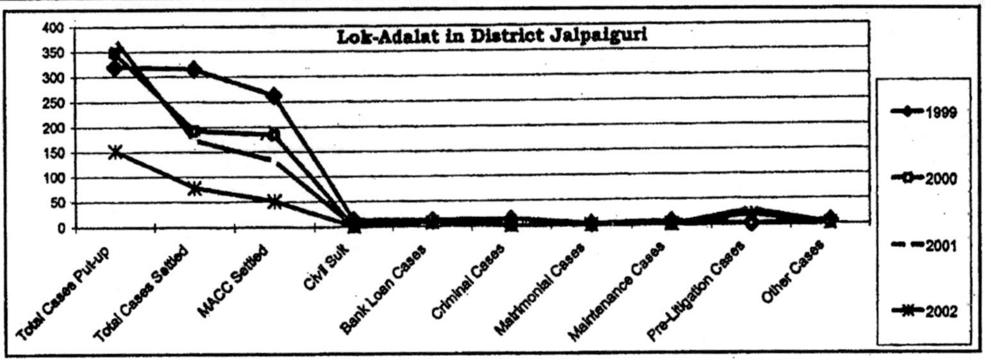

While in the year 1999 the percentage of settlements was extremely high at 98.74%, the percentage decreased to 55.17% in the year 2000 and again to 46.01% in the year 2001. The percentage of settlements in the year 2002 was 51.32%. Likewise other several Districts, in this District also, the MACC cases were the most suitable form of disputes for the institution of Lok-Adalat. Out of total 758 cases settled in the Lok-

Adalat during the last four years, MACC cases alone were 629 and an amount of 3,74,69,625/- was paid as compensation. However, the number of MACC cases also decreased substantially. During 1999 while the number of MACC cases settled were 262, the number decreased to 184 in the year 2000 and was further decreased to 132 in the year 2001 and to 51 in the year 2002. Similarly the other categories of cases also decreased tremendously. While during 1999, a total number of 13 civil cases were settled, not a single civil case was settled during 2000, 2001 and 2002. While in the year 1999 a total number of 13 criminal cases, 3 matrimonial cases, 6 maintenance cases and 6 other cases were settled, not a single such case was settled in the year 2001 and 2002. However, pre-litigation cases are new entrants in the process at this District and for the first time in 2001, 28 pre-litigation cases were disposed of in the District. In the year 2002, 18 such pre-litigation cases were disposed of.

In this District also, like several others Districts a monolithic form of dispute is being settled. Only one good element found in the functioning of Lok-Adalat in the District is the settlement of a few pre-litigation cases. In the District, some remedial measures are immediately required to be taken not only to settle more cases but also for more referral of cases and for bringing back the faith of the disputants on the institution.

Thus a multipoint strategy is required to be taken for making the institution more vibrant, for resolution of more cases by the institution. Otherwise the institution of Lok-Adalat will loose its value.

LOK-ADALAT IN DISTRICT MURSHIDABAD

The Lok-Adalat in the District is organised by Murshidabad District Legal Services Authority. The District Authority was formed by Government of West Bengal on 15th July' 1998, consisting of 14 members[34]. For the purpose of strengthening the working of the institution and to popularise the legal aid programme, the State Legal Services Authority constituted four Sub-Divisional Legal Services Committees namely, Kandi Sub-Divisional Legal Services Committee, Lalbag Legal Services Committee, Jangipur Legal Services Committee and Berhampur Sub-Divisional Legal Services Committee[35]. In the District, 878 cases were placed before Lok-Adalat during the four years from 1999 to 2002, out of which 360 cases were settled. Among those 360 cases, MACC alone were 301 and an amount of Rs. 1,55,17,500/- was paid as compensation in the District.

While in the year 1999 the total number of cases settled were 185, the number decreased to 66 in the year 2000 and was further decreased to 33 in the year 2001. However, the number of settlement slightly increased to 75 in the year 2002. Indeed, the reference cases did not decrease in a similar way. While in 1999 a total number of 227 cases were referred before Lok-Adalat the number decreased to 190 in the year 2001 but it again increased to 233 in the year 2002. The percentage of settlements decreased drastically. It is revealed by the study, that the highest percentage of settlements was achieved in 1999. During 1999 the percentage of settlements was 81.93% and was decreased to 28.94% in the year 2000 and further to merely 17.36% in the year 2001.

It is revealed from the study that only MACC cases were settled in Lok-Adalat in the district, except a few other cases. In the year 1999, while the total number of cases settled were 186, the MACC alone were 185 and only one civil case was settled in the District. Similarly, in the year 2000, while total 66 cases were settled in the Lok-Adalat, the MACC amounted to 65 and one matrimonial case was settled. The Table 8.16 and the Graph establishes such performance of the institution in the District.

Lok Adalat in Murshidabad
Table - 8.17

Period	Benches	Total Cases Put-up	Total Cases Settled	% of Settlement	MACC Settled	Civil Suit	Bank Loan Cases	Criminal Cases	Matrimonial Cases	Maintenance Cases	Pre-Litigation Cases	Other Cases	Awarded Money
1999	11	227	186	81.94%	185	1	0	0	0	0	0	0	8825000
2000	10	228	66	28.95%	65	0	0	0	0	1	0	0	3731000
2001	11	190	33	17.37%	26	0	0	0	0	4	2	2	1298000
2002	9	233	75	32.19%	25	0	0	0	11	2	4	4	1663500
Grand Total	41	878	360	41.00%	301	1	0	0	11	7	6	6	15517500

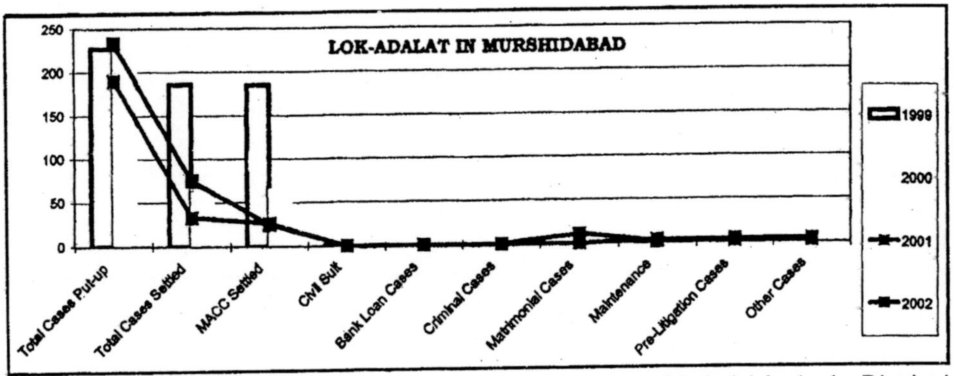

The data as well as the graph made it clear that the functioning of Lok-Adalat in the District is mainly based on MACC cases. In the year 2001, while total 33 cases were settled, the MACC were 26 and four maintenance cases; one pre-litigation case and two other categories of cases were settled. However, in the year 2002, while the total number of cases were settled was 75, the number of settlements of MACC cases were 25. Significantly, 33 pre-litigation cases were settled along with 11 matrimonial disputes, 2 maintenance cases and 4 other categories of cases. Thus a significant achievement was made in pre-litigation cases.

The number of settlements in the Lok-Adalat drastically decreased during the four years period. It is not because the reference was low but because a large number of cases were not settled even on reference. The graph clearly shows that the number of reference of cases is not as low proportionately low as the settlements of cases. This resulted in a drastic decline in the percentage of settlements.

Thus it is clear from the study that the institution of Lok-Adalat is not marching in the right direction in the District and the instrument of accessibility to justice failed to be acceded by the large number of masses. Immediate remedial measures are essential and the Sub-Divisional Committees are required to be more functional.

LOK-ADALAT IN DISTRICT BIRBHUM

The Lok-Adalats in the District are organised by the District Legal Services Authority. Birbhum. The District Authority was constituted on 15.7.98 consisting of 16 members[36]. Three Sub-Divisional Legal Services Committees were formed by State Legal Services Authority in the District namely Suri Sub-Divisional Legal Services Committee, Bolpur Sub-Divisional Legal Services Committee and Birbhum Legal Services Committee[37]. In the District of Birbhum a total number of 1509 cases were placed before Lok-Adalats out of which 433 cases were settled during the last four years from 1999 to 2002. Among such 433 cases, which were settled by Lok-Adalats, the MACC alone count for 273 and an amount of Rs 2,21,10,055/- was paid as compensation. It is revealed from the study that the highest number of cases settled in the District were in the year 1999 and subsequently the number of settlements decreased.

While in the year 1999, a total number of 167 cases were settled out of 383 cases, the number decreased to 65 in the year 2000. However, the number of cases referred to the Lok-Adalat increased to 411 in the year 2001, from 378 in the year 2000. It is further revealed from the study that the highest percentage of settlement was recorded in the initial year. While the overall percentage of settlements were 28.69%, the percentage of settlements was recorded at 43.60% in the year 1999. However, this percentage decreased to 17.20% in the year 2000, to 25.30% in the year 2001 and to 28.78% in the year 2002. The average settlement of cases per Bench of the Lok-Adalat in the District were 9. Though different categories of cases were referred before the Lok-Adalats including, MACC, civil, criminal, matrimonial, pre-litigation, but the highest number settled were MACC cases. However, the number of MACC cases also decreased subsequently in the years 2000, 2001 and 2002. While during 1999, a total number of 130 MACC cases were settled in the Lok-Adalats, the number decreased to 45 in the year 2000, 55 in the year 2001 and further decreased to 43 in the year 2002. The number of civil cases also decreased in the corresponding periods. While in 1999, 32 civil cases were settled in the

District, which included 21 money suits, it decreased to 10 in the year 2000 but again it reached 25 in the year 2001 and 35 in the year 2002. However, the number of maintenance cases increased slightly and the number reached 15 in the year 2001 from 3 of the year 1999. The District is new starter in respect of criminal cases and pre-litigation cases. For the first time, 5 criminal cases and 1 pre-litigation case were settled in the year 2001 and the number of criminal cases settled increased to 10 in the year 2002.

The Table 8.17 as well as the Graph will exhibit the declining phenomenon of the institution of Lok-Adalat in the District. It will also show the performance of the institution.

Lok Adalat in Birbhum
Table - 8.18

Period	Benches	Total Cases Put-up	Total Cases Settled	% of Settlement	MACC Settled	Civil Suit	Bank Loan Cases	Criminal Cases	Matrimonial Cases	Maintenance	Pre-Litigation Cases	Other Cases	Awarded Money
1999	14	383	167	43.60%	130	32	0	0	2	3	0	0	9238160
2000	10	378	65	17.20%	45	10	0	0	1	4	0	5	5723548
2001	13	411	104	25.30%	55	25	1	5	1	15	1	1	3681329
2002	10	337	97	28.78%	43	35	0	10	0	9	0	0	3467018
Grand Total	47	1509	433	28.69%	273	102	1	15	4	31	1	6	22110055

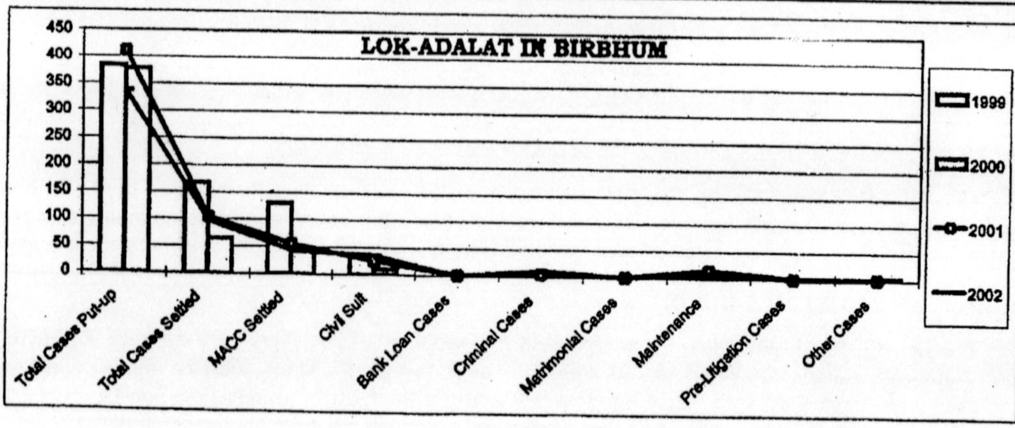

The 2001 axis will clearly exhibit the fact that the number of cases in all segments has been decreased except matrimonial cases and initiation has been made in pre-litigation cases and criminal cases. Thus if the institution of Lok-Adalat has to survive in the District, we must take some remedial measures The Sub-Divisional Committees are required to be made effective to reach the institution at the lowest level, nearer to the masses, as to make 'People's Court' a Court of general people, in reality. Otherwise, the institution will subsist in the law books and statutes and the fruit of the institution will not reach the people at large.

LOK-ADALAT IN DISTRICT COOCHBEHAR

The Lok-Adalat in the District was organised by District Legal Services Authority, Coochbehar. The District Authority was constituted on 15th July, 1998 consisting of 16 members, including the District Judge of the District Coochbehar, as its Chairman[37]. There are five Sub-Divisional Legal Services Committees established by the State Authority for the District[38]. These Sub-Divisional Legal Services Committees are Coochbehar Sub-Divisional Legal Services Committee, Dinhata Sub-Divisional Legal Services Committee, Tufangunj Sub-Divisional Legal Services Committee, Mekhligung Sub-Divisional Legal Services Committee and Matabhanga Sub-Divisional Legal Services Committee.

Though there are five Sub-Divisional Legal Services Committees constituted, the District headquarter is the main destination for the Lok-Adalats. During the four years from 1999 to 2002, total 975 cases were placed before the Lok-Adalats in the District, out of which 586 cases were settled and the percentage of settlements is quite high at 60 10% However, the number of cases referred, as well as settled, in the Lok-Adalats is decreasing continuously. While the number of cases put-up during 1999, were 353. out of which 226 cases were settled, the number of cases placed before Lok-Adalat decreased to 255 in the year 2000 and it further decreased to 158 in the year 2001. However, it increased to 209 in 2002.

Lok Adalat in Coochbehar
Table - 8.19

Period	Benches	Total Cases Put-up	Total Cases Settled	% of Settlement	MACC Settled	Civil Suit	Bank Loan Cases	Criminal Cases	Matrimonial Cases	Maintenance Cases	Pre-Litigation Cases	Other Cases	Awarded Money
1999	19	353	226	64.02%	141	15	21	9	7	0	0	33	8396097
2000	22	255	124	48.63%	74	0	26	0	18	6	0	0	5040587
2001	15	158	117	74.05%	41	0	64	1	8	3	0	0	2531377
2002	10	209	119	56.94%	50	0	50	0	19	0	0	0	2351990
Grand Total	66	975	586	60.10%	306	15	161	10	52	9	0	33	18320051

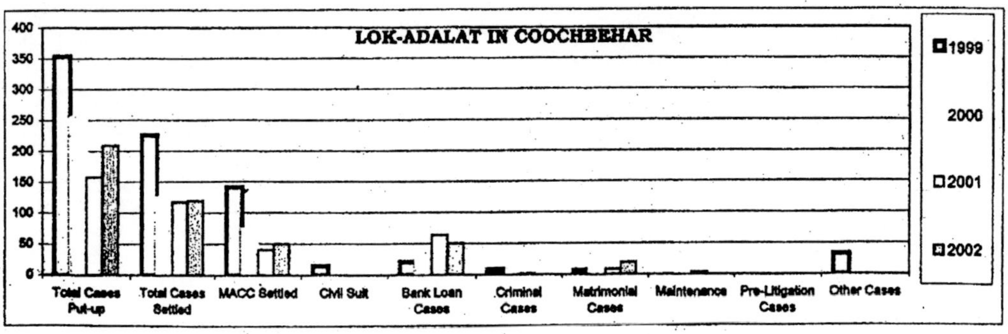

It is evident from the above data and graph that the number of cases settled in the Lok-Adalat also decreased substantially to 124 in the year 2000 and to 117 in the year 2001 However, the percentage of settlement of cases was highest in the year 2001. While in the year 2001 the percentage of settlements was 74.05%, the percentage of settlements in the year 1999, 2000 and 2002 were 64.02%, 48.62% and 56.94% respectively

Initially, the highest number of cases settled were the MACC but subsequently the civil cases marched ahead. While the number of MACC settled during 1999 was 141, it decreased to 74 in the year 2000 and to 41 in the year 2001. 50 MACC cases were settled during 2002. On contrary, while the number of civil cases settled in the year 1999 was 36 including 21 bank loan cases, it reached to 64 in the year 2001 and all of them were bank loan cases. During the last four years period, a total amount of Rs 1,83,20,051/-was paid as compensation in MACC cases. A small number of criminal and matrimonial cases were also settled in the District. While in the year 1999, only 7 matrimonial cases were settled, the number reached 18 in the year 2000 but it again decreased to 8 in the year 2001. Few maintenance cases were also settled during 2000 & 2001. The number of criminal cases also decreased to 1 in the year 2001 from 9 in the year 1999. No other case from other categories of disputes were settled in the Lok-Adalats in the year 2000, 2001 & 2002. However, in the year 1999, total 33 cases were settled under this category.

The study reveals a downward trend in the District, so far as the over all settlement of cases in Lok-Adalat is concerned. Not a single pre-litigation case was settled in these Lok-Adalats. The MACC cases, criminal cases, matrimonial cases and other category of cases have shown a downward trend The number of civil cases including, bank loan cases, settled in the Lok-Adalats were increased Indeed, it established the fact that for a large number of such civil cases, the institution of Lok-Adalat is the appropriate forum. However, from the study of the functioning of Lok-Adalat in the District, it is revealed that the functioning of Lok-Adalat in the District failed to progress, except in the civil cases. If the institution of Lok-Adalat continues to function in a similar way as it is functioning from 1999 onwards, the institution of Lok-Adalat will soon loose its existence in the District, until some immediate remedial measures are taken.

LOK-ADALAT IN DISTRICT DARJEELING

The District of Darjeeling had the privilege of organizing the first District Lok-Adalat. The first Lok-Adalat in the District was organised on 13th & 14th March'1993 at Siliguri. The magnitude of the enthusiasm can be judged from the fact that 35 para lawyers, all of whom were law students of North Bengal University, worked hard for a month before the Lok-Adalat was held. They prepared the list of the cases and studied such cases, they conducted conciliation with the disputant as a preparatory mechanism for bringing the disputants for final conciliation process at Lok-Adalat and they informed the disputants about the advantages of the conciliatory mechanism. 12 judicial officers of Darjeeling and Siliguri and 51 staff of different Courts rendered co-operation in organizing Lok-Adalat. 20 other peoples belonging to judiciary, academics and social worker were participated as president of the first District Lok-Adalat 138 cases were referred to the Lok-Adalat and an amount of Rs 65,21.182 was awarded in Lok-Adalat

However, in such a first Lok-Adalat was organised under the old scheme After the enforcement of the Legal Services Authorities Act. 1987, the Lok-Adalats in the District of Darjeeling were organised by the District Legal Services Authority, Darjeeling. The Authority was formed on 15th July' 1998 by the Government of West Bengal[39]. In order to make the institution of Lok-Adalat accessible in different Sub-Divisions of the District, the State Legal Services Authority constituted three Sub-Divisional Legal Services Committees in the District, namely Darjeeling Sub-Divisional Legal Services Committee for the Sub-Division of Darjeeling, Siliguri Sub-Divisional Legal Services Committee for the Sub-Division of Siliguri, and Kalimpong Sub-Divisional Legal Services Committee[40] The Table 8.19 and the Graph below will establish the performance.

Lok Adalat in Darjeeling

Table - 8.20

Period	Benches	Total Cases Put-up	Total Cases Settled	% of Settlement	MACC Settled	Civil Suit	Bank Loan Cases	Criminal Cases	Matrimonial Cases	Maintenance Cases	Pre-Litigation Cases	Other Cases	Awarded Money
1999	21	337	296	87.83%	145	91	29	0	4	5	0	22	21282228
2000	16	521	256	49.14%	166	30	55	0	2	3	0	0	11710442
2001	12	822	206	25.06%	120	0	77	0	5	2	2	0	10206102
2002	8	345	132	38.26%	104	0	26	2	0	0	0	0	8177934
Grand Total	67	2025	890	43.95%	535	121	187	2	11	10	2	22	51376706

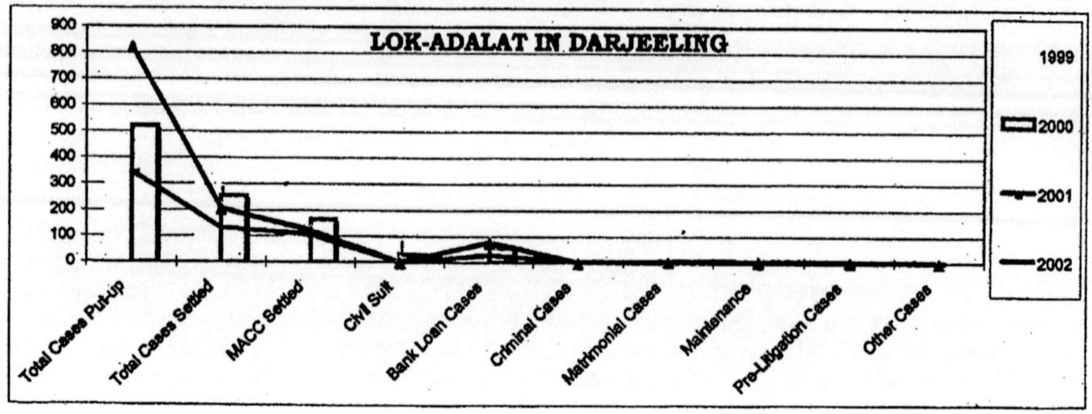

It is exhibit from the above data that during the last four years, from 1999 to 2002 a total number of 2025 cases were referred before Lok-Adalats, out of which 890 cases were settled. The number of cases referred before the Lok-Adalat increased each year until 2001. While the number of cases referred before Lok-Adalat were 337 during the year 1999, which reached 521 during 2000 and 822 during 2001. However, in the year 2002, only 345 cases were referred before Lok-Adalats. Nevertheless, the number of cases settled before Lok-Adalat decreased each year, and so did the percentage of settlements. While the number of cases settled during 1999 was 296, the number decreased to 256 during 2000, to 206 during 2001 and again 132 during 2002. Study further reveals that while the average percentage of settlements in the District was 43.95% during the last four years, the percentage was very high during 1999, which stood at 87.83%. However, this percentage decreased subsequently to 49.14% in 2000 and further to 25.06% during 2001. In the year 2002, it stood at 38.26%. Thus the number of cases settled in the District decreased continuously since its inception.

The performance of Lok-Adalats in the District was negligible in all cases except MACC and Civil. While the number of MACC cases settled during 1999 was 145, it increased to 166 during 2000 but it again decreased to 120, in 2001 and to 104 in the year 2002. Similarly, the civil cases also decreased consecutively. While the number of civil cases settled during 1999 was 120, which included 89 money suits and 29 bank loan cases, it decreased to 85 in the year 2000 and again to 77 in the year 2001. However, among those 85 civil cases settled in the year 2000, 55 cases were relating to bank loan cases and rest 30 cases were relating to money suits. Similarly all the 77 civil cases settled in the year 2001 were relating to bank loan cases. A small number of matrimonial and other cases were settled in the District, through the instrument of Lok-Adalat. Thus, while Darjeeling was the initiator of the Lok-Adalat movements in the Districts, the performance of the institution declined continuously. In these circumstances the goal of making justice available to all is not achieved in its true sense.

CRITICAL ANALYSIS OF THE FUNCTIONING OF THE INSTITUTION IN THE STATE OF WEST BENGAL

The researcher made an in-depth study on the functioning of Lok-Adalat in all the Districts of West Bengal as well as at High Court. It is clear from the above study that the institution of Lok-Adalat performed extremely well in the post 1998 period. An outstanding improvement was made during the year 1999 when 9434 cases were referred to the Lok-Adalat in which 4512 cases were settled. The institution got further impetus in the year 2000 & 2001 when the reference of cases further increased to 9616 & 9748. However, the number of settlements decreased to 4387 & 4025 in the year 2000 & 2001 but increased to 4697 in the year 2002.

It is also clear from the above study that the same declining phenomenon is not prevailing in all the Districts. On the one hand while in most of the Districts the number of settlements decreased, the number of settlements increased substantially in some Districts. The institution of Lok-Adalat has seen an increase in the Districts 24 Parganas (South), Bankura, Dakshin Dinajpur and Malda and all other Districts have shown decrease. The highest number of cases were referred as well as settled in the District of North 24 Parganas, where 4522 cases were referred in the last four years in which 3712 cases were settled. The lowest numbers of cases settled were in the Murshidabad District.

Though the institution has shown its best performance in MACC cases but a large number of other cases were also settled. Study reveals that while settling different types of disputes in the Districts, some Districts became authority in some particular cases. It had been found that some Districts were able to settle a large number of Civil cases while some other Districts have settled a large number of matrimonial cases. In Hooghly, 426 Bank Loan cases were settled, which is the highest in the State, compared to other Districts. Thus, Lok-Adalat in the District of Hooghly became specialist in Bank Loan cases. Similarly District Howrah & District Nadia settled a large number of matrimonial cases. In the same direction District Dakshin Dinajpur and District Malda were able to bring into compromise a large number of pre-litigation cases. In a similar way, the 24 Parganas South, 24 Parganas North & Murshidabad became experts in MACC cases by satisfactorily settling a large number of MACC cases. Thus, the aforesaid result on the one hand refutes the argument that the institution is proper one for MACC cases only. On the other hand it establishes the fact that the institution of Lok-Adalat has potentiality to settle a large number of other categories of cases like maintenance cases, matrimonial cases, bank loan cases, money suits, commercial disputes along with other disputes. The most important aspect of functioning of the institution is it's potentiality of settling even those cases which have not struck the door of adversarial mechanism, which is established from the data of some Districts which have settled a large number of pre-litigation cases. However, in practice it has been seen that the functioning of the institution is becoming monolithic, because in most Districts some particular forms of cases are being settled in large numbers. Nevertheless, the result from different Districts corroborate the fact that institution of Lok-Adalat as well as other ADR mechanism are appropriate forum for the cases where a long relation between the parties subsist by settling a large number of Bank loan cases and matrimonial cases. Indeed, the institution shows impressive results in cases where monetary disputes subsist and the main contentious issue would be the quantum of financial deliverance. This reason resulted in the settlement of a large number of MACC cases.

Study reveals that most of the Lok-Adalats were held in the District head quarters. Though, almost all Sub-Divisions in the State have Sub-Divisional Committees, yet excepting a few all are on papers only and those few Sub-Divisional committees, which are functioning have not contributed much towards Lok-Adalat. In the District of South 24 Parganas, five Sub-Divisional Committees were constituted but none of them are working. Similarly, in 24 Parganas North, four Sub-Divisional Committees were constituted but only two Sub-Divisional Committees have organised some Lok-Adalats. Thus, the goal of providing justice to the people at their places has not yet achieved the target. The main reasons for the non-functioning of the Sub-Divisions are the fund and infrastructure. However, fund cannot be the sole reason for non-fulfilment of the statutory obligation. One other reason for failure of Sub-Divisional Committees is the structural deficiencies. Several Sub-Divisional Committees were constituted without any Advocate. It is an established fact that the institution of Lok-Adalat cannot succeed until or unless Advocates participate in the process actively. In order to acquire active participation of the Advocates, it is essential that each Committee must have couple of Advocates. However, this may not be the sole remedy to attain active participation of Advocates though it will definitely help in bringing the Advocates nearer to the institution.

It is further clear from the above study that the large number of cases that are not settled are not because parties did not agree on settlement but because they do not bother to appear before the Lok-Adalats. It is a vital deficiency on the part of the institution. It is an established fact that the institution has shown extremely good performance in motor accident claim cases, which is a common phenomenon in all the Districts. The researcher tried to find out the true reasons for the settlement of a large number of MACC cases and non-performance of the institution in the similar way in other categories of cases. The main cause for such performance is the active participation of Lawyers. Secondly, the nature of case it self. Nature of cases, because in most of the cases disputes basically rest on the quantum of compensation. The insurance companies know that they have to pay the money either today or tomorrow. If they are paying it today they can bargain and can pay much less than what they have to pay after trial proceeding. This is because the Insurance companies have more bargaining power than the claimants. Claimants do not have high bargaining power because of the delaying adversarial proceedings. Claimants feel that even if he is getting less money, it is better to get it today instead of getting more money after 10 or 15 years. Thus, this bargaining power forces them to negotiate for quantum of compensation as per their own need. Thus, both the disputants happily settle their disputes in the Lok-Adalats.

Secondly, the active participation of the Advocates is also responsible for making the institution effective in MACC cases. However, this is because of their own interest. The researcher tried to find out the causes of active participation of Advocates in MACC cases. What the researcher finds is that, most of the cases filed for compensation were on the basis of contract between Advocates and claimants. The claimant use to pay a ratio to the Advocate out of the compensation, which vary from 15% to 25% of the compensation awarded. Thus, in MACC cases not only claimants have an interest to get money at the earliest possible time but Advocates have also the same interest of getting professional fees in such a ratio at the earliest possible date. In a large number of MACC cases, it is found that the parties verbatim settled their cases even before they put-up the case at Lok-Adalat and in those circumstances the settlement before Lok-Adalat is only a formality and provide a statutory backing. This became possible only because of the Advocates active participation. However, the noble institution of Lok-Adalat has provided this moral encouragement to the Advocates and the Insurance companies.

Apart from MACC, the Bank Loan Cases, Money Suit, Maintenance Cases and Matrimonial cases are the most successful forms of disputes for the institution of Lok-Adalat. The electricity cases and other similar cases are most successful at High Court level. Thus, if we consider the whole category of cases where Lok-Adalat has made its effect, we will find that those cases are of three categories. First, those cases where disputants knew the fate of the case. Disputants of one side knew that they have to pay the money and the disputants of the other side had firm belief of getting money. The disputes then basically came to the quantum of money. In this category of cases, the MACC cases, Bank loan cases and even maintenance cases along with a few other similar categories of disputes fall. In MACC cases the insurance companies knew that they have to pay the compensation. Similarly, the loanee knows that they have to repay the loan provided sufficient security is lying with the bank and even the Husband knows that that he has to maintain his wife, for which he has to pay the maintenance.

Secondly, those cases where one party have the right of access to service while the others have the duty to provide service. Electricity disputes and other consumer-oriented disputes are examples of this category of cases. The Electric Company knows that they have to provide service to the consumer and the consumer knows that they have the right to get service because it is an essential service. This is the cause of a large number of cases relating to electricity are being settled in the Lok-Adalats.

Thirdly, those cases where an ongoing relationship subsist between the parties. The maintenance cases, matrimonial disputes, bank loan cases and commercial disputes are a few examples of this category of cases. The reason for the success of this category of cases is that the ongoing relationship can be maintained. Suppose, in maintenance cases or matrimonial disputes between husband and wife, the decision at adversarial proceeding can be only on evidence and rational arguments backed by legal instruments. In the process of proving and disproving the case, the proceeding becomes the battlefield, full of allegations and counter allegations, which results in the complete disbanding of relationship[41]. The end product would be the order based on rational argument and evidences, which might be based on truth less story. In these circumstances the purpose of justice is frustrated. Will the adversarial mechanism can do better justice than the Lok-Adalat in these forms of disputes? Whether, in a dispute for maintenance between father and son or between husband and wife where both are able to settle their disputes with the help of conciliators is not qualitatively better than making allegation and counter allegation? In Bank loan cases and commercial disputes where the parties have hope to continue their on going relationship, the Lok-Adalat and the ADR mechanism are the best fora for resolution. That is why a large number of matrimonial cases, Bank loan cases and commercial disputes being settled in the Lok-Adalat.

The other issues, which require analysis, are the reasons for failure of the institution to succeed in a large number of those cases where parties appeared but failed to settle. The most important reason is the non-participation of lawyers in the proceeding because of the fear of their professional loss. However, if the disputant agrees to settle the cases; then lawyers have a minimal role to play, for which a change in the mind set of the people is essential. This mindset of the people as well as of lawyers depends upon various factors. Faith on the institution of Lok-Adalat, understanding the controlling process during conciliation proceeding, the expectations of end result, proper understanding of their interest and most important is the alternatives available to them. The alternative available to them have a vital impact, while taking decision for settling disputes or to be abstaining from settlement.

Once Lord Keynes said,[42] 'Men will do all rational things but only after exploring all other alternatives'. The important words of Lord Keynes are still having the same importance. The different scholars reiterate the theory that the human beings take decisions on available alternatives[43]. This implies on the process of Lok-Adalat also. It is a common view that the institution of Lok-Adalat is effective because the adjudicatory system fails in providing quick justice with minimal expenses. Though the initiation of the institution made out of concern that the justice delivery system fails to provide goods and because of the docket of cases it is on the verge of collapse, but on jurisprudential aspects it is a established fact that the adjudicatory system is not the fit institution for all forms of cases, for which the Lok-Adalat is the best forum. Thus, in those cases for which the Lok-Adalat is the best forum, the institution cannot be able to provide the fruit of conciliation proceedings effectively until the adjudication system became effective. However, this view of mine may be contrary to several views. In my view, the adjudicatory system must require to be effective in order to make the institution of Lok-Adalat more productive.

In one Bank loan case in Lok-Adalat at Hooghly District, the borrower declined to compromise with the Bank because he had a firm belief that after the return of the case to the adjudicatory proceeding, it will take further 14-15 years to decide and there also he has to pay in a lengthy instalment. The loan was for a lorry and the amount with interest stood at around three lakhs. Bank agreed to deduct a good portion of hefty interest but the borrower was agreeing to pay only the principal amount and that also in instalment. Borrower had an injunction in his favour that he will operate the vehicle. The cause for borrower's stand was that the vehicle became 13 yrs old and according to the new rule, which is supposed to be implemented, the vehicle above 15 yrs old cannot ply in the city like Kolkata. He even agreed to return the vehicle to the Bank but the price of vehicle became much lower than the due amount. Thus, in this case the borrower had more bargaining power because of three reasons. Firstly, the amount of security is much lower than the amount of dues. Secondly, he knows that in the present scenario, Bank will not seize the vehicle because of the value and reason behind this was that since long he has an injunction in his favour from court of law. Thirdly, the important reason is the available alternatives, which is more fruitful for the borrower because if the case will return to the court it will take further 5 to 10 yrs to decide and in the meantime the vehicle will become valueless. However, if the available alternatives had been active, the bargaining power would have changed. If the borrower knows that if he is not settling disputes today in Lok-Adalat he has to pay a hefty amount within a short span when the adjudicatory proceeding will end, the scenario of negotiation would be different.

Similarly, in other cases when any party does not settle disputes, it is only because of their available alternatives. The parties who will benefit out of the delay in the adjudicatory proceeding, do not agree to settle. In the insurance cases when the Insurance companies are not willing to settle disputes they have the alternatives, where though they have to pay higher amount in adjudicatory proceedings but it is only after a span of 5-10 yrs. Thus, the interest out of delay makes them aloof from settlement in some cases. Similarly, when the claimant does not agree to settle the disputes they have an alternative where they will get much more money than the settlement amount. Though, it may take a long time but the interest of more money prevails over the interest of time. Thus, it is clear that the decisions of the disputants in the Lok-Adalat as well as other places are based on the available alternatives. In such circumstances, if the alternatives would become much more active, in other word if the adjudicatory proceeding become much more effective, the bargaining power will change and people will prefer to settle their disputes, instead of uncertain out comes of the disputes. However, this requirement of fast resolution of disputes on alternatives may be remedied by 2002 amendment of the Legal Services Authorities Act, 1987, where parties will have the impression that if they would not settle the disputes, an uncertain out come will be imposed on them but only in Permanent Lok-Adalat for public utilities service.

There are several other factors, which the study reveals and are some how responsible for the poor performance of the institution at several places. First, the most important aspect is non-participation of a percentage of lawyers in the process. A large number of lawyers are sceptical about the institution. While in America and other developed countries a large number of legal professionals have expertise in mediation and a separate class of legal professionals have emerged there. On the contrary, in India we are waiting for a class of professionals who will have the expertise in the field of ADR like Lok-Adalat. Thus, the change in the legal professionals' attitude is important to make the institution much more effective.

Secondly, the lack of active people's participation. The active participation depends upon different things, awareness about the institution, belief in the institution, continuous legal awareness programme, training of the para lawyers, involvement of NGOs in the process. Indeed, High Court Legal Services Committee attempted to popularise the institution and the Lok-Adalats were widely covered by the media but that is not an adequate measure for the institution in whole of the state. Law Schools can play a important rote. In this direction LASWEB played an important rote in the State. They organised camps for law students each year and the students persuaded the parties for the resolution of disputes through conciliation.

Thirdly, some technical reasons also appeared as hurdle in the process of settlements. In one motor accident compensation case, the adjudicatory proceeding ended with an exparte award of Rs 50,000/-[44]. The insurance company filed Misc Case for setting aside the exparte award. The matter was referred to the Lok-Adalat for resolution of disputes. Parties agreed to settle the matter on 49000/-. The learned judges of the Lok-

Adalat declined to record settlement on the ground that the matter was referred to Lok-Adalat for Misc petition only. The matter had to be referred back before Lok-Adalat for resolution. Thus in this case the petitioner, who is waiting for justice for last 17 years, have to wait further. In my opinion the technical ground must not become a hurdle during the process of settlement.

Thus, as a whole, though the institution of Lok-Adalat significantly increased after the constitution of different authorities in the State but much more is needed to make the people's Court for the people by the people. Two vital deficiencies have been established by the research. First, the institution of Lok-Adalat is losing popularity in most of the places, which resulted in declining of the number of settlements in those places. Even, the number of settlements at State level has been decreasing in the year 2000 & 2001. Secondly, compared with the other contemporary States the functioning of the institution is at far low scale. One comparative example will show the low magnitude of performance of the institution in the State. In West Bengal, while 16196 cases were settled during the long period of one decade, the State of Rajasthan successfully settled 199416 cases during a single year of 2001. Similarly, the State of Gujarat settled more than 5 lakhs cases in single year of 2000.

Thus, in order to provide a cost effective and a time effective dispensation of justice and to make access of justice meaningful for the large number of masses, there is still much more needed, to be done.

RESPONSES TO THE QUESTIONNAIRE FROM THE PEOPLE ASSOCIATED WITH THE INSTITUTION OF LOK-ADALAT AS WELL AS DISPUTANT

The researcher has distributed a questionnaire to 75 different people belonging to legal profession, retired and service judges, social activists and the disputants, including the people belonging to Insurance companies. However, 52 people responded, including several dignitaries of the State who are actively involved in the Lok-Adalat movement. The Researcher, enlightened from the experience of Justice D. Basu, who can be considered as the pioneer of the Lok-Adalat movement in West Bengal, and Justice Malay Sengupta who was also actively involved in the Lok-Adalat movement and participated himself as judge in several Lok-Adalats in the State.

The researcher held many discussions with various members of the different Legal Services Authorities, including the Member Secretary of the State Legal Services Authority, Mr B.Biswas about the functioning of the institution of Lok-Adalat. Researcher also visited several Lok-Adalats in order to gather experience over the functioning of the institution and to obtain responses of the persons associated with Lok-Adalat as well as disputants.

On questioning about the requirement of changes, at least to make the presence of the parties mandatory, out of 52 people 46 people stated in the affirmative to make the necessary changes in the Act, 4 people said that it is not essential and two people did not say any thing. Among those 46 people 8 people said that mere presence of a party might not serve the purpose as the party may disagree to compromise even after appearance. However, they made a suggestion that appearance should be ensured by any means. On questioning, that what criteria should be kept in mind while selecting the place of holding Lok-Adalat, 29 people said that the Court premises where the case has been instituted. On query whether the Lok-Adalat is required to be held in public place instead of court premises to create court free environment, 32 people answered in the negative in which 3 people including Justice Malay Sengupta said that the court records are necessary for disposal of cases and the court will not agree to part with the records. However, 5 Advocates asserted in the affirmative, in which two said that it could be implemented, provided that infrastructure could be made at other places. Other 5 disputants belonging to Insurance companies said in the negative while the other disputants said in the affirmative.

It is revealed from the study that it is customary in West Bengal to appoint a retired judicial officer as a member Judge and accordingly all the respondents corroborated the fact. On questioning whether the concerned authority would face difficulties in finding judges from Advocates and social workers, all the response came in the negative. On query, whether judges are trained enough, a mixed response appeared. 39 people responded in the positive, among them, six people said that they are trained enough, though no specific training is arranged and one person said that not all the time the judges are trained. However, 13 people responded in the negative. On the question, whether cases are postponed if judges think that the case can be settled, if some time is allowed to the disputants, 35 people said yes in which 6 people said on rare occasions, ten people said in the negative and 7 people did not respond.

On query about what opportunity is provided to the disputants to establish their cases before any compromise is arrived at, 11 people said persuasion of judges in which three people said after hearing the parties and their agent/officer, 33 people said argument of the Advocate and persuasion of judges and rest of the persons concurred with the above two, including arguments of parties. It is revealed by the study that 35 responded reasoned, lack of awareness regarding the Lok-Adalat among the disputants, for the reference of a small number of cases to the Lok-Adalat. 15, who responded, said that lack of initiatives by Advocates and by judges are the reason for the small number of reference. However, one respondent pointed out the lack of infrastructure is responsible for the low references and one respondent observed that the lack of initiatives on the part of concerned officials of the District level authority is responsible for such minimal references. On questioning, in which category of cases the institution of Lok-Adalat has shown an encouraging performance, all the respondents said that the compensation cases, among them 22 people said Marriage cases & Bank loan cases along with compensation cases. On questioning whether Advocates of respective parties create obstacles during the process of negotiation, 45 respondents replied in the negative while 7 respondents replied in the affirmative. However, on questioning the different disputants about how they got information about the institution of Lok-Adalat all of them said they were informed by their respective Advocates. On the question, because of the active involvement of Advocates in MACC cases such a large number of MACC cases, are settled and at the same time because of their inactive participation in other categories of cases, the settlement of other cases are negligible, 35 respondents said in the affirmative and made lawyers responsible for the failure of institution to settle effectively the different categories of cases while 17 persons responded in the negative. On asking for suggestions for the increase of the number of references before the Lok-Adalat, 26 respondents suggested to generate awareness about Lok-Adalat. 15 people suggested for awareness along with development of confidence building measures, 4 respondents said that personal initiatives along with awareness and confidence building measures and the rest 7 respondents suggested the personal initiatives of lawyers along with awareness and confidence building. On asking whether the senior Advocates provide encouragements, 39 respondents said in affirmative while 13 said in the negative.

Interestingly, on questioning about primary object of holding Lok-Adalat, 33 respondents said the speedy disposal of cases and less expenditure on the process, while 7 respondents said only the speedy disposal of cases. 7 respondents said, to develop harmony and peace among the disputants along with speedy and inexpensive disposal of cases while 5 said to develop a democratic attitude towards dispute resolution, along with speedy and inexpensive resolution of disputes. On asking whether the process of decision making in the Lok-Adalat is democratic, all of the respondents responded in the affirmative except two respondents who responded in the negative. On questioning whether the popular faith on the institution of Lok-Adalat resulted because of the failure of judicial system to provide justice cost effective and time effective, 37 people responded in the affirmative while 7 people responded in the negative. On questioning whether the participation of women in the functioning of Lok-Adalat can assist in better performance, 43 respondents said in the affirmative while 9 people did not respond. On questioning, whether any one of the parties became a loser in the process at the end of process when the cases are settled, the answer came in the negative. Respondents affirm that the process of Lok-Adalat is such where each of the parties becomes a winner.

One important question, which the researcher asked the respondents, was whether the time effective functioning of regular judicial system would help in more disposals of cases by Lok-Adalats? It is mainly because human behaviour is such, which takes decision on the basis of available alternatives, and in the present situation the available alternative in adversarial mode of dispute resolution is heaven for the disputant having bad faith. 45 respondents agreed with the views of questionnaire while 7 persons replied in the negative. Indeed, it has established the fact that there is always scope of co-existence of Lok-Adalat with adversarial system and each other is co-related. The effect of failure of one institution will always be on the other. Even, when the adversarial mode will became more effective at the same time Lok-Adalat will also become more productive. On questioning whether the respondents agreed that at present the cases are referred to the Lok-Adalats at a stage when the relation between the parties are totally broken and for which the need is to refer the cases at an early stage, 32 respondents replied in the affirmative in which three respondents said that they have partially agreed and rest of the respondents replied in negative.

Interestingly, on questioning whether it is required to make mandatory for some cases like MACC, matrimonial and other similar cases to be referred before Lok-Adalat in the initial stage because the Lok-Adalat is the best forum for resolution of such disputes, 38 respondents said in the affirmative while 14 respondents said in the negative. On being asked what steps do they suggest to create awareness about the functioning of Lok-Adalat at village, 42 respondents said to take all the steps as mentioned in the questionnaire namely, effective awareness camp, use of mass media, person to person contact by the legal aid members, effective participation of the NGOs in the process and involvement of Law Schools. Three of the respondents said the effective awareness camp at remote places with the assistance of NGOs & para lawyers. Two respondents said the effective awareness camp while three respondents suggested person-to-person contact by legal aid members, effective participation of the NGOs and effective awareness camp and two respondents suggested the involvement of Law Schools along with active participation of NGOs and awareness camps. On questioning whether the number of cases settled in the Lok-Adalat is decreasing continuously and secondly is it becoming monolithic, 29 people responded in the affirmative while rest in the negative. On asking whether implementation of Sec. 89 will provide a new life in the Lok-Adalat movement, 38 people responded in the affirmative and 12 in the negative.

Thus, mixed responses came from the respondents. The responses were some time based on respondent's own interest as on asking whether the Lok-Adalat be organised at Panchayat level or at village level the disputants said in the affirmative while mostly Advocates said in the negative. Similarly, a large number of Advocates did not make themselves responsible for minimal disposals in cases other than MACC. However, apart from the suggestions for making the institution more effective, most of the respondents agreed with the views of the researcher on two aspects. First, in the process of Lok-Adalat none of the parties are a loser and the end product made both of them happy. Secondly, there is scope of subsisting both the systems of administration of justice, first by adversarial mode of dispute resolution and secondly the alternative mechanism of Lok-Adalat. Both the institutions are co-related with each other and can affect on the functioning of the other institution. The improvement of the working of the adversarial mode of dispute resolution will improve the functioning of Lok-Adalat. So the requirement is not only to improve the functioning of Lok-Adalat but also the adversarial mode of dispute resolution.

CONCLUSION

The institution of Lok-Adalat is successfully providing justice to the large number of people in the country for the last two decades. Millions of cases were settled and millions of people utilized this instrument of dispensation of justice effectively. Study reveals that the institution was intercepted in the State of West Bengal after one decade of its foundation. The institution is gaining popularity continuously since initiation. In Bengal too the institution successfully spread over the State within a few years The extremely good performance in the State has been seen during the year 1999, when more than 10 times growth of the institution has been recorded, compared to the corresponding years.

A large number of cases belonging to MACC and other categories were settled in the state. Study on the one hand refute the presumption that the institution is proper only for MACC cases, by settling a large number of different categories of cases in the State. On the other hand it is established that the institution of Lok-Adalat is neither a secondary means of dispute resolution nor a sub-standard dispute resolution mechanism. Qualitatively what would be better than the parties settling their disputes themselves with the help of independent conciliators? The parties concerned have control over the process. It saves the parties from allegation and counter allegation.

The study established that the three categories of cases are appropriate for this noble institution of Lok-Adalat. First, where the disputes are involving money and one party knows that he has to pay the money and the other party knows that he has a reasonable claim or right to receive the money. Secondly, where ongoing relationships subsist between the parties and thirdly where party of the one hand have duty to provide service and the party of the other hand have right to obtain service. Thus, the institution of Lok-Adalat effectively settled a large number of cases in all the aforesaid categories. However, the highest number of cases settled belongs to the compensation claims. In West Bengal, more than 73% cases settled in the State were belonging to this category. Indeed, all the Districts of the State have shown an encouraging performance in MACC cases but at the same time they settled a large number of other cases also. However, the similar situation is not prevailing in all the States of the Country. In most of the States the percentage of MACC cases varies from 5% to 15%, which is comparatively much lower than the percentage of settlements of MACC cases in West Bengal.

One most negative aspect of the functioning of institution of Lok-Adalat is its declining phenomenon in West Bengal. Although similar situations have been recorded in few other States also. Even in Gujarat the number of settlements decreased in the year 2001 and in a similar way the declining performance has been in the State of Rajasthan. Even though the number of settlements in a single year of 2001 of the State of Gujarat is ten times more than the entire settlements of the West Bengal. The decrease in West Bengal is thus not comparable with that of the State of Gujarat because the institution of Lok-Adalat in West Bengal is still in a developing stage. Though, some Districts have performed extremely well and the number of settlements increased substantially but the number of settlements is decreasing in most of the Districts. The lack of active participation of most of the lawyers has cost most to the institution. Lack of legal awareness is also responsible for minimal disposals. Though 47 legal awareness camps were organised during the year 2001 yet it is not sufficient for the State of West Bengal.

In Haryana, the Rules made the provision for appointment of Director for legal literacy and training of para lawyer. Similar attempt is needed in West Bengal in order to popularise the institution of Lok-Adalat and provide training to the para lawyers. Only a few NGOs are involved in the legal literacy programme and popularising the Lok-Adalat. The Legal Services Authorities Act and the Rules made thereunder have the provision for encouragement of NGOs but little has been done in the State to this end.

Permanent and continuous Lok-Adalats were established in Kolkata but it failed and only after a few months of its operation, it became un-operational. The Permanent Lok-Adalat as provided in 2002 Amendment, is yet to be established. However, after the establishment of the permanent Lok-Adalat for Public Utilities Services, a large number of cases will be settled by this means and the burden of the regular Court will decrease to a large extent.

Thus the institution of Lok-Adalat has shown both upward and down ward movement in the State. White on the one hand it improved extremely well in post 1998 period, it failed to sustain its improvement. Compared to the other contemporary states the institution has done little in West Bengal. Now time has come to take immediate steps not only to safeguard from the declining phenomenon and sustain improvement but also to make it more active in order to provide effective justice to attain the Constitutional goal of access to justice to all. A joint effort by lawyers, judges, para lawyers, other legal fraternities, social workers, NGOs and the people at large will be able to make the institution fruitful for the billions of the people of the Country. Otherwise this noble institution will also loose the faith of the people and as a result the institution will again dip into eclipse instead of providing participatory justice to billions of people.

REFERENCES

1. Legal Aid Services West Bengal (LASWEB), a reputed NGO of West Bengal, played important role in the Lok-Adalat movement in West Bengal. This NGO can be considered as pioneer in Lok-Adalat movement in the State. In fact the first Lok-Adalat by this NGO was organised long back in the year 1991' 14th & 15th December at High Court, Calcutta. Indeed this was the first Lok-Adalat in the State of West Bengal, so far the available information suggests.
2. Legal Aid Services West Bengal,(LASWEB) Souvenir, (1991).
3. Legal Aid Services West Bengal (LASWEB) can be considered pioneer in the State for the Lok-Adalat movement. Several Lok-Adalats were organised under (he auspices of LASWB in which a large number of cases settled. The first Lok-Adalat was also organised by LASWEB.

4. See Legal Aid Services West Bengal, Souvenir published on the occasion of 5th Lok-Adalat.
5. Calcutta Gazette, No. 6505 J, 19-04-1994.
6. Calcutta Gazette, No. 7116 J. 27-07-1998.
7. Calcutta Gazette, No. 6861 J, (15.7.1998), 17-07-1998.
8. The Calcutta Gazette, No 6846-J (15-7-98), 17-07-1998.
9. The Calcutta Gazette, No 732 - 736/SLSA-80/99 (18-4-2000), 18-04-2000.
10. The Calcutta Gazette, No 6860-J (15-7-98),. 17-07-1998.
11. The Calcutta Gazette, No 738/SLSA-80/99.18-04-2000.
12. The Calcutta Gazette, No 6844-J (15-7-98), 17-07-1998.
13. The Calcutta Gazette No. 692/SLSA-80/99, 693/SLSA-80/99. 694/SLSA-80/99, 18-4-2000. All the three Sub-Divisional committees were constituted on 12-4-2000 consisting of 9 members of each district.
14. The Calcutta Gazette, No 6848-J(15-7-98), 17-07-1998.
15. The Calcutta Gazette, No 940-944/SLSA-80/99, 17-05-2000
16. The Calcutta Gazette. No 6845-J (15-7-98), 17-07-1998.
17. All the four Sub-Divisional Legal Services Committees were constituted on the same day on 18th April, 2000 by virtue of Sec. 11A of the Legal Services Authorities Act, 1987. The Committees were formed for the Sub-Division of Hooghly, Chandannagar, Arambagh and Srirampur. See The Calcutta Gazette, No. 707-/10/SLSA/80/99 (15-7-98). 17-07-1998.
18. The District Authority was constituted on 15th July, 1998 by Government of West Bengal consisting of 16 members including the District Judge of Howrah, who will function as the Chairman of the Authority. See The Calcutta Gazette No. 6849-J (15-7-98). 17-07-1998.
19. The two sub-Divisional Committees were constituted on 18th April'1998, namely Howrah Sub-Divisional Legal Services Committee and Uluberia Sub-Divisional Legal Services Committee consisting of 10 and 9 members respectively. See The Calcutta Gazette, No. 705/SLSA-80/99 & 706/SLSA-80/99. 18-04-2000.
20. The Calcutta Gazette, No. 6854-J(15-7-98). 17-07-1998.
21. In family disputes or other similar disputes where parties have continuing relationship, the conciliatory mechanism for resolution of disputes is the best tool. However, the cases, which normally appeared before the Lok-Adalat, are basically after long legal battle, which resulted in the complete breakdown of the relationship. Under these circumstances it became difficult for conciliator to pursue the matter constructively towards settlement and chances of settlement were minimal in those circumstances. However, if the matter appeared before the conciliator in the beginning stage of dispute the chances of resolution of dispute is much more higher.
22. The District Judge entrusted to associate with the Authority as its Chairman. The other member of the authority includes. District Magistrate. Superintendent of Police, Chief Judicial Magistrate, Public Prosecutor and Government Pleader. See The Calcutta Gazette, No. 6847-J (15-7-98). 17-07-1998.
23. The Calcutta Gazette, No. 713-718/SLSA-80/99, 18-04-2000.
24. Government of West Bengal constitutes the District Authority by virtue of Sec 9(2) b of the Act on 15th July 1998 consisting of 16 members. See The Calcutta Gazette, No 6857-J (15-7-98), 17-07-1998.
25. The Sub-Divisional Legal Services Committees were constituted on 18th April, 2000 by the State Legal Services Authority, by virtue of power conferred under sec. 11A(1) of the Act. See The Calcutta Gazette, No. 731/SLSA-80/99. 730/SLSA-80/99, 18-04-2000.
26. The District Legal Services Authority was constituted on 15th July 1998 by Government of West Bengal by virtue of Sec. 9(2)b of the Legal Services Authorities Act, 1987, consisting of 16 members including the District Judge of District Nadia as Chairman of the Authority. See The Calcutta Gazette, No. 6850 J (15-7-98), 17-07-1998:
27. All the four Sub-Divisional Legal Services Committees are formed on 18th April' 2000, by the State Legal Services Authority, West Bengal by virtue of Sec 11A of the Legal services Authorities Act 1997. Each of the

four Sub-Divisional Committees consist of 10 members. See The Calcutta Gazette, No. 722-725/SLSA-80/99, 18-4-2000.

28. The District Legal Services Authority was constituted on 15th July' 1998 by the Government of West Bengal by virtue of the Sec. 9(2)b of Legal Services Authorities Act. 1987, consisting of 15 members, See The Calcutta Gazette. No. 6858 J (15-7-98), 17-07-1998.

29. Both Sub-Divisional Committees were constituted on 18th April 2000 by State Legal Services Authority, West Bengal. Both sub-Divisional Legal Services Committees consist of 10 members. See The Calcutta Gazette, No 703/SLSA-80/99, 704ySLSA-80/99,18-04-2000.

30. The District Authority was constituted on 15th July, 1998 consisting of 16 members. See The Calcutta Gazette, No 6856 J (15-7-98), 17-07-1998.

31. The Sub-Divisional Legal Services Committees were,constituted by the State Legal Services Authorities, consisting of 10 members in each committee. See The Calcutta Gazette. No 726-729/SLSA-80/19, 18-04-2000.

32. The District Legal Services Authority was constituted on 15th July 1998 consisting of 16 members. See The Calcutta Gazette. No 6855-J, (15.07.1998), 17-07-1998.

33. The Calcutta Gazette, No. 711/SLSA-80799 & 712/SLSA-80/9.18-04-2000.

34. The Calcutta Gazette. No. 6852-J (15-7-98), 17-07-1998.

35. The Calcutta Gazette, No. 719-721/SLSA-80/99, 18-04-2000.

36. The Calcutta Gazette. No. 6851-J (15-07-1998), 17-07-1998.

37. The Calcutta Gazette, No. 695-697/SLSA-80/39, 18-04-2000.

38. The Calcutta Gazette. No 6853-J, (15-07-1998), 17-07-1998.

39. The Calcutta Gazette, No 698-702/SLSA-80/99, 18-04-2000.

40. The Calcutta Gazette, No 6859-J. (15-07-1998), 17-07-1998.

41. The Calcutta Gazette, No 936-939/SLSA80/99, 17-05-2000.

42. The researcher being an Advocate has an experience of a maintenance case, where a young couple having one baby were confronted with some disputes. Wife filed maintenance case against her Doctor husband. Husband's lawyers filed reply with counter allegation against wife having illicit relationship with her father. During evidence wife made certain allegations against husband's family. This allegation and counter allegation created a situation where no one of them can live together any further. Though, wife is getting maintenance but her family is broken fully. The allegation or counter allegation was not the whole contention of the parties but lawyers input made it irreconcilable.

43. Justice S.B. Sinha, *Alternative Dispute Resolution, Souvenir* LASWEB, (1996). Para 7. The Souvenir was published on the occasion of 5th Lok-Adalat held on 13th & 14th January, 1996. In order to understand further about the importance of alteratives in decision-making process, See Study Material, *ADR workshop:* 24-29 Sep'2001, LASWEB See also. Ury & Fisher, Getting to yes, Penguin Publication.

44. The author had opportunity to participate a weeklong workshop on the Mediation technique. Charles B. Wiggins, an American Mediator provides a in depth analysis of the importance of alternative in decision making. See also, Ury & Fisher, Getting to yes. Penguin Publicafon.

45. *Smt Bela Rani Manna* V. *National Insurance Company Ltd,* No 428 of 1983. The matter appeared before Lok-Adalat on 27-07-02 at City Civil Court Kolkata.

CHAPTER 9

Findings and Suggestions

The study established the fact that the People's Court of ancient times, which was identical with the institution of Lok-Adalat, was in existence from time immemorial with different nomenclature. During the ancient period, disputes were resolved by the guilds of different professions with people's participation. The Kula, Sreni and Gana courts effectively administered justice during such periods having specified hierarchy. All forms of disputes, except cases of offences of grievous nature, were dealt with in those People's Courts and the King had minimum role to play in the administration of justice at grass root level. The People's Court remained a distinct institution even during the Moghal rule in India. The indigenous dispute resolution mechanism was effective until the advent of British regime. One of the findings of the study is that the Islamic jurisprudence as well as Hindu polity preferred resolution of dispute through Panchayat of relatives or neighbours. Holy Quran specifically mandate for appointment of mediator or conciliator for resolution of family disputes. The genesis of the institution of Lok-Adalat is found in the ancient Panchayat system.

Introduction of the Anglo-Saxon jurisprudence inducted the technicalities in the process of dispute resolution. As a result it detached large number of masses from the administration of justice. The British administration of justice replaced the ancient dispute resolution mechanism with the adversarial mode of dispute resolution. Thus our traditional participatory form of dispute resolution mechanism faded into insignificance in many parts of the country; which resulted in denial of access to justice to large number of people from the towns and villages who cannot afford to pay for costly justice for their grievances.

When the British system of administration of justice failed to provide access to justice to all, the search was started for alternative means for resolution of disputes. Even the British realised about the impact of the adversarial mode of dispute resolution, which made the process technical, lengthy and costly. They initiated the alternative means of Arbitration but for the commercial disputes only. In post-independence period, the legal fraternity tried to explore alternative means for resolution of disputes. Endeavour to find out alternatives to adversarial form of disputes resolution were being researched upon in other Countries as well. As a result several alternatives including Arbitration, Conciliation, Mediation, Med-Arb, Medola and Mini-Trial came into existence. However, In India, Arbitration and Conciliation were utilised effectively in post Independence period in commercial disputes, labour disputes and family disputes. Those alternate modes of arbitration and conciliation were utilized effectively in few forms of disputes. The arbitration was used in commercial disputes where prior agreement existed. Conciliation was utilised in family disputes and labour disputes but on few specific occasions only. Such alienation of arbitration and conciliation from large number of disputes makes it alien to large number of people. As a result those system could not provide relief to the large number of masses.

Administration of justice was ineffective because on the one hand adversarial mode of dispute resolution failed to provide access to justice to the large number of people and on the other hand the alternative means like arbitration and conciliation failed to fulfil the hopes and aspiration of large number of masses. The situation was so aggravated that the legal fraternity started crying that the administration of justice is on the verge of collapse. Even, the general masses in order to ventilate their grievances began to look up for the services of the under world. The need was felt not only to the alternatives of the adjudication but also to the so-called alternatives in the form of arbitration and conciliation to supplement them with new means. Thus during 80's, taking clue from the traditional dispute resolution mechanism, the institution of Lok-Adalat was projected as an alternative means for resolution of disputes. The institution of Lok-Adalat was emerged in the first stage as a legal aid strategy in order to provide access to justice to all by providing justice speedily and inexpensively.

The basic principle and underlying idea of the Lok-Adalat is to provide cheaper and quicker justice at the doorstep of the people so that access to justice become meaning full to all the people of the country irrespective of their resources. The spirit behind the Lok-Adalat is 'Live' and 'Let Live', 'Give' and 'Take'. It is a participatory form of dispute resolution mechanism; which is in reality, a revival of traditional form of dispute resolution mechanism. The aim at the proceedings before the Lok-Adalat is to bring the dispute to an end, which are hard to be achieved in adversarial mode of dispute resolution.

The institution of Lok-Adalat is functioning on the democratic basis. The disputants have control over the process of negotiation, which makes the process consumer friendly. In Lok-Adalats all the parties, their counsels, conciliators cum judges sit together with one single aim to bring the parties to amicable settlement so as to initially satisfy both the parties and bring the dispute to its logical end. The institution of Lok-Adalat has succeeded in setting thousand of cases in single day, which otherwise would have taken years to resolve. Until now the institution of Lok-Adalat could settle millions of cases. Study revealed that until 1999, more than 97 lacs cases were settled through Lok-Adalats in which Rs 2306,07,32,170/- (Rs Two thousand three hundred six crores seven lacs thirty two thousand one hundred and seventy) only was awarded as compensation to the claimants in Motor Accident Compensation Claim cases alone. The reason for its success lies in its process, which is simple, less formal, cheap and expeditious. It is simple because the legal formality has little role to play and cheap because no court fees or other charges are required for resolution of disputes in Lok-Adalats. On the other hand incentives has been provided in the form of return of the court fees if paid at the time of filing of the case before court of law. It is expeditious because the matter settled within single or couple of hearings at Lok-Adalat that save the parties from unmanageable expenses which would otherwise have to be incurred during the long process of adjudication including professional charges.

The justice delivery mechanism as adopted in Lok-Adalat is neither inferior in quality compared to the adjudication process nor it is a compromise on the part of the poor. Even the process as adopted in the Lok-Adalat and its out come is qualitatively superior to the adjudication process specifically in certain categories of cases. The underlying rationality of Lok-Adalat coming into existence and be successful is the experience which tell us that an adversarial adjudication will leave one party the victor and other the loser, does not remove the dispute from the society and may lead to further disputes or tension. The process of Lok-Adalat make both the parties winners because the out come of the process was of their own. In certain categories of cases, specifically in the disputes where parties have a continuing relationship, it saved the parties from making allegation and counter allegation against each other. It attempted to bring peace and harmony among the disputants. Accordingly, matrimonial disputes are successfully resolved, bringing the broken homes back to harmony.

The institution of Lok-Adalat had functioned effectively for more than a decade without any explicit legislation. However, Lok-Adalat too had legal instrumentalities during that time in the form of Constitutional directives and the guidelines prescribed by the judiciary. It is evident from the study that the institution of Lok-Adalat has been enshrined as an instrument to fulfil the Constitutional obligation of providing equal justice to all and to make access to justice meaningful for the down trodden people. Thus, the institution of Lok-Adalat is nothing but a means to fulfil the Constitutional obligation as enshrined in the Preamble, Art. 14, Art. 39A, Art. 40 and other provisions of the Constitution.

The legislative mechanism in the form of Legal Services Authorities Act, 1987 eliminates the vacuum created because of the non-availability of explicit legislation for Lok-Adalat. Indeed, it was further strengthened by 1994 Amendment and C.P.C. Amendment, 1999. The institution of Lok-Adatet got further impetus by Legal Services Authorities Amendment Act, 2002, which supplemented the institution of Lok-Adalat with permanent Lok-Adalat. In fact both adhoc and permanent Lok-Adalat are going to be in existence. One having former characteristic that will function solely as conciliatory body without having power to pass decree on merit if the parties failed to settle their disputes and the other is Permanent Lok-Adalat, which has power to pass decree on merit if parties failed to settle their disputes. However, study revealed some deficiency in the provisions of the Legal Services Authorities Act. Firstly, the Act does not prescribe any mandate for the parties to appear before the Lok-Adalat. Secondly, no remedy has been prescribed when the parties deliberately do not appear before Lok-Adalat. Thirdly, The Legal Services Authorities Amendment Act 2002 empowered the Lok-Adalat to pass the decree on merit if parties failed to settle their disputes but the Act did not prescribe any provisions for appeal against order passed on merit. Thus, certain amendment in the Act as discussed in earlier chapters will remedy such deficiencies and will help in functioning the institution effectively. Apart from that, provisions of procedural laws namely C.P.C, Cr.P.C and substantive law like IPC may be Invoked to summon the parties and witnesses to Lok-Adalat which will strengthen the process before Lok-Adalat.

Since the inception of the institution of Lok-Adatet the judiciary played a vital role. It not only influenced the enactment of the law but also made effort for proper implementation and enforcement of the Legal Services Authorities Act, 1987. It works as watchdog for the institution of Lok-Adalat The study points out that the formation of Permanent Lok-Adalat for public utilities sector by virtue of Legal Services Authorities Amendment Act, 2002 is nothing but materialisation of the judicial pronouncement In this regard Art. 141 of the Constitution came into play when a committed Judiciary decreed liberal guidelines for future action.

The institution of Lok-Adalat effectively provided justice to a large number of people since its inception in 1962 at Gujarat. Millions of cases were settled at national sphere through this conciliatory mechanism. The growing popularity of the institution can be established from the fact that while until March, 1996, only 13061 Lok-Adalats were held in different parts of the country in which 57,38,423 cases were settled and an amount of Rs 861,27,79,423. was awarded as compensation, the number of settlements increased to 97,20,289 in 49415 Lok-Adalats held until 1999 and an amount of Rs 2306,07,32,170/- was awarded as compensation in motor accident compensation claim cases alone. The highest number of Lok-Adalats were organised in the State of Gujarat where 10165 Lok-Adalats were held until 1999. The organisation of Lok-Adalat in the State of Gujarat was further increased to 24763 until Sep. 2002 in which 17,09,869 cases were settled. In the State of Uttar Pradesh 36,08,531 cases were settled in Lok-Adalats until 1999. Study further revealed that the performance of the institution of Lok-Adatot is not similar in all the places. In some places like Chandigarh, Tripura, Lakshadweep, Andaman & Nicobar Lok-Adalats are newborn institutions. Indeed, In some places like Arunachal Pradesh, Manipur, Meghalaya, Mizoram and Sikkim, performance of the institution was not impressive. In almost all the States, a large number of motor accident compensation claim cases were settled which varies from 5% to 20% in different States. A large number of other categories of cases also settled in the Lok-Adalats. The trend is encouraging that this institution has came to stay as an effective alternative to adversarial system of dispute resolution.

It is found that Lok-Adalat was initiated in West Bengal much later than in several other states. The first Lok-Adalat in the State was organised at the end of 1991. Until March'1996, only 39 Lok-Adalats were organised in the State in which 2400 cases were settled and an amount of Rs 591,47,700/- was awarded as compensation. Study further revealed that the institution of Lok-Adalat performed extremely well in post 1998 period. An out standing performance was made in the year 1999 when 9434 cases were referred before the Lok-Adalat in which 4512 cases were settled. The number of reference of cases further increased in the years 2000 and 2001 but the number of settlements has decreased slightly in these two years. However, number of settlements further increased in the year 2002. In West Bengal different categories of cases were settled which include MACC cases, maintenance cases, matrimonial disputes, bank loan cases, title suit, money suit, petty criminal cases, pre-litigation and other categories of cases. However, highest percentage of settlement recorded are in MACC cases, which is alone 73% of the total cases settled. Thousands of people belonging to all Districts were benefited out of this result-oriented institution. The highest number of cases referred as well as settled were in the District of North 24 Parganas where 4522 cases were referred in the last three years in which 3712 cases were settled. The lowest number of cases settled was in Murshidabad District. However, compared to other contemporary States the performance of Lok-Adalat is not satisfactory but then the institution is in growing stage in West Bengal. Constant encouragements and consistent educative process of awareness programmes are warranted.

It has come to light that while in some Districts Lok-Adalat is gaining popularity steadily and the number of reference and settlement increased significantly, the number of settlement decreased in several districts. The institution of Lok-Adalat has constantly registered increase in the Districts 24 Parganas south, Bankura, Dakshin Dinajpur and Malda but all other districts have shown decrease in performance. A probe into the reasons of disparity in performance in various districts will bring to the fore the causes which can be effectively tackled by appropriate measures. Some such reasons for decline of the number of cases in different Districts are inactive participation of Advocates, managerial deficiencies, unawareness among the disputants and the concentration of Lok-Adalat in the district headquarters.

It is revealed from the study that some districts have been able to settle large number of civil cases while some other districts have settled a large number of matrimonial cases. In Hooghly 426 bank loan cases were settled, which is highest in the State compared to other districts. Similarly, Howrah & Nadia settled a large number of matrimonial cases. In the same direction Dakshin Dinajpur and Malda were able to bring into compromise in large number of pre-litigation cases; the 24 Parganas South, 24 Parganas North & Murshidabad scored well in MACC cases. Thus, the aforesaid results on the one hand refute the argument that the institution is effective only for MACC cases. On the other hand it established the fact that the institution of Lok-Adalat have potentiality to settle a large number of other categories of cases like maintenance cases, matrimonial cases, bank loan cases, money suits, commercial disputes etc. Indeed, the institution of Lok-Adalat established that it has potentiality to settled large number of such cases, which have not entered in the roll of adjudicatory proceedings. Accordingly, a large number of pre-litigation cases were settled in different Districts. However, such potentiality has not been utilised in most part of the State. Of the total settlements in the State of West Bengal, MACC cases were alone 73%, which is much higher than that of several other States.

A remarkable finding of the study is that in three distinct areas Lok-Adalats were particularly successful. First, the cases where the disputants knew the fate of the case. Disputant of the one side knew that they have to pay the money and the contestant on the other side have firm hope of getting money. Thus, the dispute basically centres round the quantum of money. MACC cases, bank loan cases, cheque bounce cases and even maintenance cases are example of this form of disputes. Secondly those cases where one party has right to have access to service while the other has duty to provide service. Electricity disputes and other consumer-oriented disputes are examples of this form of disputes. Third where ongoing relationship subsist between the parties. The matrimonial cases, maintenance cases, bank loan cases are examples of this form of disputes.

Yet another meaningful finding is that although the institution of Lok-Adalat is functioning in all the Districts of West Bengal, except in few cases, almost all Lok-Adalats in the State were organised at District Headquarters. Though Sub-Divisional Legal Services Committees were established in most of the districts yet all such Sub-Divisional Committees are on papers only. Such non-activation of Sub-Divisional Committees resulted in deprivation of countryside people to obtain the fruit of the institution. Different authorities established in the State failed to organise 'People's Court' at 'people's places'.

It is revealed that majority of people have shown satisfaction on the functioning of Lok-Adalat. A mixed response came from the respondents whom the researcher served questionnaire. The response was some times based on respondent's own interest as on asking whether the Lok-Adalat be organised at peoples places instead of court premises, the disputant replied in affirmative while most of Advocates responded in the negative. Similarly, large number of Advocates did not make themselves responsible for minimal disposal of cases. However, apart from the suggestions for making the institution more effective, most of the respondents agreed with the views of researcher on two aspects. Firstly, in the process of Lok-Adalat none of the parties is loser and the end product made both of them happy as end justifies the means. Secondly, there is a scope of continuance of both the systems of administration of justice, firstly by adversarial mode of dispute resolution and secondly by the alternative mechanism of Lok-Adalat. Both the institutions are co-related with each other and can effect on the functioning of other institution. The improvement of working of the adversarial mode of dispute resolution will improve the functioning of Lok-Adalat. So the requirement is not only to improve the functioning of Lok-Adalat but also to expedite the adversarial mode of dispute resolution. In fact the effective functioning of the adversarial mode of dispute resolution will make the institution of Lok-Adalat more functional.

The NGOs played substantial role in initiation of Lok-Adalat. In fact the seed of the institution of Lok-Adalat in the State of West Bengal was sown by NGO's, which organised several Lok-Adalats after initiating it in the year 1991. The Advocates, Judges, Para-Lawyers, Social Workers and other legal fraternity played important role in making the institution successful. However, some of the Advocates have shown keen interest in some category of cases like MACC, which resulted in the settlement of large number of such cases. Indeed most of them keep themselves aloof from the institution. It is fact that without the active participation of the

Advocate the institution like Lok-Adalat cannot be successful. So it is essential for the betterment of the institution that much larger percentage of Advocates should become active towards participation in the institution. NGOs' attempt to train para-lawyers in the field of Alternative Dispute Resolution mechanism can create a new category of professionals having friendly attitude towards Lok-Adalat. But very little progress have been made in this direction. Although the social workers are part of the panel of the judges of the Lok-Adatets they need to be identified and trained in the art of conciliation and awareness about the institution so that access to justice become meaning full to the less privileged masses.

SUGGESTIONS

In order to make the institution of Lok-Adalat more effective and result oriented the following suggestions are made:

1. It should be made mandatory for certain categories of cases to be filed before Lok-Adalat and on failure of the parties to settle the dispute there, the case may be transferred for adjudication in regular court. Motor Accident Compensation Claim cases, Matrimonial Disputes, Maintenance Cases, Electricity Service Dispute, Bank Loan Cases and other such cases which pro-suppose continuing relationship between the parties are such categories of cases, which can be filed before Lok-Adalat at initial stage. Indeed, The Legal Services Authorities Amendment Act, 2002 opened the scope for filing of electricity disputes, insurance claims and other public utilities sector cases before the permanent Lok-Adalat. However, in those places where the permanent Lok-Adalat have not been established such cases can be filed in Lok-Adalat of former types and if parties failed to settle their disputes then only the matter can be entertained by the adjudicatory forum. This dual reference system w ill not only make the parties committed to settlements but also open up the forum of regular courts as the final arbiter.

2. The Bar Council of India has decided not to participate in any Lok-Adalat matter, to protest against the Legal Services Authorities Amendment Act, 2002. In a resolution passed on 23rd October, 2002, the BCI decided to abstain from all event held to observe Legal Services Day and observe hunger strike a day earlier. The opposition is on imaginary ground; (1) the amendment stipulates that the Permanent Lok-Adalat will be presided over by a retired District Judge and there will be two other members and the BCI is wary of having non-legal person on the panel as they can easily passed influenced judgement by overriding the views of the retired judge, (2) amendment takes away the right of a party to file a civil suit. This is the worse of the two apprehensions for which the Advocate oppose the Permanent Lok-Adalat. They fear that their bread and butter is denied by settling lakhs of cases outside law courts. It is suggested that the Advocates Act, 1961 be suitably amended incorporating provisions to make it the duty of every Advocate, enrolled under the said Act, to participate in the Lok-Adalats.

3. In order to make the institution of Lok-Adalat more effective the researcher suggest certain amendment in the Legal Services Authorities Act, 1987. Firstly, the Act must specifically mandate for the appearance of the parties and if the parties do not appear before Lok-Adalat some remedial measure should be adopted. The remedy can be in two ways. Either the Lok-Adalat should be empowered to proceed further if parties failed to appear before it, or the court from where the case has been referred can proceed further under Order IX of the Code of Civil Procedure treating such non-appearance as failure on the part of parties to appear at the time of hearing. Secondly, the Act must prescribe clearly that if a judge in service is appointed as a judge of the Lok-Adalat no record from his court can be referred for conciliation at such Lok-Adalat Thirdly, some provisions for appeal should be incorporated in the Act against the order passed by the Permanent Lok-Adalat on merit The appeal provision can be incorporate in such a way that the appeal can be made before division bench of High Court, so that, no further appeal can lie before High Court.

4. Under the present scheme the award passed by the Lok-Adalat is a decree, which can be executed in civil court. In order *to* ensure effective execution of the decree passed by the Lok-Adalat a

definite procedure should be evolved for follow up actions that the decision is executed immediately in accordance with the settlement. Lok-Adalat must be empowered to execute its own award.

5. The aim of providing access to justice to all cannot be achieved until and unless the institution of Lok-Adalat is able to provide access to justice to the countryside people. Most of the Sub-Divisional Committees in West Bengal are not functioning and are on paper only. Sub-Divisional Committees in collaboration with village Panchayat can play important role in providing access to justice to all. Though each Sub-Divisional Committee has members of the Zilla Parishad but such inclusion also failed to activate the Sub-Divisional Committee. In order to make the institution effective and to provide opportunity to the people of the far-flung areas to avail the fruit of the institution of Lok-Adalat, Sub-Divisional Committees are required to be made effective. A joint effort of the Bar, Bench, Social Workers, Village Panchayat and the legal fraternity is essential in this end.

6. Without the active involvement of lawyers the institution of Lok-Adalat cannot succeed in achieving its goal. It has been revealed from the study that the representation of lawyers is minimal in different Committees. The Secretary of each District Bar Association must be an ex-officio member of the District Authority. At least two Advocates from the Bar of Sub-Divisional Court must be appointed as members of the Sub-Divisional Committees. One of them must be the Secretary of such Sub-Divisional Bar Association. In order to attract active participation of the Advocates some sort of incentives should be Introduced. They may claim income tax rebate by way of notional compensation for the loss of income they have suffered for appearing before Lok-Adalat, as they would have earned much more by defending cases in other courts than what they are likely to receive for appearing in Lok-Adalats. The Income Tax Act may be amended to allow tax concession; A lot of concession in other cases are given in the Income Tax Act, 1961.

7. In order to make the institution of Lok-Adalat more effective it is essential that Lok-Adalat should be manned by experienced and talented persons. Although the Judges of the Lok-Adalat are appointed from among the retired Judicial Officers, Advocates and Social Workers and most of them are talented in their field but still some training is essential in order to make them understand the interest of the parties and the basic cause of disputes. Similarly, the training of the Para Lawyers is also essential because it will not only help in creating a trained pre Lok-Adalat conciliator but also help in making a new class of legal professionals having friendly attitude towards alternate means of Lok-Adalat. A regular training programme for Judges, Lawyers, Para-Lawyers, Social Workers, NGO's, and other legal fraternity will help in improving the functioning of the institution of the Lok-Adalat. In this direction a unique attempt has been made by the Hanyana State Legal Services Authority, which created a post-called Director for Legal Literacy and Training of Para Lawyers. Similarly in Gujarat Permanent Legal Aid Clinic provided regular training. Similar attempt in West Bengal and other places will improve the functioning of Lok-Adalat and people can be aware about the Lok-Adalat scheme.

8. Each District Authority as well as State Authority have made a panel of the name of the persons from Bar, Retired Judges and Social workers from whom the judges of the Lok-Adalats are appointed. Insimilar way a panel should be made at Sub-Divisional level. The State Authority should review such panel at interval of one or two years and according to the performance of the panel members the panel may be modified.

9. NGO's have played important role in the functioning of Lok-Adalat. In fact the initiation of Lok-Adalat was done by NGO's. Only few NGO's are involved in legal aid and Lok-Adalat movements. At least one NGO at each District should be accredited and such NGO's should be entrusted with the responsibility to make aware the general masses about the Lok-Adalat and Legal Aid movements.

10. The Law teachers and Law students should be encouraged to take active part in the process of Lok-Adalat. Students can be engaged in pre Lok-Adalat conciliations. The teachers can guide them.

Indeed, it will be helpful for the institution if some Lok-Adalats in each year can be organised at Law College Campuses or other similar places where a large number of students and Law teachers can actively participate in the process. They can undertake preparatory survey and research work and can extend supportive services in its efficient execution. However, the involvement of political parties and politicians should be discouraged so that the institution of Lok-Adalat is not abused for political motives.

11. The procedure in Lok-Adalat should be informal, flexible and legal technicalities should not become a hurdle for settlement. The Judges must themselves interact with the disputant instead of hearing argument of Advocates. The Judges must attempt to understand the interest of the parties and persuade both the parties towards settlement. Indeed Advocates should also be allowed to participate actively.

12. A Code of Conduct for the Judges of the Lok-Adalat should be evolved and they shall maintain professional integrity. Protection to the Judges must be provided for privileged communication.

13. The Government must provide adequate fund to the different functionaries involved in Lok-Adalat movement. In West Bengal one of the reasons for non-activation of the Sub-Divisional Committee is lack of adequate budgetary provisions. Thus from Sub-Divisional Committee to the Central Authority, adequate fund should be provided for organisation of the Lok-Adalat, legal awareness camp, NGO's funding, training of the Para-Lawyers and other functionaries of the Lok-Adalat scheme and other expenditures.

14. A monitoring cell under the State Authority should be established to ensure proper implementation of the Lok-Adalat scheme at all level in general and at Sub-Divisional level in particular and for proper accounting and strict financial discipline of the Lok-Adalat.

15. The researcher is of the view that proper rewards should be given to such authority or committee, which implement the Lok-Adalat schemes most successfully. Similarly, the NGO's, Lawyers, Judges and other members associated with the Lok-Adalat should be rewarded for their effective contribution towards Lok-Adalat movement. Such reward may be the acknowledgement in form of certificate and medal, to be distributed by the State Authority on yearly function at State Level.

16. The place of holding Lok-Adalat should be decided on the basis of the cases of the concerned area. It is advisable that few Lok-Adalats are held in each Sub-Division in court free environment like Village Panchayat, School Premises and College Campus etc so that general people can participate in the process and the Lok-Adalat on such occasion can be observed as 'Festival of Justice'. This form of organisation of the Lok-Adalat will provide a new life and enthusiasm in the movement.

17. Permanent Lok-Adalat of former characteristic should be established in each district so that pending cases can be referred to the Lok-Adalat regularly. These Lok-Adalats will not only be able to settle large number of pending cases but also pre-litigation cases. Simultaneously, permanent Lok-Adalat for public utilities service shall also be established. Such permanent Lok-Adalat will be able to dispose of plenty of cases relating to public utilities service.

18. The researcher is of the view that a wide publicity should be given for the institution of Lok-Adalat through Radio, Television, Press Briefing, Use of Cinema Slides, Publication of Books and Periodicals, free distribution of such Book and periodicals including leaflet to each village panchayat and social welfare organisation. This will help in creating awareness among the people of the grass root level and the ignorant people living in the far-flung areas of the State will able to know the significance of the Lok-Adalat and can reap the benefit from the institution.

19. Permanent Conciliation Board should be established at Block level. Such Board will function under either the District Authority or Sub-Divisional Committee. Such Conciliation board will attempt to settle the cases in the beginning and will work as pre Lok-Adalat conciliation body. People shall

have access to the board for their grievances. Indeed, the West Bengal government placed a bill, in the Assembly for formation of Block Level Conciliation Board. In my opinion, such permanent Conciliation Board at Block level should be established under the supervision of Sub-Divisional Legal Services Committee, so that settlement reached at by such Board can be in unison with the functioning of Lok-Adalats in the Sub-Division.

20. The Lok-Adalat movement can be successful only if the general masses will participate on voluntary basis in the functioning of the Lok-Adalat. The researcher suggests that a co-ordination committee at each village panchayat level can be established. Such co-ordination committee will function as intermediary between Block level Board and Village Panchayat. It will help in bringing more people towards Lok-Adalat, which will in result make the 'Lok-Adalat' in reality a 'People's Court'.

BIBLIOGRAPHY

BOOKS

1. Austin, Granville, The Indian Constitution: Cornerstone of a Nation, (1966). Oxford University Press.
2. Altekar, A S, State And The Government in Ancient India, (1979), Motilal Banarsidass, New Delhi.
3. Bhattacharya, Sibnath: Rural Poverty in India, (1989)
4. Baxi. Upendra, The Indian Supreme Court and politics, (1980), (M.C. Sharma)
5. Chitkara, M. G., Lok Adalat and Poor, (1993) Ashish Publishing House, New Delhi.
6. Chisti, M. Anees, Committees and Commission in pre-independent India, Volume 4, P 79, (2001), Mittal Publication.
7. Deshta. Sunil, Lok-Adalat in India: Genesis and Functioning, (1995), Deep & Deep Publications. New Delhi.
8. Dhavan. Rajeev, R. Sudarshan & Salman Khurshid, Judge and Judiciary power, (1985) (M.C.Sharma)
9. Gifford, Donald. G, Legal Negotiation: Theory and Application, 211 (1989), West Publishing Co.
10. Goldberg, Stephen B, Frank-E.A. Sander, & Nancy H. Rogers, Dispute Resolution : Negotiation, Mediation and other processes, P6-9 (1992).
11. Gupta, Subhash Chandra, OMBUDSMAN; AN Indian Perspective, 1995), Manak Publication.
12. Iyer J, V. R. Krishna, Our Courts on Trial, (1987), B. R. Publishing Corporation, Delhi
13. Iyer J, V. R. Krishna, Law Versus Justice: Problems and Solutions, (1981), Deep & Deep Publications, New Delhi
14. Johari, H. C, Arbitration and Conciliation Act, 1996, (2002), Kamal Law House.
15. Jois J, M. Rama, Legal and Constitutional History of India, 348 (2001)
16. Kane, P. V. History of Dharmasastra, Vol III (1973), Bandera Oriental Research Institute.
17. Mackie, Karl, David Miles & William Marsh, Commercial Dispute resolution: An ADR Practice Guide, (1995), Butterworth Publication.
18. Majumdar, R.C, The History and Culture of the Indian People, The Mughal Empire, (Second Edition), Vol VII, Bhartiya Vidya Bhavan, Bombay.
19. Majumdar, R. C, An Advanced History of India: The Delhi Sultanate And The Mughal Empire, Part II (1967) MacMillan St. Marthin' s Press.
20. Mishra, Anil Dutta & Madhev Shivappa Dadage, Panchayat Raj—Gandhian Perspective, (2002)
21. Mohta, V. A, Arbitration and Conciliation, Introduction (2001), AIR Publication.
22. Moududi, Syed Abul Ala, Tqfhimul Quran, Vol-1,
23. Narayan J. P.S, Law Relating to Lok-Adalat, (2002), Asia Law House.
24. Nath. Brindra, Judicial Administration in Ancient India, (1979), Janaki, Patna
25. Paul, Solil & Anupam Srivastava, Mulla: The Code of Civil Procedure, 1908, (Sixteenth Edition, 2001), Butterworth Publication.
26. Pramanik, Swapan Kr. & Prabhat Datta, Panchayat and people- The West Bengal Experience, (1994).

27. Rao J, M. Jagannadha, Law's delays world over-need for a change in our mindset-Towards permanent Lok-Adalat, Nyaya Deep- April - June'2000 Pg
28. Rao, P. C & William Sheffield, ADR what it is and how its works, (1997), Universal Law Publishing Co Pvt Ltd, Delhi
29. Sahai. R. S, Panchayat Raj in India, 95, (1968),
30. Sampath,D. K, Mediation, (1991) NLSIU Publication.
31. Sarkar, Sir Jadunath, Moghal Administration, (1935), Orient Longman, Bombay.
32. Sharma, Mool Chand, Justice P.N. Bhagwati, Court Constitution and Human Right, 1, (1995), Universal Book Traders
33. Sharma, S. D. Administration of justice in ancient India, (1988), Harman Publishing House, New Delhi
34. Srivastava, A. L, Akbar the Great, P 279, Vol-II (1972), Shiva Lal Agarwala, Agra.
35. M.K. Sharan, Court Procedure in Ancient India, (1978), Abhinav Publication. New Delhi.
36. Supakar, Shraddhakar, Law of Procedure and justice in Ancient India, (1986), Deep & Deep Publications.
37. Ury & Fisher, Getting to yes, Penguin Publication
38. www.councilforjustice.org/fiuiction.htm

ARTICLES

1. Anand J. A. S, Fifty years of Indian Judiciary- Its achievements & failures, Nyaya Deep, April-June 2000
2. Bakshi, Upendra and Marc Galanter, Panchayat Justice : An Indian Experience in Legal Acces, In M. Cappellitti (Ed), 344, Vol III (1979).
3. Collar, Carman & Gerry Spolter, International I.P. Dispute.Resolution: Is Mediation a Sleeping Giants? LL.M ADR Study Material, Bond University.
4. Chandra, Sarvesh, ADR: Is Conciliation the Best Choice?, in, P.C. Rao & William Sheffields, ADR, What it is & How it works, P83 (1997).
5. Chitkara J, M. G, Accessibility of Justice, P82, Nyaya Path, Souvenir-2000.
6. Dharmadhikari J, D. M, Lok-Adalat, P30, Nyaya Path, Souvenir (2000).
7. Fuller, Lon-L, The forms and limits of Adjudication, Harvard Law Review, P 369, Vol 92:353, (1978)
8. Grove, Peter, Mediation & Arbitration: Alternatives for intellectual property disputes, http://www.beicac.com/cfm/index/cfm?L= 157&P= 167.down loaded on 24.11.01.
9. Gupteshwar. K, 'The Statutory Lok-Adalat: Its structure and role', JILI, vol.-30, April-June, 1988,Pg.-174
10. Majumdar J, S. B., Profile of legal Aid Schemes in India post and presents Nyaya Path. Souvenir (2000).
11. Menon, N. R. Madhava, Lok-Adalat: Indian contribution to world jurisprudence, Nyaya Path, Souvenir, (2000)
12. Menon, N. R. Madhava, Justice Sans Lawyer: Some India Experiments, India Bar Review, Vol-2 (1985).
13. Menon, N.R.Madhava, Law Commission and grass root level justice, Indian Bar Review, Vol 12(4), (1985 Editorial)
14. Menon, N. R. Madhava, Lok-Adalat in Delhi: A Report from a legal educational perspective, Indian Bar Review, Vol 12 (4) 1985,
15. Menon, N. R. Madhava, Lok-Adalat: People's Programme for Speedy Justice, Indian Bar Review, Vol. 13(2): 1986,Pg. 132
16. Veerraju G., Panchayati Raj-A Gandhian Perspective, In, Anil Dutta Mishra, Mahadav Shivappa Dadaye, Panchayati Raj - Gandhian perspective, (2002), Mittal Publication
17. Moorje, M. N, Lok-Nyalaya: A place for common man in a changing society, AIR 1984, Journal 68.

18. Nariman, F.S, Arbitration and ADR in India, in P.C. RAO, ADR what it is and how its works, (1997) Pg.45, Universal Law Publication.
19. Pandey, Janardhan, Gandhi & Panchayat Raj, In Anil Dutta Mishra & Madhev Shivappa Dadage, Panchayet Raj -Gandhian Perspective, (2002)
20. Ramaswamy J,K, Settlement of disputes through Lok Adalat is one of the effective dispute resolution on statutory basis, In, P.C.Rao & William Sheffield, AD.R: What it is and How its works, (1997).
21. Rao J, M. Jagannadha, Laws delay world over- need for change in our mindset- towards permanent Lok-Adalat. P24, Nyaya Path, April-June 1999.
22. Rao, P. C, Alternative to litigation in India, In , P.C.Rao & William Sheffield, ADR - what it is and how it works, P24, (1997)
23. Reddy, K. Jayachandra, Alternative Dispute Resolution, In P.C.Rao & William Sheffield, ADR: What it is and how it works, 79 (1997)
24. Shah J, M. B, Effective Fast Track Justice System, Nyaya Path, Souvenir, (2000).
25. Sinha J, S. B, Alternative Dispute Resolution with special reference to Civil Procedure (Amendment) Act, 1999, Souvenir published by LAS WEB (2001)
26. Sinha J, S. B, Alternative Dispute Resolution, Souvenir LASWEB, (1996).
27. M.V. S. Sitalaxmi, Family Court and the Goal of Speedy Settlement of Matrimonial Disputes; LLM Dissertation, NLSIU, 1992.
28. Wade, John H, Arbitration of Matrimonial Dispute, Bond Law Review, P 395(1999)(11).

COMMISSION & COMMITTEES REPORTS

1. Law Commission of India, Alternative Forum for Resolution of Disputes at Grass-roots Level, 114th Report (1986).
2. Law Commission Of India, The role of legal profession in strengthening the system of administration of justice, 131st Report, 31st August' 1988.
3. Law Commission Of India, The High Court Arrears: A Fresh Look, 124th Report, 29th February' 1988.
4. Law Commission Of India, Urban Litigation: Mediation As Alternative to Adjudication, P 1, 129th Report.
5. Judicare: Equal justice - Social justice report, (1977)
6. Legal Aid Committee Report (Government of Gujarat), 1971 pare13.12
7. The Report on Processual Justice to the people (1973),
8. Committee for Implementation of Legal Aid Scheme(1980).

JOURNALS & OTHER MATERIALS

1. Constituent Assembly Debate, Book 1, (1947).
2. Nyaya Path Jan-Mar, (2000)
3. Nyaya Deep, Jan-Mar 1999.
4. Nyaya Deep, April-June 2000,
5. Nyaya Deep, Oct-Dec. 1999
6. Nyaya Deep, Jan-Mar. 2000
7. Legal Aid News Letter, Vol XI, Part 2&3, July-Dec. 1991
8. Legal Aid News Letter, Vol-XII, Part 1, April-June 1992
9. Legal Aid News Letter, Vol-XU, Part 2, July-Sep. 1992
10. Legal Aid News Letter, Vol DC Part 1-4, May 1989- Feb. 1990

11. Legal Aid News Letter, Vol X (Part 1 & 11) May- August
12. Legal Aid News Letter, Vol XI, page 4, January- March 1992
13. Legal-Aid News Letter, May-August, 1990, P 15
14. Nyaya Path, Souvenir (2000), Year 1, Issue 4.
15. Nyaya Path, April-Sep' 2001, Year: 2, Issue: 5&6.
16. Nyaya Path Sep' 2002, Year 3, Issue 9,10th & 11th.
17. LASWEB, Study material on Mediation skills, 24-29th Sep 2001, Kolkata.

INDEX

B

C